BARKER PLAYS EIGHT

Howard Barker

PLAYS EIGHT

The Bite of the Night

Brutopia

The Forty

Wonder and Worship in the Dying Ward

OBERON BOOKS
LONDON

WWW.OBERONBOOKS.COM

First published in this collection 2014
by Oberon Books Ltd
521 Caledonian Road, London N7 9RH
Tel: +44 (0) 20 7607 3637 / Fax: +44 (0) 20 7607 3629
e-mail: info@oberonbooks.com
www.oberonbooks.com

A catalogue record for this book is available from the British Library.

PB ISBN: 978-1-78319-087-4
E ISBN: 978-1-78319-586-2

Cover photography by Eduardo Houth

Contents

THE BITE OF THE NIGHT

Characters

MACLUBY	a soap boiler
CREUSA	a woman of Troy
SAVAGE	a scholar
BOY	his son
OLD MAN	his parent
HOGBIN	his pupil
HELEN	a defector
FLADDER	her husband, King of the Greeks
GUMMERY	a soldier
EPSOM	a soldier
SHADE	a soldier
A BOY	of Troy
GAY	a daughter of Helen
HOMER	a poet
BOY	son of Savage (adult)
ASAFIR	a Truce official
JOHN	their servant
CHARITY	daughter of Gay
SCHLIEMANN	an archaeologist
YORAKIM	a labourer
ASAFIR	a labourer
OFFICERS	
YOUTHS	
PUBLIC	

First Prologue

MACLUBY: They brought a woman from the street
And made her sit in the stalls
By threats
By bribes
By flattery
Obliging her to share a little of her life with actors

But I don't understand art

Sit still, they said

But I don't want to see sad things

Sit still, they said

And she listened to everything
Understanding some things
But not others
Laughing rarely, and always without knowing why
Sometimes suffering in disgust
Sometimes thoroughly amazed
And in the light again said

If that's art I think it is hard work
It was beyond me
So much of it beyond my actual life

But something troubled her
Something gnawed her peace
And she came a second time, armoured with friends

Sit still, she said

And again, she listened to everything
This time understanding different things

This time untroubled that some things
Could not be understood
Laughing rarely but now without shame
Sometimes suffering disgust
Sometimes thoroughly amazed
And in the light again said

That is art, it is hard work

And one friend said, too hard for me
And the other said if you will
I will come again

Because I found it hard I felt honoured

Second Prologue

IT IS NOT TRUE THAT EVERYONE WANTS TO
BE
ENTERTAINED
SOME WANT THE PAIN OF UNKNOWING
Shh
Shh
Shh
The ecstasy of not knowing for once
The sheer suspension of not knowing
Shh
Shh
Shh
Three students in a smoke-filled room
Three girls on holiday
A pregnancy on a Saturday night
I knew that
I knew that
I ALREADY KNEW THAT

The marriage which was hardly
The socialist who wasn't
The American with the plague
I knew that
I knew that
I ALREADY KNEW THAT

We can go home now
Oh, car seat kiss my arse
We can go home now
Oh, underground upholstery
Caress my buttock
I loved that play it was so true
Take your skirt off
I loved that play it was so
Take your skirt off
What are theatres for

TAKE YOUR SKIRT OFF

THIS HAS TO BE THE AGE FOR MORE MUSICALS
Declares the manager
The people are depressed

THIS HAS TO BE THE AGE FOR MORE MUSICALS
Declares the careerist
Who thinks the tilted face is power
Who believes humming is believing

No
The problems are different
They are
They really are
I say this with all the circumspection
A brute can muster

I ask you
Hatred apart
Abuse apart
Boredom in abeyance
Politics in the cupboard
Anger in the drawer
Should we not

I KNOW IT'S IMPOSSIBLE BUT YOU STILL TRY

Not reach down beyond the known for once

I'll take you
I'll hold your throat
I will
And vomit I will tolerate
Over my shirt
Over my wrists
Your bile
Your juices
I'll be your guide

And whistler in the dark
Cougher over filthy words
And all known sentiments recycled for this house

CLARITY
MEANING
LOGIC
AND CONSISTENCY

None of it
None

I honour you too much
To paste you with what you already know so

Beyond the slums of England
Tower blocks floating on ponds of urine
Like the lighthouse on its bed of mercury

Beyond the screams of women fouled
Who have lost sight and sense of all desire

And grinning classes of male satirists
Beyond
The witty deconstruction of the literary myth
And individuals in the web of class

NO IDEOLOGY ON THE CHEAP
NO IDEOLOGY ON THE CHEAP

You think a thing repeated three times is a truth
You think to sing along is solidarity

NO IDEOLOGY ON THE CHEAP

Apologies
Old spasms
Apologies
Old temper
Apologies
Apologies

I charm you
Like the Viennese professor in the desert
Of America
My smile is a crack of pain
Like the exiled pianist in the tart's embrace
My worn fingers reach for your place
Efficiently

IT'S AN OBLIGATION…!

Act One

SCENE ONE

The ruins of a University.

CREAUSA: Lost in Troy. *(Pause.)* Listen, getting lost. *(Pause.)* That also is an infidelity *(Pause.)* I walked behind. Wife bearing the food. The flask. The diapers. Wife under the bundle. The clock. The colander. The old man's vests. Through flaming alleys by clots of rapists whose glistening arses caught the light. The chess set and the fruit cake. Wives under the soldiers. The flannel and the toothbrushes *(Pause.)*
Turks in Smyrna
Romans in Carthage
Scots in Calais
Swedes in Dresden
Goths in Buda
Japs in Nanking
Russians in Brandenburg

Unbelted and unbuttoned they thrust their arms into the well of skirt

I did prefer
I did
To continuing this marriage in another place
Prefer to get lost
The gutters bubbling with semen notwithstanding
The spontaneous stabblings of intoxicated looters notwithstanding
I slipped down Trader's Avenue and hid
AND HE CAME BACK
I will say this
I will give credit where it's

He did
He did come back
A dozen paces boy in hand and dad on back
His eyes shouted
His mouth hung speechless as a ripped sheet
I could have
I wanted to
That grey and never happy face

CREU-SA!

Once my name heaved out his gob and stuck to falling arches
Once
His last call
Only once
It drifted down with burning papers
It sailed on draughts like embers of old Frocks
And turned away
Triangle of males
The three degrees of man

I vomited my shame into the shop
On all smashed things I added pounds of self disgust
And wiping on a dead man's curtain stood up frail
But light

Widowhood is grief but also chance
And falls of cities both finishes and starts

SCENE TWO

A MAN and A CHILD.

SAVAGE: I WILL END UP KILLING YOU.

BOY: Yes.

SAVAGE: I think we know that, don't we? I will end up killing you?

BOY: Yes.

SAVAGE: And burying you in the coke. Under the power station floor. Or sling you in a rusty truck…

BOY: Yes.

SAVAGE: One eye hanging from some almighty blow. WE DO KNOW THAT, DON'T WE?

BOY: Yes.

SAVAGE: *(Sits.)* Through no fault of your own…

BOY: Not really, no…

SAVAGE: My character being what it is. And the times being what they are. The state of the world and my temper. I think murdering you is inevitable. Kiss me. *(THE BOY kisses him.)*

BOY: You have to have freedom

SAVAGE: I must have it. I am forty and I must have it.

BOY: Everything's against you.

SAVAGE: Every fucking thing.

BOY: And I'm a constant irritation.

SAVAGE: Not constant.

BOY: Not constant, but an irritation.

SAVAGE: Children are.

BOY: We are, and then there's grandad. We're both an irritation and we are obviously holding up freedom.

SAVAGE: Yes…

BOY: You're forty and freedom's like a muscle, if it isn't used it at-it at –

SAVAGE: Shut up.

BOY: It atrophies –

SAVAGE: SHUT UP. *(Pause.)* Kiss me. Kiss me! *(THE BOY kisses him. An OLD MAN enters with a pot.)*

OLD MAN: Done the potatoes.

BOY: What does atrophy mean?

OLD MAN: Done the potatoes.

SAVAGE: Oh, the gnawed bone of my mind…the bloody, gnawed bone of my mind… *(Pause. They look at him.)* Dirty butcher's bone in the gutter no dog would stoop to lick… *(Pause.)*

BOY: You always say that.

SAVAGE: I do. I do say that

BOY: You put your hands to your head and you say the gnawed bone of my mind…

SAVAGE: Yes…

BOY: What's the matter with it?

OLD MAN: Lucky to find potatoes… *(He goes off.)*

SAVAGE: I woke in the night. I woke in the night and the sky was purple with the bruise of cities. I thought of avenues where they sleep the sleep of family love, the pillowcase, the nightdress, the twitching of the poodle. YOU CALL THAT LIFE?

BOY: Call that life?

SAVAGE: The dozing daughter in the dormitory town has tossed off the eiderdown. Down it goes, hiss to the nylon carpet and piles like warm shit from the sphincter of the dog. YOU CALL THAT LIFE?

BOY: Call that life?

SAVAGE: Every dead clerk is a slab on the causeway to liberty.

BOY: Down with the clerks! Down with the documents!

SAVAGE: I taught Homer here… *(HOGBIN enters.)*

HOGBIN: Sorry I'm late. *(Pause.)* Am I late? *(Pause.)* Am I sorry? *(He sits.)* I had an excuse, and then I thought, he does not care if I have an excuse or not. I thought in fact, if I do not appear he will not notice, so I would only demean myself by inventing an excuse in the first place. Why appear at all, in fact? HOMERIC FUCKING GREECE, WHAT DOES THAT SAY TO ME? Sitting on the bus this was, at the back eye-deep in soup of fags and women's underwear. HOMERIC FUCKING GREECE?

SAVAGE: You barren filth.

HOGBIN: Now, then…

SAVAGE: You ephemeral spewing of suburban couplings.

HOGBIN: Of course I am ephemeral. So are we all.

SAVAGE: Abuse and more abuse.

HOGBIN: *Merci.* I didn't do the essay. But here's the notes.

SAVAGE: The notes?

BOY: He doesn't want your notes!

HOGBIN: I heard the reggae through the wall. The beat bored into me. I looked at Homer. Dead letters swum before my eyes. Old Europe struggling with the beat. The beat! The fucking beat! GIVE US KNOWLEDGE, DOCTOR SAVAGE! *(Pause.)*

SAVAGE: The Trojan War. *(Pause.)* The Trojan war occurred because a married woman lent her body to a stranger. *(Pause.)* That's all for today. *(Pause.)*

HOGBIN: I knew that.

SAVAGE: Excellent.

HOGBIN: I KNEW THAT, GIT.

SAVAGE: You read it. You did not know it. Knowledge is belief. *(He gets up to go.)*

HOGBIN: DON'T GET UP. *(Pause.)* The seduction of Helen. The seduction of Helen is a metaphor for the commercial success of the tribes of Asia minor and the subsequent collapse of the Peloponnesian carrying trade. Only a military alliance of the Greek states restored the monopoly. In classical fashion the outcome of trade wars is the enslavement of populations in the interests of cost-free labour and the eradication of the infrastructure of the rival enterprise, namely the razing of cities. *(Pause.)*

SAVAGE: No. It was cunt.

HOGBIN: Cunt's the metaphor, trade's the –

SAVAGE: HELEN'S CUNT. *(Pause.)*

SAVAGE: That's it for today, Mr. Hogbin. *(Pause.)*

HOGBIN: I hate my father. He is a big-bollocked snob who walks the streets in shorts and stares at women. Intellectuals he calls bums. Bums, he calls them. He has foreign holidays and speaks American. What does bums mean? Bums means arses but I think he means tramps. GIVE US YOUR INTUITIONS AND STUFF THE FACTS. *(Pause. He gets up.)* Cunt, was it… *(He goes out. MACLUBY enters, looks at SAVAGE, describes:)*

MACLUBY: Been crouching here since the final tutorial. The door shut and they left. Down slid the timetable with the rust. The tinkling of drawing pins, the descent of postcards. Then the lampshade crashed. The splintering of fluorescent lances in cracked corridors. The mole's disdain of plastic tiles. And then the landscape yawned, and chalk breathed out, undoing the keystone of the library arch. WE ALL HEARD THE LIBRARY CRASH.

SAVAGE: I heard it.

BOY: I heard it! Books blew everywhere!

MACLUBY: And you stayed put. While demolition cowboys ripped the wiring out.

SAVAGE: KNOWLEDGE!

MACLUBY: While they smashed the basins kept your seat.

SAVAGE: KNOWLEDGE!

MACLUBY: Their curses, their pornographic sentiments.

SAVAGE: KNOWLEDGE!

MACLUBY: The clatter of their arid minds and mundane politics.

SAVAGE: *(Pause.)* It was a paper overcoat against their spit… *(THE BOY holds SAVAGE.)* I lost his mother. She could not stomach me. My whine and bite. My sitting in the edge of the chair. PUT YOUR ARSE BACK IN THE CHAIR! I could not. My whine and bite…

MACLUBY: Give us the kid. *(Pause.)*

SAVAGE: Give you the –

MACLUBY: Give us him, why don't you? *(Pause.)*

SAVAGE: Who are –

MACLUBY: Harry Macluby. Soap boiler.

SAVAGE: Soap boiler?

MACLUBY: Well, do you want him or not? *(Pause.)* On your sick bed, writhing like a worm on baking bricks, shouting the whole length of the ward, I DID NOTHING WITH MY LIFE,

BECAUSE OF THEM, THEY WEIGHED ON ME. Your cry of misery would lift the gutters off the hospital… *(Pause.)*

SAVAGE: SOAP BOILER?

MACLUBY: Ashes of Roses. *(Pause.)*

SAVAGE: My mother ditched me also…

MACLUBY: There you go…

SAVAGE: A poor boy will find his benefactress…

MACLUBY: Inevitably, and what use are you?

SAVAGE: No use…

MACLUBY: All your kisses papered over hate…

SAVAGE: I DRINK HIS FONDNESS AND RESENT HIS LIFE.

MACLUBY: You know, you see, you do know…

SAVAGE: Love of children, what is it? Self-love. The clinging of a desperate mortality. You have to understand the feeling. Not just feel the feeling or you are a mollusc. What are you, a murderer?

MACLUBY: Silly.

SAVAGE: And in five years he will not lend me one stale breath…

MACLUBY: It's so, it is…

SAVAGE: *(To THE BOY.)* THIS MAN WANTS YOU.

BOY: Wants me?

SAVAGE: He says.

BOY: What for?

SAVAGE: Apprenticeship in the soap trade.

BOY: Soap?

SAVAGE: SOAP, YES, SOAP! *(Pause.)* Get your things. *(Pause.)*

BOY: I think, in spite of everything, although you will probably murder me, I would prefer to stay with –

SAVAGE: Toothbrush. Flannel. And clean pants.

BOY: Rather die from you bashing me in one of your fits than –

SAVAGE: Pyjamas if you've got some –

BOY: LIVE WITH ANYBODY ELSE. *(Pause. SAVAGE refuses to look at him.)* I LOVE YOU.

SAVAGE: Love, he says. That word. Emaciated syllable. *(He looks at him.)* Replace the word love with another. And you will see how thin it is.

BOY: There is no other.

SAVAGE: MOLLUSC!

BOY: You are always calling me a mollusc…

SAVAGE: Yes… *(Pause.)*

BOY: You are so unhappy. And I can't help… *(Pause, then THE BOY goes off.)*

SAVAGE: You see, how I have become his child, and he is burdened with me. I make him suffer for me. *(He looks at MACLUBY.)* Teach him Ashes of Roses. The man who can smother mortality in scent, or wash blood off the hands of killers will not lack for friends. *(THE OLD MAN enters with a plate of dinner. He looks at SAVAGE, pitying him.)*

OLD MAN: *(To MACLUBY.)* I said to him, travel. Travel the world, go on.

MACLUBY: He hates the world…

OLD MAN: The merchant navy, for example. See things while you have the power.

MACLUBY: The Taj Mahal. The pyramids…

OLD MAN: The Taj Mahal. The pyramids…

SAVAGE: The truth is not all in that junk, you –

MACLUBY: Old Moscow's onion domes… *(THE BOY returns, with a small bag. He stands waiting. SAVAGE looks at him, suddenly weeps. THE BOY goes to touch him.)*

SAVAGE: No…! *(Pause, then MACLUBY leads the way and THE BOY follows. Pause.)*

OLD MAN: Football, is it? *(He puts the plate down, starts to go.)*

SAVAGE: I owe you nothing, do I? *(He stops.)* Because you grated on my mother, what's the debt?

OLD MAN: No debt, son.

SAVAGE: And because one not-so-very-mad night I squirmed against his mother, to the ticking of the wedding present and the clatter of the drunkards in the sick-swamped street, so setting in motion the torture of paternity, I OWE NO DEBT, ME NEITHER, DO I? *(Pause.)* Argue. Argue for your rights to me.

OLD MAN: No rights.

SAVAGE: No rights… *(THE OLD MAN turns to leave again.)* And what is intimacy anyway?

OLD MAN: Search me…

SAVAGE: I clung to her and it was two pebbles clashing. *(THE OLD MAN looks.)* When I was in her, hard against her womb, some razor slashed my head, some miniature blade designed to kill conception YOU DON'T EXPECT TO FIND KNIVES IN THERE OF ALL PLACES. Anyway, it failed, and he was born…

OLD MAN: *(Nodding after THE BOY.)* Football today, is it? *(A hiatus of pity.)* Did I ever thank you for the books?

SAVAGE: Books?

OLD MAN: On Homeric metre. By Dr. Savage of the University. To My Father on that great big empty page.

SAVAGE: Christ knows why I –

OLD MAN: An introduction to the Iliad. In Memory of my Mother.

SAVAGE: Barmy reflex of a clever son –

OLD MAN: No, I –

SAVAGE: DON'T LICK FEELING OFF THAT LINE OF ARID PRINT. *(Pause.)*

OLD MAN: Wha'? *(Pause.)*

SAVAGE: The binding was so poor the leaves fell out. As if they were ashamed to hang with such a dedication –

OLD MAN: Wha'?

SAVAGE: THE SENTIMENTAL LIAR I HAVE BEEN.

OLD MAN: Kind thought I thought…

SAVAGE: Kind thought? I hated you. Your mundane opinions. Your repetition of half-truths. Straddling my back. You burden. You dead weight. HE'S GONE SO WHY DON'T YOU. *(THE OLD MAN turns.)* No one is here for long. Who knows, some death might be already on me. Some growth in the dark, deep wet. Give us some time for my own needs. Old bones. Old pelt. *(THE OLD MAN withdraws some yards behind SAVAGE, and sits.)* We can have knowledge, but not in passivity. Knowledge exists, but the path is strewn with obstacles. *(THE OLD MAN breaks the plate.)*

These obstacles we ourselves erect. *(He takes a shard.)* The conspiracy of the ignorant against the visionary can be broken only by the ruthless intellect. *(He undoes his vest.)* Pity also is a regime. *(He attempts to cut his throat.)* And consideration a manacle.

OLD MAN: Trying…

SAVAGE: Manners –

OLD MAN: Trying…

SAVAGE: Loyalty –

OLD MAN: Trying, fuck it –

SAVAGE: Responsibility, IRON BANDS ON THE BRAIN. *(HOGBIN enters with a book.)*

HOGBIN: Helen was a whore in any case, it says – *(He sees THE OLD MAN.)* Oi.

SAVAGE: KNOWLEDGE IS BEYOND KINDNESS YOU KNOW –

HOGBIN: OI!

SAVAGE: Shut up… *(THE OLD MAN succeeds, gurgles.)*

HOGBIN: Hey! Fucking hey!

SAVAGE: I know. I know he is. *(HOGBIN stares at him. THE OLD MAN dies. SAVAGE suddenly seizes HOGBIN, in a horrified embrace.)* KISS ME, THEN! MY TRIUMPH! KISS ME, THEN!

HOGBIN: Oh, fucking –

SAVAGE: KISS ME!

HOGBIN: Oh, bloody 'ell –

SAVAGE: MY LIBERTY! MY APPALLING LIBERTY!

HOGBIN: *(Tearing from his embrace.)* Oh, shit and shit –

SAVAGE: Don't leave me.

HOGBIN: HE – LP

SAVAGE: *(Grasping him tightly.)* Did it…did it…did it… *(They rock to and fro. Pause.)*

HOGBIN: Blood's tickling my toes…warm tickle… old man's contents…old man's drain… *(He shudders.)*

OLD MAN: We left the lorry on the road, looking for crashed bombers on the scarp, sun in, sun out, behind these towering clouds and dark drenches of rain, I was alone and saw the tailplane in a smudge of trees, or wing was it, with roundels of the R.A.F., and my boots went swish towards it, swish through downland flowers while the wind creaked faintly in the beached boughs of the thorny trees, alone and hot, smell of tunic, smell of blanco, swish went the poppy heads, alone and hot UP SHOT LIKE RABBITS FROM A DIP TWO NAKED ARSES brown as polish, gipsies fucking to the rhythm of that wing in scattered tracer belts and navigation clocks, swish the pelting of their feet, leaving her arse print in the turf, her shoulder blades were printed in the turf until with little jerks the grass stood up again. *(Pause.)*

SAVAGE: The death of my father necessitates the cancellation of our next tutorial.

HOGBIN: For grief, is that?

SAVAGE: Grief, yes.

HOGBIN: The socialized consequence of death is naturally bereavement but under grief the individual might conceal some inexplicable delight. *(Pause.)* I pose the question only –

SAVAGE: I SAID YOU HUNGRY ADOLESCENT NO TUTORIAL.

HOGBIN: Not a tutorial, no, but –

SAVAGE: My old man's dead, whose dry hand was the only proof of goodness I knew yet, I carried him through Troy! *(Pause.)* 'To think my boy taught brilliance here', he said, to reprimand the red-backed bastards ripping off the roof. He never read books but still he hated televisions, he chucked them out the windows of the flats, some instinct he had for shattering mendacity, the incorruptible old sod...

HOGBIN: The spontaneity of violence is surely the formal resistance of the proletariat to –

SAVAGE: WON'T TEACH. *(He goes to arrange THE OLD MAN.)*

HOGBIN: Give us yer handkerchief... *(SAVAGE gives him a rag. He wipes the blood from his feet.)*

SAVAGE: I'm sorry I was born, and sorry I was cured, sorry I fell in love, and sorry I was married, sorry and sorry again for every choice I –

HOGBIN: *(Wiping himself.)* Yeah, but was it a choice? You presuppose the possibility of refusals –

SAVAGE: Oh, you arid youth, I think the young are barren as a shaft of concrete in the Sahara sun.

HOGBIN: Bollocks, you rhetorical shitter –

SAVAGE: WISDOM, not cleverness. KNOWLEDGE, not retorts. TRUTH, not wit. One bit of truth felt in the veins!

HOGBIN: You are a pile of metred drivel, why I sit here fuck knows, when –

SAVAGE: One truth! One truth! NOT A LOT TO ASK IS IT!

HOGBIN: Read Buka on the nature of hyperbole, it's 'ere somewhere – *(He pulls filthy pages from a pocket. SAVAGE kicks it across the floor.)*

SAVAGE: GOT TO SUFFER!

HOGBIN: *(Gathering the precious pages.)* You are a plastic bag of urine –

SAVAGE: SUFFER, YOUTH!

HOGBIN: Tossed against a corrugated fence – there, now I'm doin' it. *(MACLUBY appears. Pause.)*

MACLUBY: I gave the boy a ball. His eyes went big. He's nine and he can't catch.

SAVAGE: I hate balls. The ball returns the idea after every revolution. No effort, no struggle of the intellect. Give him a polygon to kick. *(MACLUBY turns to go.)* A FATHER ALSO LOVES BUT THROUGH A GRATING. Tell him that…

SCENE THREE

HELEN with A HUSBAND, seated.

HELEN: I'm back. *(Pause.)* My arse in the marital chair. *(Pause.)* My piss in the marital pan. *(Pause.)* WELL, BE DELIGHTED. *(Pause.)* You ache to touch me, but you won't. And silence is your knife. Twist away! *(Pause.)* Troy was full of intellectuals. I saw their corpses. Their corpses hung on wires. DO HIT ME IF YOU WANT TO, OTHERS DID. *(Pause.)* And all of them kept diaries, always their diaries in a miniature hand like lice had crept through inkwells. ANY PALTRY THOUGHT THEY DEEMED IMMORTAL. Fevered note-takers and every scrap was burned by troops, every leaf! *(Pause.)* The comedy of history. *(Pause.)* BURST MY FACE OR I SHALL GO ON TALKING. *(Pause.)* I saw one on his knees to drunken squaddies who said not SPARE MY LIFE, not like the shopkeeper who offered them his wife to whip to pulp, but I BEG YOU SMUGGLE OUT THIS BOOK. I saw the thing kicked down a gutter, the pages bound in fat and sweat, the banality, the futility! I AM PHILISTINE AND LOVELESS... *(Pause.)*

FLADDER: Helen fucks the wounded in the wards, they said. *(Pause.)* Which aroused me. SHAMEFULLY. *(Pause.)* Or dogs, some ventured to suggest. Which aroused me. SHAMEFULLY. *(Pause.)* The filthy infantry. The long lick of their dreams. *(Pause.)* I crept to the canvas in the dew, sodden and erect, to eavesdrop what malpractice their knotted maleness would inflict on you. *(Pause.)* Our suffering. Our ecstasy. *(SOLDIERS enter, with CREUSA.)*

GUMMERY: Every light bulb. Every cage bird.

SADE/EPSOM: PULVER!

GUMMERY: Pity was our banner, as you wrote in final orders. So the tarts we spared...

EPSOM: And infants, if they did not cry too loud.

GUMMERY: Troy's gone. Nothing to block the wind off Asia now. ARSEHOLES TO THIS BITCH. I must say that. *(He bows to HELEN.)* Your servant, etcetera.

SHADE: Ten years goes by in a flash...

EPSOM: That final bugle made my heart sink. I never smelled depression like it, even in defeat. It hung over the trenches like a fog, and the champagne corks were miserable squibs. No one could work up any speeches, we drifted past old weapon pits and put out our lips against the hinges of burnt tanks. Go home? My wife is fucking with the priest, I had it from my brother. What did he think, I'd put a pistol in my gob and make him heir to seven dirty acres? Not that I blame him. Nor the priest, him neither. I blame no one.

ARSEHOLES TO THIS BITCH, HOWEVER. *(He bows to HELEN.)* I must say that. *(He sits on the floor.)*

CREUSA: *(Looking at her.)* Helen…!

FLADDER: *(Pause.)* The word. *(Pause.)* HELEN. *(Pause.)* The idea. *(Pause.)* HELEN. *(Pause.)*

CREUSA: Alive!

FLADDER: She stinks like a horse. I say this, I announce this, I announce this because the idea has got around she is ethereal. No, I assure you it is not the case. I know she stood naked on the battlements in the seventh year –

GUMMERY: The eighth –

FLADDER: The eighth year, was it, stood naked and the wind sneaked round her parts, the cool wind out the Caucasus, fresh with snow and hibiscus, but still she had the odour of the mare, why did you do that? The army laughed, seeing you less than perfect. Seeing your body rather flawed. Of course they knew sex is not in the proportions, but still they laughed, calling the cooks out of their tents, staring and jabbering, why did she do that? *(Pause.)*

CREUSA: I've been passed round a bit myself…not bad…not the worst thing in the world, to have no choice. *(Pause.)* Not the worst thing.

EPSOM: *(Nudging his neighbour.)* Oi…

CREUSA: The worst thing is –

GUMMERY: *(Indicating FLADDER, who weeps.)* Oi…

CREUSA: To imagine choice exists… *(Two of the soldiers go to FLADDER placing their hand on his shoulders.)*

HELEN: Oh, the solidarity of weeping men… *(HOGBIN enters, stops.)*

HOGBIN: Europe's a mess… *(They look at him.)* I say the only ideology is total scepticism…That's not an ideology, he says. *(He looks them over.)* What's this..? *(They examine him.)* This is a university, so point yer firearms downwards, there's a love… *(They make no move.)* What's this…? *(Pause. He is undeterred.)* Ruins or not, it's still a seat of learning and so is any place where questions are still asked. Balls to chancellors and piss on economics. THE TROJANS DID NOT SCATTER, why should we? Some remained, he says so, fat guts says they fucked their conquerors, MESSAGE FOR THE OPPRESSED! *(SAVAGE enters. HOGBIN bows mockingly.)* The wobbling residue of culture! *(He rises.)* He imitates the amoeba, which cannot be squashed by jeeps.

HELEN: I know him.

HOGBIN: She knows you…!

HELEN: Staggering through courtyards under books. Boiled in your sweat. A stew of anger and unhealthy fat…

HOGBIN: She knows you…!

HELEN: And looking along the wires of dangling intellects I thought, the fat one has escaped my husband's spite…

SAVAGE: Eventually the camps will shut, and rusty execution sheds fall down in gales, and guards retire to plants begonias. ALL FORGOTTEN! *(Pause.)* But one still excavates the files, plucks memoirs out of bonfires, and keeps testimony safe in his archival head… *(EPSOM moves to threaten SAVAGE, who shrinks to the frowns.)* Don't spill the head! *(EPSOM stops, bemused.)* It contains the agony of others, like a cup… *(He looks up.)* You are Helen of Troy… *(She weeps suddenly, cradling him in her arms.)*

HELEN: Yes…and now…obscurity…! *(Pause. SHADE picks up his kit.)*

SHADE: Home, James…!

FLADDER: Home?

SHADE: Bands playing on the quay. And similar shit. Flags in babies' gobs. And similar shit. *(To CREUSA.)* Carry my loot, you!

FLADDER: This is home.

SHADE: Wha'?

FLADDER: Where so much hate has concentrated, that must be home also.

SHADE: *(To CREUSA.)* Mind my mirror!

GUMMERY: IT'S HOME HE SAYS. *(SHADE stops.)*

SHADE: Wha'? *(Pause.)*

GUMMERY: I never knew a Trojan, nor heard of Troy. And yet, no sooner had my boot touched Trojan pebble but –

FLADDER: You hated.

GUMMERY: Just like that. Peculiar.

SAVAGE: Not peculiar. *(Pause. They look at him.)*

HOGBIN: Careful, clever…

SAVAGE: May I speak?

HOGBIN: CARE – FUL…! *(Pause.)*

SAVAGE: The war was already in you. Do you think hatred has no life? It's born with you. It howls in your first howl. Impatient loathing coiled behind your tongue which on the pretext ROLLED OUT LIKE A PYTHON, a hundred feet of scales… *(Pause.)* The kind man racks his mind how thousands might grapple in the mud for a single woman. The disbelief! Or the lout stab the pensioner's eyes! The kind man should stare down his own throat… *(Pause.)*

SHADE: *(In realisation.)* Whad' yer mean, this is his home?

FLADDER: *(Leaping up.)* Nobody goes!

SHADE: Fuck that –

FLADDER: GENDARMES! *(GUMMERY goes to grab the mirror from CREUSA.)*

SHADE: MY MIRROR!

FLADDER: Home the lie, home the sentiment!

SHADE: *(Grabbing one end of the mirror.)* My mirror!

FLADDER: The knife under the pillow, the long, cold marital stare…

EPSOM: *(Wading in.)* STUFF IT, BARRY! *(GENDARMES rush in, pin back SHADE's arms. A breathless pause.)*

FLADDER: Home? What's that? The dead eye of the widow who finds she is no widow? The child's sullen resignation of its place? HOME WHAT'S THAT. *(Pause.)* Go, if you wish. *(THE GENDARMES release him. SHADE goes to take the mirror from GUMMERY.)* No mirror. *(He stops.)*

SHADE: No mirror? *(He looks about him.)* I SUFFERED FOR THAT MIRROR. IT'S MY PRIZE! *(Pause.)*

FLADDER: The ship goes hooooooo… *(Pause.)* The ship goes hoooooooo… *(Pause, then SHADE dumps to the ground. GUMMERY returns the mirror.)*

HELEN: First Troy is under the ashes. Second Troy now. *(She goes to leave.)*

GUMMERY: Second Troy? Of what, lady? Paper?

FLADDER: Paper, yes. Paper Troy now! No more weapons! No more walls! Write everywhere our shame! *(HELEN goes out and FLADDER rises.)* CONSTITUTION WRITERS! *(To SAVAGE.)* How's your spelling?

SAVAGE: Adequate.

FLADDER: Spell agony.

SAVAGE: H – E – L – E

FLADDER: You'll do! *(He sweeps out, followed by GUMMERY and EPSOM. CREUSA remains, staring at SAVAGE. Pause.)*

CREUSA: So there you are…

SAVAGE: Don't start –

CREUSA: There you fucking are –

SAVAGE: DON'T START I SAID –

CREUSA: THE IMAGINATION, THE INTELLECT –

SAVAGE: The rattle of your mundane prejudice and –

CREUSA: BARMY NOTIONS –

SAVAGE: DOMESTIC TRIVIALITY YOU –

CREUSA: POSTURING AS VISIONS YOU –

SAVAGE: MICROSCOPIC OBSESSIONIST!

CREUSA: SNOB! *(A pause of exhaustion.)*

SHADE: It's mine, now. *(He indicates CREUSA with a nod.)*

SAVAGE: Yes.

SHADE: The arse. The cry. The dream. Mine. *(Pause.)*

SAVAGE: Yes. *(CREUSA looks at SAVAGE, pitifully.)*

CREUSA: Oh, you mad and forlorn bastard…I couldn't take any more of you! *(Wearily, she takes the mirror and bundle from SHADE and goes off. SHADE looks a long time into SAVAGE.)*

SHADE: I also have a mind. *(SAVAGE turns to look at him.)*

SAVAGE: You –

SHADE: I also have a mind. *(Pause.)* I don't exhibit it, like a balloon. THE MIND. *(Pause.)* I don't wag it.

SAVAGE: No…

SHADE: But it exists. And it has archways, upon archways. And cisterns, and reservoirs also. Fuckall books and fuckall songs but. And anyway, what are those things? They are daggers, also. SONG IN THE EYES! *(He feints at SAVAGE and goes off, watched by HOGBIN.)*

HOGBIN: *(Fearfully.)* Get out of 'ere…

SAVAGE: Why?

HOGBIN: This crew. This regiment. 'alf off their 'inges, gates swinging in the 'urricane, MIND YER GOB!

SAVAGE: Why?

HOGBIN: MAD GATES BANGING!

SAVAGE: GO WHERE ANYWAY? *(Pause.)* Go, he says… the spontaneous retort if things degenerate… nomadic instinct of the urban boy…what are you, a sparrow, off at the first pin drop? A rabbit, pelting at the shadow of the cloud? Nomads have no written culture, you know that…

HOGBIN: Fuck your comprehensiveness…

SAVAGE: NO KNOWLEDGE ON THE HOOF.

HOGBIN: Yes, but this – *(Pause.)*

SAVAGE: To go beyond. That's our hunger, that's our thirst. To go beyond, you must stand still. FIRST PARADOX OF ALL GREAT JOURNEYS.

(He opens his arms.) Kiss me, I have told you something.

HOGBIN: You always wanna be kissed –

SAVAGE: DO IT OUT OF GRATITUDE! *(HOGBIN pecks him.)*

HOGBIN: Who was that, your Mrs who got lost? I think you shoved your cold chisel in 'er cracks and drove a decent woman barmy. Did you? But I think she's kind, as all blasphemers are…

SCENE FOUR

A tumult of paper. Men folding. HOGBIN on his knees, copying. HELEN enters with A DAUGHTER.

HELEN: WILL WHOEVER BRINGS DEAD MEN'S RIBS AND THINGS INTO MY BEDROOM STOP!

FLADDER: *(Entering.)* Second Troy has paper walls because they offer no defence. All the energies of the inhabitants will be directed towards the examination of our errors. Write reconciliation everywhere, and artists, if there are any, stick pictures on it!

HELEN: It is an offence to tamper with war graves in any case, who is doing it, do you know…?

HOGBIN: Not the foggiest…

HELEN: Someone is, I'm not imagining it.

FLADDER: WHERE'S SAVAGE? HAS HE MADE THE LOVING CONSTITUTION YET?

HELEN: A bit of thigh, or skull with weird red hair on it? Perhaps the dogs do it?

HOGBIN: Maybe dogs…

HELEN: No shortage of dogs in Second Troy.

HOGBIN: Dogs all over the shop…

HELEN: No, it isn't dogs, it's men. A CORPSE IN THE BED WILL BE NEXT. *(SAVAGE enters.)*

SAVAGE: The Seven Principles of New Troy.

FLADDER: Seven is it...good...

SAVAGE: The poor will apologize. The rich will forgive. The thief will be compensated. The victim accused.

FLADDER: Of what?

SAVAGE: Tempting the thief.

FLADDER: Good.

SAVAGE: All governors will swim rivers at seventy.

FLADDER: Why?

SAVAGE: To prove their minds are still good.

FLADDER: Yes...

SAVAGE: The sick will dictate morality. The healthy will never be paid.

FLADDER: They have health.

SAVAGE: They have health, yes. The intellectual will be revered until he speaks. The passionate will be in receipt of pension books. *(Pause.)*

FLADDER: That's eight, surely? *(SAVAGE bows.)*

HELEN: When I was fourteen I could tell jokes. And men said, you tell jokes better than a man!

GUMMERY: I don't call that a constitution...

HELEN: But for all their laughing, not one of them would lay a hand on me. Not one!

GUMMERY: Do you Les?

HELEN: So I stopped telling jokes. And they were all over me! Breaking one another's jaws, and scrapping in the gutter.

GUMMERY: *(To SAVAGE.)* I DON'T CALL THAT A CONSTITUTION.

HELEN: There is a time for jokes, but it's not now.

SAVAGE: *(To GUMMERY.)* Nail it to the doors, and all the citizens of Paper Troy will be outraged and stamp their feet, and go around shouting 'Never!' *(Pause.)* Which is good, and the proper condition for a populace to be in.

FLADDER: PAINT IT. THE SEVEN PRINCIPLES OF PAPER TROY.

ESPOM: *(To WORKERS off.)* PAINTS!

GUMMERY: *(Confused.)* Seven? You said eight…

FLADDER: Seven, yes! *(To SAVAGE.)* You see, they gawp at your magnificence… *(GUMMERY stares at the paper.)*

SAVAGE: *(Patiently, to GUMMERY.)* This gives you freedom…

GUMMERY: Freedom?

SAVAGE: To break the stranglehold of the consecutive. You can write seven twice. Or not number them at all.

GUMMERY: *(Shaking his head.)* Confusing…

SAVAGE: Yes!

GAY: My mother called me Gay. Do you know why? I don't know why, I'm sure. And I had a sister called FELICITY. What was that about? Felicity died, naturally, and of such a painful illness! But I am going to be gay. I am. *(HELEN leans fondly over her daughter.)* DON'T TOUCH ME WITH THOSE GNAWED AND KNEADED TITS. *(Pause. She smiles, kissing her mother fondly.)*

SAVAGE: Knowledge is a suite of rooms. Dirty rooms, unswept as museums in the provinces. And to enter each room you must leave with the woman at the door some priceless thing, which feels part of yourself and your identity, so that it feels like ripping skin. And the keepers sit in piles of discarded treasures, like the pelts of love or children's pity, and at each successive door the piles are less because few stagger such long distances, until there comes a door at which there lies a small, white rag stained as a dishcloth, which may be sanity. AND IF YOU THINK THAT IS THE END YOU ARE MISTAKEN, IT IS THE BEGINNING. *(Pause.)* And people say, 'I know myself'. Have you heard that? Never! They know the contents of one room. *(Pause.)*

FLADDER: But who'd want knowledge if knowledge meant I could simply look at her, and looking see only a hundred pounds of flesh, which by virtue of its shape defines her beautiful? If knowledge is to be so cool I'd say stuff knowledge WHAT DO YOU FIND HELEN, DR SAVAGE? SHE MADE ME THINK APPALLING THOUGHT. *(Pause.)* Lay down for my inspection every inch of you infatuation. *(Pause.)* What, no words, and you a teacher? *(Pause.)* You see, if she is not impossible to see without she wrecks our peace, what did we suffer for? IMAGINE THE TEMPER IN THE WAR CEMETERIES! *(Pause.)*

SAVAGE: All my life I have searched out Helen of Troy. And if you stuck a bin of offal there and called it Helen, I should have to stoop to it. *(The fraction of a pause.)*

FLADDER: BIN! *(He goes out.)*

SHADE: *(Calling off.)* A BIN!

HELEN: Oh, doctor, they will chain you to it and you will suffocate on stench for uttering one solid truth upon another… *(A bin is manoeuvred on.)*

CREUSA: *(Entering).* Oh God, what has he done?

HOGBIN: Been a silly bugger all over again – *(THE SOLDIERS chain SAVAGE to the bin by his wrists. GAY sits down on the floor.)*

GAY: The amount of killing I have seen! My father, for example, on the floor and skinned. Paris! Yes, it's true! They skinned him. And my grandfather was INSIDE OUT. I have seen the lot, I can assure you, and I thought to myself, Gay, they want you to go INSANE. So I decided there and then I would not. I DECLINED TO BE INSANE. *(Pause.)* I think Paper Troy won't last. And then what? Another pile of murders and a skinning or two! *(Pause.)* My mother gave birth to me with my father's thing in her gob I JUST KNOW IT. He took his clothes off while she contracted and lay beside her. I JUST KNOW HE DID THEY WERE LIKE THAT. So I've seen the lot, really, and am I insane? QUITE THE CONTRARY. *(She skips out.)*

HOGBIN: *(A crablike move to SAVAGE.)* Too fucking clever –

SAVAGE: Away you skinny newt –

HOGBIN: Night's coming in and storm clouds full of freezing rain –

SAVAGE: You book-snapping terrier –

HOGBIN: You will perish of exposure you unhealthy sod of fat –

SAVAGE: You whimpering abortion of a greyhound's toss –

HOGBIN: NOW, THEN, TRUTH-TELLER! *(He rolls about on the floor.)* No chains! *(He somersaults.)* No bin! *(He goes towards CREUSA, who has drawn a paper over herself. A storm rumbles. HOGBIN gets under with her. He pokes out his head.)* Adopt the nature of the chameleon. *(He withdraws. A ragged book flies out. Then HOGBIN's head.)* Borkman and Salberstein. *(He goes back in.)*

SAVAGE: Oh, rain on, oh, dark on, and gales roar up the beach like bombers levelling the streets. I know what Helen is, I know what Helen is! Another shell in the boiling breech! Oh, to be at sieges, at every siege that ever was, and throw in death from the hills, the breakfast goes, the kitchen goes, the crockery went up a hundred feet, the horse stood at the traffic lights and then down came its parted hooves, one in the garden of the spinster, one in the orphanage, I trawl, I dig, I excavate! Under your half-truths! The lecturer's voice is a whip. The vicar's lectern is a rack for thrashing youth! Who trusts the smiles on the library steps? Razor blades in the dictionary! I know! I know what Helen is! She's all that's unforgivable! *(FLADDER enters in an overcoat. He sits.)*

FLADDER: I like the night. I feel what in the day I must deny has every right to full consideration. Say you understand me. *(He looks at the paper tent.)* What is going on in the paper house?

SAVAGE: My student is struck dumb by the body of my wife and theoryless for once, explores her with his tongue. And she's another man's thing, by which he risks castration at the least. A real cocktail of pleasures, but you'd appreciate it, what's love without the risk of death?

FLADDER: *(Implacably.)* I wish to be tried, and if necessary, executed. *(Pause.)*

SAVAGE: *(Astutely.)* On no charges, presumably?

FLADDER: No charges.

SAVAGE: And the verdict?

FLADDER: Guilty. And I prosecute myself.

SAVAGE: So new Troy opens with the execution of the governor?

FLADDER: I'll demand the ultimate penalty.

SAVAGE: And I'll grant it. I take it I'm the magistrate?

FLADDER: Who else? Are you not the only criminal? *(He goes out.)*

SAVAGE: If every man is ashamed, and you are not ashamed. If every man is guilty, and you refuse guilt…WHAT THEN!

CREUSA: *(Emerging, adjusting her clothing.)* He says…*(A small, dry laugh.)* He says…I drive all anger from his mind…he says…listen to this…to see me naked kills his ambition…the peace, the peace, he says…

SAVAGE: Listen, I have –

CREUSA: NO, YOU LISTEN. *(Pause.)* He says incredible things no man ever said of me. But he's impotent as yet. UNDERSTANDABLE! If you put such store by one woman, to come erect at once would be no compliment, would it? I'm honoured by his crisis. *(She looks at herself, bemused.)* I've been through hell, but you were hell as well…what happened to our son? *(Pause.)* Oh, look, I ask as casually as one might for a book or newspaper! I had all the instincts but I learned to suffocate them in a bag, I don't threaten you with maternal rages, so where did he, you can tell…*(Pause.)*

SAVAGE: He. *(Pause.)*

CREUSA: It's me who broke the bond, and watched the three of you stagger out of my life, no claims and no reproaches, what's a child in any case, we stepped across whole ditchfuls, I remember... *(Pause.)*

SAVAGE: He. *(Pause.)*

CREUSA: The product of a joyless copulation, no I have no temper, boot the sentiment, boot the mother stuff, HE WHAT. *(Pause.)*

SAVAGE: Whatever you imagine is as likely as the truth. As painful, or as painless.

CREUSA: Still, I want to know, however futile –

SAVAGE: Dream it instead –

CREUSA: I do, I dream it often but –

SAVAGE: WHAT DIFFERENCE DOES IT MAKE.

CREUSA: IT MAKES A DIFFERENCE! *(Pause.)* Tell me, I'll swallow it. Down, like a single pill, gollop, and gone! Life continues, under Hogbin's fascinated stare or beaten by the Greeks, today it's rheumatism, tomorrow, plague, the sticky belt of crisis but first what happened to my son? *(Pause.)* The mundane bit of life I mundanely delivered... *(Pause.)*

SAVAGE: I don't know. I lost him. *(Pause.)*

CREUSA: Lost him...

SAVAGE: Lost him, yes...

CREUSA: Mislaid him...

SAVAGE: Mislaid him, yes, no, I lost him.

CREUSA: Lost him?

SAVAGE: LOST, YOU KNOW THE WORD, IT HAPPENED ALL OVER EUROPE. Drifting infants, in dead men's uniforms...

CREUSA: You –

SAVAGE: LOST MY CHILD AND HELPED MY FATHER DIE!

CREUSA: Oh, you –

SAVAGE: And not guilty!

CREUSA: You –

SAVAGE: NOT GUILTY, NO! *(She stares at him. Pause.)*

CREUSA: Hold my hand, you terrible mouth, biting the concrete, your gums all shredded and your lips all torn…terrible mouth on you… *(She hold his hands. HOGBIN emerges and looks. To HOGBIN, not turning.)* It's all right…these are old bruises we have to bruise again… *(She gets up, goes out.)*

HOGBIN: Funny, ain't it, any bastard can serve a woman properly but me. Any phlegm-stained criminal to do a violation of a child is rigid as a tree branch. Any dancing manikin dribbling on a deb gets seven inches on request. WHAT ABOUT ME!

SAVAGE: Patience…

HOGBIN: PATIENCE…!

SAVAGE: She is. *(Pause.)* It's only a space.

HOGBIN: A space?

SAVAGE: A mobile space.

HOGBIN: A MOBILE SPACE?

SAVAGE: You think by parroting you diminish truth you hate to entertain –

HOGBIN: IT'S OBLIVION! *(Pause.)*

SAVAGE: So's a grave. A space enclosing oblivion. *(Pause.)*

HOGBIN: Want it anyway. So did you, once… *(HELEN enters, holding a fragment.)*

HELEN: Neck bone. *(She lifts the lid of SAVAGE's bin, drops it in, replacing the lid.)* I think they do this because they desire me. I may be wrong.

It could be hatred, but then, what's hatred? I think it's desire also, what do you say? *(She looks at HOGBIN.)*

HOGBIN: *(Cautiously.)* I wouldn't disagree with you –

HELEN: Oh listen, I am so sad tonight, so stuff your tact. I want a conversation.

HOGBIN: Stuff it, yes…

HELEN: I get no sleep. I go to my room, and even as I go towards the door I think to myself, oh, the futility of this…

HOGBIN: Know the feeling…

HELEN: I fling the sheet aside and there – WHY DO YOU ALWAYS AGREE WITH ME? *(Pause. HOGBIN shrugs.)* I fling the sheet back and – *(Pause.)* Of course I suffer all the consequences. More lined. And more bad tempered. The face becomes a landscape of insomnia and yet the overall effect is that I am MORE DESIRABLE. Yes! It's true! Do you think I am insane? Do you think, poor thing, she is deluded? There is no point in the conversation if you hold that opinion, none at all, no, I tell you the truth because you are unhappy, I ditched modesty decades ago and so would you, I have had nine children, my belly's a pit, or as the poetically-inclined say when they're lapping me, a sandy strand from which the tide receded leaving feathered frontiers. Ugly, but who's deterred? You see, for compliments I have a perfect memory… *(Pause.)* This is not a conversation, is it? I am doing all the talking. *(EPSOM and GUMMERY rush in with FLADDER between them, stripped and beaten.)*

FLADDER: I am the murderer! I am the victim!

HELEN: *(Horrified.)* WHAT HAVE YOU DONE TO HIM!

FLADDER: I am the killer! HANGMAN IN ATTENDANCE, PLEASE!

HELEN: WHAT HAVE YOU DONE TO HIS FACE!

GUMMERY: He told me to!

FLADDER: *(To SAVAGE.)* SENTENCE ME, THEN!

HELEN: His face, look…

GUMMERY: HE TOLD ME TO…!

FLADDER: Innocent squaddies! *(She goes to wipe away his blood.)* DON'T TOUCH THE ASSASSIN'S FACE! *(She stands back.)* I asked them to hurt me, and all they could think of was their fists, what other tortures do they know about? Love? NO CHAIR FOR THE ACCUSED, I kneel, no, that's too comfortable, I squat, what was the sentence, death?

SAVAGE: Yes…

FLADDER: Didn't hear it.

SAVAGE: It goes without saying.

FLADDER: CACOPHONY IN COURT! Listen, the destruction of cities, the wrecking of fleets, the burning of crops, infanticide by numbers, all this is so much TRIVIA. War crimes, rubbish, no. In Paper Troy the only crimes are crimes against the self.

HELEN: I think you are the most insatiable exhibitionist.

FLADDER: *(Glaring at her.)* Exhibitionism you would know about, who hung your cunt out to all youth, I'VE SEEN HER DO IT LIKE THE BUTCHER SHOWING MEAT.

HELEN: Get up and wash your face, will you…?

FLADDER: What we do against others is no sin, it's self-murder I prosecute, the only crimes are crimes against the self, that's the source of cruelty.

HELEN: Wash your face, please…

FLADDER: Wash it, why? Wash yours, it's black with terror. YOU THINK TO SHOW YOUR ARSE IS REVELATION? *(She slaps him. Pause.)*

HELEN: You see, you bring out the worst in everyone. *(Pause. FLADDER hangs his head.)*

GUMMERY: He was such a bugger once, a proper head-hacker, I saw him swallow blood hot from severed arteries, the head still rolling in the fosse…

HELEN: Terrible decline… It comes from having Helen back…

SAVAGE: *(Briskly.)* No executioner. Pity. Paper gaol, then, until such time as paper death sets in.

FLADDER: *(Seeing SHADE enter.)* HERE'S THE MAN TO DO IT. *(The look at SHADE.)*

EPSOM: Go 'ome now, Barry, if yer wish. And take the mirror. *(Pause.)*

SHADE: Home? What's that?

FLADDER: In him, even, whose mouth is a brass purse of pain, some rotted quality of personal perfection must persist, all gnawed and spoiled by terror and abuse, DEEP THOUGH! *(Suddenly, SHADE flies at him.)*

HOGBIN: *(Horrified.)* Hey…!

SAVAGE: *(Looking.)* Not looking…

HOGBIN: Oi, you're the –

SAVAGE: NOT LOOKING –

HOGBIN: MAGISTRATE!

HELEN: *(As SHADE works on FLADDER).*
His little sob at coming

His great shout at coming
His little spilling
His great splash of fluid
His snivelling at betrayal
His great cataclysms of despair
His skittering with infants
His flinging of the baby at the wall
WHAT COULD YOU MAKE OF THAT BRUTE AND BOY. *(Pause.)*
No man made me more eager to betray him or more willing to come back… *(Pause.)*

HOGBIN: He ain't dead… *(Pause.)*

HELEN: Not dead? *(She laughs, as SHADE walks away from the kneeling FLADDER.)*

SHADE: The worst thing that can happen to a compulsive apologist I think, is to lose his tongue…

HELEN: Lose his…

SHADE: Finish Paper Troy.

HELEN: His tongue…

SHADE: *(Tossing it away.)* And paper knives –

HELEN: NO TONGUE –

SHADE: *(Holding a vile thing.)* I had to rip it up by its roots. NO PRIVATE LIFE IN NEW TROY! NO CLAMOUR OF APOLOGY! *(Pause.)*

HELEN: Put it back…

SHADE: *(Turning to her.)* Put it back? Why, did it please you very much, lapping your sour flavours? *(EPSOM laughs.)* NO MORE OF THAT EITHER. He only watches now, his eyeballs do the talking.

HELEN: Put it back…

SHADE: *(Thrusting it at her.)* You.

HELEN: The voice. The words. Are what desire is. The message is arousal. Or we're cattle. You have castrated him.

SHADE: No, I left those shrivelled things intact.

HELEN: YOU HAVE CASTRATED HIM. *(Pause.)* He could mutter me into upheavals no shoving hip could copy, earthquakes by his bawdy –

EPSOM: LEND US THE TONGUE, THEN!

HELEN: Oh, you sham male dog on its hind legs dancing –

EPSOM: LEND US IT!

HELEN: Parody of masculinity –

SHADE: *(Flinging the tongue to EPSOM.)* Bury it, with honours, since it commanded us at epic slaughters, or pickle it for youth to gawp at. And this fat one, let him record its wit from recollections, in eight volumes. As for this bitch, new queen now, for new Troy. Where's my looted woman?

CREUSA: No thank you.

SHADE: NEW QUEEN I SAID. *(To HELEN.)* And you, her slut. *(He goes to the kneeling figure of FLADDER, puts his hands on FLADDER's shoulders, embraces him.)* Don't think cruel men have not also suffered, or victims spluttered terrible savagery in tears… *(Pause.)* I'm looking for a god. *(Pause. He turns to SAVAGE.)* Could it be you?

SCENE FIVE

A Beach, GAY, with a stick. A BOY, seated.

GAY: Reasons for the fall of Paper Troy. One! *(THE BOY hesitates.)* Come on, oh, do come on, or I will beat you!

BOY: Erm…

GAY: One! The degeneracy of the aristocracy and their flirtation with the arts. Two! The martial ardour of the warriors could find no satisfaction in origami! Three! Are you listening, I don't think you try at all, this is HISTORY I'm teaching you! And stop fidgeting, or I will beat you! *(Exasperated pause.)* I sometimes think, people are such swine, such inveterate swine. And then I think, no, you can make them better.

BOY: By beating them?

GAY: By beating them, yes! How else? *(She sees a figure, off.)* Oh, no, here comes that horrid old man again! Don't encourage him. Because he's blind we all go silly, he knows that, he uses it to exploit us. *(HOMER enters, blind.)* YOU ARE NOT TO PUT YOUR HAND INTO MY DRESS AGAIN. *(He stops.)* I think the beach should be a place for children to be children and not poked about by peculiar old men.

HOMER: You are not a child.

GAY: I am a child. I am thirteen. Obviously I am a child.

HOMER: You are not a child, and I am not an old man.

GAY: Conundrum.

BOY: What?

GAY: Conundrum. He says all these things, these conundrums and things, and the next thing you know –

HOMER: Stop –

GAY: Hand up your –

HOMER: STOP. *(She concedes.)* I am not an old man because I know nothing. And you are not a child because you know it all. Now give me your hand. *(She extends it. HOMER draws it quickly to his crutch.)*

GAY: There! I knew that would happen!

HOMER: A GOD LIVES THERE.

HELEN: *(Entering.)* The author of the *Iliad.*

GAY: HE IS TRYING TO MAKE ME INSANE! *(She pulls away, runs off.)*

HOMER: The young…! No charity! So cruel, which is their fascination…

BOY: She beats me with a twig!

HOMER: Lucky fellow…

BOY: Right round the face sometimes, whip. Because I don't know ten reasons for the fall of Paper Troy.

HOMER: There are not ten reasons.

BOY: That's what I say! *(He hurries off.)*

HELEN: I hate your songs. Do you mind this? The ripping livers and the splash of brains. The prosody is marvellous but, I must say this and fuck the consequences. The torrents of intestine and the ravens picking skulls I AM SO VIOLENT, were you always blind? When their attacks were beaten off we maimed the wounded. With kitchen knives, me and the Trojan women, hacked them in the ditch, trimming the features off their heads like turnips for the market and their cocks we cropped. DON'T SAY YOU NEVER HEARD OF THIS were you born blind or was it horror spread some merciful film across your retina, and what's pity, I do think pity is no substitute for truth –

HOMER: Helen –

HELEN: I REFUSE TO CLAP YOUR SONGS. *(Pause.)* I loved Troy, because Troy was to sin. Why did you never say that? But him who took me there was not a sinner, only an exhibitionist, and not my equal. DON'T YOU KNOW THE HELL IT IS TO FIND NO MAN YOUR EQUAL? Say that, in your next book. That was the agony of Troy, not slippery swords or old men massacred, but Helen's awful loneliness in dream…

HOMER: Helen…

HELEN: Do what you like with my daughter – when history gets to a child no mother can be of the least relief.

HOMER: *(Holding out his arms.)* Helen! *(He encloses her. She weeps. SAVAGE appears with HOGBIN pushing the bin.)*

SAVAGE: I said, if I am the god, why do I have to drag the bin? Put wheels on it, he said…

HELEN: *(Pulling free of HOMER.)* What are you?

SAVAGE: What am I?

HELEN: You come here, first a clerk and now a god – it's obvious you want to destroy me –

SAVAGE: Me –

HELEN: WHAT ELSE ARE YOU HERE FOR!

HOGBIN: *(Demonstratively.)* The Interlude of the Bin! Within the bin – *(He removes the lid.)* The fruits of the hospital! I construct – I demonstrate – the vital elements of the Suffering Biped – ONE! *(He reaches into the offal.)* It's a – *(He looks at a shapeless thing.)* Call it a foot – *(He places it on the ground.)* This transports the lie around – the biped is manoeuvrable, it is not still, no, it stamps in unison, the foot being also for DANCING, a futile repetition aimed at creating social unity, ANOTHER LIE and also, KICKING, the ecstasy experienced by the biped in inflicting pain, TWO! *(He dips in again.)* The knee! *(He looks at a shapeless thing.)* Call it a knee –

SAVAGE: *(Staring at HOMER.)* Listen –

HOGBIN: Why not a knee –

SAVAGE: Listen, will you?

HOGBIN: *(Laying the piece down.)* I'm talking –

SAVAGE: This is him who –

HOGBIN: I'M TALKING, AREN'T I? *(Pause.)* Knee. For kneeling with. To imaginary forces such a God, or actual forces such as the party, the murderer, etcetera, a complex joint enabling the biped to grovel most convincingly –

SAVAGE: HO – MER! *(He throws himself at HOMER's feet and kisses the hem of his garment.)*

HOGBIN: Also, for driving into softer organs such as the stomach or the genitals, to render ineffective the thing I number THREE – *(He dips in again at random.)* The organ of increase! *(He pulls out a shapeless thing.)* Call it a dick – why not a dick – and with the other bit – two elements with which… *(He stares at the thing.)* the biped…in a extravaganza of futility…pretends to…shake off consciousness…or fails to…RIBS! *(He reaches in, stops in mid-movement. To SAVAGE.)* You mustn't do that…he may be the very wickedest of bastards…

SAVAGE: THE GREAT MAN LENDS US HOPE…

HOGBIN: You say that because you sense you are a great man yourself, but undiscovered…

SAVAGE: *(To HOMER.)* We squabble, my student and I, my desperate and sadistic student, we – but you would know, you with your flocks of followers –

HOGBIN: Creeping…

SAVAGE: Clustering around you for the least perception which –

HOGBIN: Creeping…

SAVAGE: LET ME WORSHIP SOMEBODY! *(Pause.)* So barren isn't it, a life without prostration? *(To HOGBIN.)* AND THAT GOES FOR ALL JUVENILE ICONOCLASTS! *(Pause. To HOMER.)* Savage, PhD, lecturer in classics, theses on metre and the first six books… *(Pause.)* Beloved genius… I call you genius…though he would say there's no such thing…THERE IS AND THIS IS IT… *(Pause.)* Speak to me…a little philosophical deduction…no, that's a lot to ask, a real impertinence, forgive me… anything would do… *(Pause.)* Not anything, that's silly, not anything, not the time of day, no, but a little distillation? Or is distillation now impossible? *(Pause.)* COME ON, I WROTE TWO BOOKS ABOUT YOU!

HOGBIN: Ribs! *(He pulls a shapeless thing from the bin.)* Call it ribs, all right? *(He places it down.)* In the shelter of which the biped hides his HEART, formerly conceived as the organ of feeling, passion, etcetera, but now exposed as leathery and boring PUMP.

HOMER: I hate the young. When I was young even, I hated the young… *(Pause.)*

SAVAGE: *(To HOMER.)* You are the greatest poet in the world. Of any time. Of any culture. *(Pause.)* I wonder if you heard? I said –

HOMER: You imagine you compliment me.

SAVAGE: Don't I?

HOMER: And having complimented me, you expect the compliment to give me pleasure.

SAVAGE: Doesn't it? *(Pause. Suddenly, shockingly HELEN leaps on HOGBIN and wrestles him.)*

HOGBIN: Oi! *(HELEN and HOGBIN roll about. She bears him down.)* Oi! *(She laughs with delight.)* Oi! *(They roll over the floor.)*

HOMER: The great artist drifts beyond the common consciousness, like a child carried to sea by a raft. The beach gets further, the paddlers get further, the weak swimmers, then the strong swimmers, all out of reach, until – YOU ARE WRITING IT DOWN!

SAVAGE: No, I –

HOMER: LIAR. HEARD THE PEN.

SAVAGE: *(Innocently.)* Was I?

HELEN: *(To HOGBIN, climbing off him.)* Be my lover.

HOGBIN: No!

HELEN: They say no now! Listen! No, he says. Look, I plead…!

HOGBIN: Don't wanna…

HELEN: We will have a child and call it – *(To HOMER.)* DON'T LOOK AT ME LIKE THAT I AM NOT INFERTILE. *(HOGBIN scrambles to his feet.)*

HELEN: Listen…! *(She cups her ear.)* The daily chant of Laughing Troy…

SHADE: *(Entering.)* The word. *(He looks at them.)*

The word today is Us.

All say it.

Us.

It soothes the soul, it calms the temper, can't hear you.

Us. *(HOMER starts to leave.)*

I thought you were blind, not dumb. *(He stops.)* I also have a mind.

HOMER: Us.

SHADE: Excellent. I think with vast and bloated genius, to stoop is healthy. *(He turns to the others.)* Everybody!

ALL: Us. *(Pause. He turns to leave.)*

SAVAGE: Excuse me, am I still a god?

SHADE: Why not? Aren't you still ugly? *(He goes to leave again.)*

SAVAGE: Tomorrow's word then! *(SHADE stops.)* If you're looking for suggestions... *(Pause.)* MUST.

SHADE: Must...?

SAVAGE: US and MUST. The twin pillars of history... *(SHADE goes out. Pause. They look at SAVAGE critically.)* I did not come here to sit on a beach... *(They stare at him.)* Where's knowledge? Where does it lie? In meditation? The lillies and the rhyming couplets? The whispering sandal in the aromatic garden? NO POET EVER TOLD US ANYTHING. *(HOGBIN looks at HOMER.)* And why? BECAUSE HE NEVER GOVERNED. That's why he's blind, he only looks inside. ALL RIGHT MR HOMER YOU CAN ABUSE ME NOW. *(Pause.)* I'm waiting, in a lather of submission... *(Pause.)*

HELEN: You are not a very great man, Dr Savage...

SAVAGE: His lashing, please...

HELEN: Or even very dignified...

SAVAGE: His lashing, not yours…! *(Pause, then HOMER goes off.)* I am beneath contempt…

HELEN: Yes, but he's looking for my daughter. *(She turns to go, stops, looks at HOGBIN, who is replacing the offal in the bin.)* What's the matter, do you love another woman? *(HOGBIN shrugs.)* I hope I shan't hate you. I'm such a hater. It's the burden of my life.

HOGBIN: I'm sorry, I–

HELEN: Don't! *(Pause, to SAVAGE.)* He was going to apologize! Or is that right? Perhaps he knows, if he really tried, he could love me? *(She goes out. MACLUBY appears.)*

MACLUBY: The Pruning of Helen. *(SAVAGE and HOGBIN fill the bin, replace the lid.)* The pruning of Helen may have been – this is the nature of political decisions – spontaneous. A flash of intuition or a stab of malice.WHAT DO YOU THINK HISTORY IS, DELIBERATION? On the other hand it may have been the outcome of long and acrimonious debate within the ruling circle, WHAT DO YOU THINK HISTORY IS, SPASMS? *(To SAVAGE, who is going out.)* Oi! *(SAVAGE stops.)* He also sins who only writes the words. But you know that. *(MACLUBY goes out. CREUSA enters.)*

CREUSA: Slave one day. Queen the next. Would you believe? The transformations! But happy by order, and to be illiterate. Difficult, when I was not illiterate in the first place. This Troy to be in single syllables. Difficult. Or hard, should say. *(She exerts her imagination.)* MY – PLAIN – FACE – TO – BE – THE – BADGE – OF – TROY! Done it! *(She tries again.)* AND – IN – MY – LIFE – THE – CROWD – WILL – SEE – AND – LOVE – ITS – SELF – NOT – STOOP – TO – SNOBS – NOR – LICK – THE – ARSE

– OF – BEAUTY – Beauty's two… *(Pause.)* Shade's Troy. *(She parrots.)* I also have a mind…! *(Pause. She looks at HOGBIN.)* Will you talk to me, I have given up all hope of a quiet life, and a quiet life when I had it I despised, it was not quiet, it was clay, it was not quiet, it was mud, quiet is something else, not dense but light I think. I left notes for you in so many places, my scrambling love, my rodent, I was burrowed, I was tunnelled, all my dark exposed to daylight, a tent uptipped, a parcel with your fingers at the strings, the haste, the impatience, the breathless hunt, and your great wail of desperation, did you get my notes, every tree trunk I left letters in and every litterbin, no, I exaggerate, some I did pass by, do I embarrass you at all, you look so, I am so rarely this enthusiastic and you look, OH, FUCK I HAVE OFFENDED HIM, calm down, calm down, there I'm calm now, I am so glad to see you, there, statement of extreme reserve, DON'T YOU WANT TO FUCK NOW, shh! I could, almost, I could, yes, I could almost BEAT YOU, I ALSO HAVE A MIND, please speak or don't I leave you room, I don't, do I, here's room. *(She stops. Pause.)*

HOGBIN: Cold today… *(Pause.)*

CREUSA: Cold today. You? Ah. Shh! Could let out such a torrent. Could let out such a volley but no, shh, I have done everything. I have been everythinged, and you – a balding and precocious youth can WHO'S IMPOTENT AT THAT – for which no criticism – can make me who has done everything and been everythinged – *(Pause.)* If I believed in gods I'd say some godlike bugger had sprinkled me with what – delirium – to entertain himself – cold, is it? All right, just sit, to sit with you would be enough, and say a few words, or nothing if you – *(He sits.)* Thank you. *(Pause.)* I thank him. *(Pause.)*

HOGBIN: Cold today…

CREUSA: We are like that. We are! We are so inconsistent. We are liars without meaning it. And now I'm cold as well. Excellently cold. Excellently off the idea. Excellent. I could no more have you than. I am to speak in words of single syllables I must remind you. It is the function of my majesty. *(Pause.)* Arse is one syllable. Cunt obviously. It is a miracle when two moods coincide. It is a sacrament. THREE SYLLABLES! *(A long pause, then she lets out a cry.)* Oh, God… *(Pause.)* Oh, God, you have met someone else… *(Pause.)*

SCENE SIX

The Government. EPSOM carries on the mirror.

SHADE: Gather round me. Come on, gather round me, comrades in arms, etcetera, treaders of the bowel carpet and the brain mat – *(He opens his arms to them. He clutches them round the shoulders. They stare into the mirror.)* Oh, we are ageing! Oh, we are shedding! Look, the ploughed up skins, we are hanging off our cheek bones and our eyes are dim. Look deep, look deep, we slew arbitrarily and we pitied arbitrarily. Look deep. Speech, Les.

EPSOM: Speech?

SHADE: Speech! Yes! This is the frame of greatness, did you think battle was your forte? Never, battle's for the bullock this is where proper violence belongs. WORDS! Les!

EPSOM: Can't –

SHADE: He can't, he can't, Brian, you –

GUMMERY: Must I?

SHADE: You must, old friend.

GUMMERY: Look at yourself then, Barry –

SHADE: Brian, I do –

GUMMERY: Look 'ard and tell us, is it a healthy face is looking back at you?

SHADE: Not healthy, no –

GUMMERY: Or noble?

SHADE: Noble, no –

GUMMERY: Regard the beak, the way the eyes protrude –

SHADE: They do, and I forgive your rudeness –

EPSOM: Yellow skin –

SHADE: Thank you –

EPSOM: And puffy round yer lids –

SHADE: Oh, Les, you have discovered speech –

GUMMERY: Is there pity in the eyeball?

SHADE: Pity? None –

GUMMERY: Mercy?

SHADE: Mercy? KEEP THE MIRROR STILL we're looking for my – what –

GUMMERY: Mercy –

SHADE: No, can't see it, Brian, unless that bloodshot vein is it… I think sometimes, they want me to be cruel. They bay at cruelty, but still I think they want me to be cruel. I think even the beaten man wants to be beaten. Why is that?

SAVAGE: *(Entering.)* The governor is the nightmare of the populace… *(Pause.)*

SHADE: Leave me with the doctor. We must define new life, the gutters and the ceilings of New Troy. How laughter might be made as sharp as wire and dancing a new drill… *(GUMMERY and EPSOM leave. SHADE looks into SAVAGE. Pause.)* SUPPOSING WE TRUSTED ONE ANOTHER! *(Silence.)* Supposing. *(Pause.)* Just supposing. *(Pause.)* I used the word trust loosely. Because I imagine there is trust and trust. Trust I think I fathom but TRUST…! What's that? *(Pause. GUMMERY comes back in. SHADE detects him in the mirror with alarm.)* DON'T RETURN WITHOUT WARNING ME! *(GUMMERY freezes.)* What is it, Brian, you made me jump.

GUMMERY: Old Helen of Old Troy.

SHADE: What about her?

GUMMERY: Is carrying 'er 'usband round the 'ouse on 'er back. 'e croaks on 'er like a sun-burned frog. Down alleys and through the estates. And 'is saliva everywhere, buckets of, the tongueless dribble, it appears, in excess, and it's making puddles where women exercise their dogs…

SHADE: All right…

GUMMERY: This was the cause of ten years' bleeding and now look at 'er, bare legs and filthy black – It makes a pig of everyone who raged for ten years at the gates if she's to be a slut with unwashed legs –

SHADE: I can see you're anxious –

GUMMERY: History, Barry!

SHADE: History, yes, but even Helen ages –

GUMMERY: Quicker than most, but dignity would help. *(He goes out.)*

SHADE: I take his point. And once they sold her piss in little bottles. Well, so it was said by servants who crossed to our lines with buckets of the stuff. Could have been the cat's for all we knew. One piss is just like any other. *(Pause.)* Or isn't it?

SAVAGE: No.

SHADE: Some smeared their wounds with it. Some swallowed it with cordials. The very depth of barminess. Or was it?

SAVAGE: No. *(Pause.)*

SHADE: What do you want, Doctor Savage?

SAVAGE: Knowledge.

SHADE: How?

SAVAGE: Through you.

SHADE: Through me? But aren't I coarse and stupid?

SAVAGE: Yes. But stupidity's my instrument.

SHADE: *(Smiles.)* It's night, I let all insults fly, like vermin coming through the floorboards RAT ON THE GOB!

SAVAGE: You hate all kisses which aren't quick –

SHADE: Yes, I admit it.

SAVAGE: And whispers of impossible intentions –

SHADE: I admit that too! Night's the time for filth and for confessions. LOATHSOME INSECT IN THE SINK! You think I will like you if you abuse me. Intellectual's privilege? *(He goes to SAVAGE, close.)* I think my whim, my unrestrained and brutal impulse, spewed from the depths of my defective character and made by you into the monosyllables of late Trojan law, would in their essence be no worse than all the caring calculations of fifty trembling humanists, do you agree or not? *(Pause.)*

SAVAGE: Reserve my judgement.

SHADE: Reserve your judgement – *(He sees EPSOM in the mirror.)* WHAT IS IT LES YER MADE ME JUMP! *(EPSOM enters.)* Still up, old son? What is it, indigestion?

EPSOM: She's placed these adverts. *(He holds out some postcards.)*

SHADE: Must I look?

EPSOM: In corner shops.

SHADE: Must I? You read. *(He goes to the window.)* Look, the very paring of a moon, a nail of moon, against the plague pit of the sky, the word tonight is HACK. You could hack pods of pregnancy with the moon's hook…

EPSOM: *(Reading.)* Helen, formerly of Troy –

SHADE: Don't you love moons, doctor? They teach us all is shit, by shining on the good and bad alike…

EPSOM: Model, seeks interesting work part-time…

SHADE: STOP THAT!

EPSOM: *(Stops reading.)* I mean, if she's no better than a whore – then what did we – ten years of – *(Pause.)*

SHADE: She was a whore! Why else did we go there? I think the sex thing is such a punishment to us. I think you cattle. Don't you? Copulating cattle? Seeing the rear end of a cow I think, its hips are not unlike a stooping tart, and us likewise no doubt, our bits droop like a dog's. HUMAN DIGNITY WHAT'S THAT.

SAVAGE: I don't know.

SHADE: Don't you?

SAVAGE: I think it's love.

SHADE: What love? You chuck words up like a dead men's ashes, what love? The love of criminals in cars or bankrupt marriages? WHAT?

SAVAGE: I don't know! I'm frightened to know!

SHADE: The love of old men for their benches, what?

SAVAGE: I'M FRIGHTENED TO KNOW!

SHADE: Stare in the glass! *(He fetches the mirror.)* Stare in the glass.

SAVAGE: *(On his knees still.)* I don't like mirrors…

SHADE: No one does. *(He places it close to SAVAGE.)*

SAVAGE: Avoided mirrors all my life –

SHADE: Because you're ugly –

SAVAGE: Am I? Yes I –

SHADE: Ugly, yes, go on –

SAVAGE: Shaved without one, you can see –

SHADE: Go on –

SAVAGE: Lots of hairs get missed, my wife, she used to say you are the most ungroomed and unprepossessing man I ever – do you think it honours you to be dishevelled – I shun fashion like a –

SHADE: Digressing, doctor –

SAVAGE: As if for some reason there was sin in elegance –

SHADE: Digression on digression –

SAVAGE: I do find speaking to a mirror very –

SHADE: Now your eyes are shut –

SAVAGE: Are they – my eyes –

SHADE: Shut, yes–

SAVAGE: I THINK IF LOVE LIES ANYWHERE IT'S ON THE OTHER SIDE OF SHAME. *(Pause.)*

CREUSA: *(Who has entered.)* Don't believe him, will you? His confessions? The routine torrent of his preposterous sins… *(SAVAGE looks at her, very long.)*

SAVAGE: *(Pause.)* This – vilifying hag – obsessed me with her fundament. The breath turned lead, went solid in my lung, to see her knicker on the stair… I have to say this, she moved me to oaths and superlatives, so I won't speak. Knowledge compels stillness.

SHADE: This private life! I do shudder. This stew of knotted flesh! I do writhe. *(Pause. He turns to SAVAGE.)* How can we make the new man? *(Pause.)* I think he must live in the street. In public always, where nothing uncommon can be done. Can you do this?

SAVAGE: Yes…

SHADE: Laughing. Dancing. I think he should move and think in crowds. Can you write this?

SAVAGE: Yes…

SHADE: Once, when I saw men in the streets with miserable faces, staring at the ground, I nutted them. In streets in Attica where I ran yobbish prior to the war I said cheer up you cunt and if they did not grin to order I rammed my forehead through their gristle. This was instinct but now I see it also must be politics. *(Pause.)* New Troy. The land of laughter… *(Pause. He looks to SAVAGE.)* Write it, then…

CREUSA: And Helen? *(They look at her.)* Helen who is all clandestine fuck? *(Pause.)*

SHADE: I see no place for Helen, do you, Dr Savage? No place for her in Laughing Troy? Her ego and her filthy legs? Her mouth and acts of endless privacy? She is all I and this is the age of we…

SAVAGE: I has no arms. *(Pause. He looks up, half-curious.)* Does it? The letter? *(Pause.)* I is a single stem? *(Pause.)*

CREUSA: *(With rising horror.)* Oh, God, he's –

SHADE: *(To SAVAGE.)* Go on. More cogitation. Further elaboration of the infant thought…

CREUSA: Listen –

SHADE: I THINK BECAUSE I HAVE TO.

SHADE: Oh yes, you do, you do.

SAVAGE: AND HAVING THOUGHT IT – OUT THOUGHT! VILE OBJECT, OUT FOR SCRUTINY! *(Pause.)* Helen, who has grown so wild, Helen might be – *(He struggles.)*

CREUSA: Listen, I said –

SHADE: SHUT UP, YOU. *(Pause. He goes to SAVAGE.)* Won't help the thought to birth. You birth it, you conceived…

SAVAGE: Yes…

SHADE: TERRIBLE LABOUR OF THE THOUGHT!

SAVAGE: Pruned… *(Pause.)*

SHADE: Pruned? *(Pause. He walks up and down. Suddenly SAVAGE lets out a terrible cry.)*

SAVAGE: KNOWLEDGE! *(SHADE hurries out, bundling CREUSA with him. SAVAGE rocks on his knees. MACLUBY appears.)*

MACLUBY: Knowledge… *(SAVAGE turns, sees him. He scrambles to his feet.)*

SAVAGE: Helen – got to – Helen – Where's she?

MACLUBY: Wrong way.

SAVAGE: Is it? *(He turns to go the other way.)* Can't move with this –

MACLUBY: Solidarity Street.

SAVAGE: Where's that?

MACLUBY: Near the Us Museum.

SAVAGE: Which way's –

MACLUBY: Quick!

SAVAGE: *(Tugging at the bin.)* How can I, with this thing! *(Pause. SHADE enters again, with the key to the manacles. He unlocks them.)*

SHADE: Genius can't be encumbered, can it? Genius? *(He goes out again. SAVAGE rubs his wrists.)*

MACLUBY: Moon's gone again... *(Pause.)* Never find yer way...

SAVAGE: Free concerts block the avenues...

MACLUBY: *(Gazing into him.)* Unfortunately... *(Pause. Suddenly SAVAGE confronts his horror.)*

SAVAGE: All right! *(Pause. He crawls to the mirror SHADE has left, and looks in it.)* All right...! *(MACLUBY goes out.)*

SCENE SEVEN

The Street. Sound of a conga. HOGBIN rushes in.

HOGBIN: Oi! *(The conga appears, the dancers in sacks.)* Somebody! *(They chant.)*

THE CONGA: Got – to – be – so – glad – now –
Got – to – be – so – glad – now –
Oh – so – glad –
Oh – so – glad –

HOGBIN: Listen, will yer! *(They pass by.)* I must stop doin' that. I shout oi! And no one shifts. Why should they? The Redundant Oi, by Kevin

Hogbin. *(He sees HOMER.)* Oi! *(He runs up to him.)* I saw three geezers drag a woman off!

HOMER: The first duty of the poet is to survive. *(Pause.)*

HOGBIN: Is it…? *(The conga returns.)*

THE CONGA: Got – to – be – so – glad – now –
Got – to – be – so – glad – now –
Oh – so – glad –
Oh – so – glad –

HOGBIN: *(In despair.)* Can't think, can yer? CAN'T FUCKIN' THINK! *(The conga departs.)*

HOMER: Testament… Not participation…testament!

HOGBIN: An 'alf of me says 'dance, Kevin! The beat!' And 'alf says 'put wax in yer ears! Tie down yer feet!'

HOMER: How hard that is! *(He grabs him.)* Listen, my third book.

HOGBIN: THIRD book?

HOMER: I sing you my third book.

HOGBIN: Third book…?

HOMER: Listen, I give it to you! Listen! *(Pause.)* The Heroic Life of the Citizens of Sacked Cities.

HOGBIN: Long title for you.

HOMER: *(Pause.)* The Ruinad. *(Pause.)* I sang it once before. And they left, singly or in groups, like men who had forgotten to post letters, until at the end, I was singing to myself… *(He suddenly sobs.)*

HOGBIN: All right…all right…so what…if it's true – *(The conga reappears.)* OH, FUCK THEM…! *(HOMER begins to sing, but is drowned by the conga.)*

THE CONGA: Got – to – be – so – glad – now –

Got – to – be – so – glad – now –
Oh – so – glad –
Oh – so – glad –

HOMER: You ask me to believe,
You ask me to believe,
In the mercy of the gods,
I say their mercy is only
A refreshment of their malice…
(He fades, falters.)

HOGBIN: What? *(Pause. HOMER is peering blindly, off.)* 'omer? *(Pause.)* I'm still 'ere. *(Pause.)* As long as one child is 'alf attentive, you 'ave an audience. *(Pause.)* 'omer. *(Pause.)* I COMMAND THE POWER OF YOUR GENIUS! The people's right to your imagination…give us it! *(Pause, then EPSOM passes through.)*

EPSOM: Old times… Suddenly, what seemed like always and forever, is old times…

HELEN: *(Entering, supported by FLADDER, and bandaged.)* Murder me. *(She looks around.)* MURDER ME.

HOMER: *(Who sees nothing.)* Murder Helen? Why?

HELEN: MURDER! *(Pause.)*

HOMER: You don't mean that.

HELEN: I do. I do mean it.

HOMER: Then why ask? There are cliffs. And ponds. Railway tracks, and dynamos –

HELEN: I want to die –

HOMER: Liar –

HELEN: LOOK AT ME.

HOMER: LIAR. *(Pause.)*

HOGBIN: *(Who has been transfixed by the sight of her wounds.)* Giggle…! Want to giggle…! Try to be grown up but want to giggle…! *(He throws himself at HELEN's feet, clasping her ankles.)*

GAY: *(Entering.)* Has anybody got the doctor?

HELEN: It was a doctor who did it.

GAY: Oh, good. Oh, good, because… Let's face it, we have seen some awful things and the presence of trained specialists is comforting…it is! I hate bad hangmen, for example. Ask the hanged, they will tell you, *merci, merci,* for a trained professional…! *(She goes to FLADDER and puts her arms around him affectionately.)* She can always grip with her thighs, and her tongue, which they say is of such great versatility, that could become as tensile as a cable… *(THE BOY enters, staring.)*

BOY: Woman got no arms… *(They ignore him. He addresses HOMER.)* Why did you cut her arms off?

GAY: No, it wasn't him.

BOY: Must have been, he –

GAY: No, he only –

BOY: YES HE DID. *(Pause.)*

HOMER: If I had not made Helen, Helen would not have been disfigured… *(Pause.)* But Helen had to be made…

GAY: SHE DID NOT HAVE TO BE MADE! *(She claps her hand to her mouth.)*

Oh, I –

Oh, I – now that was – really, that was so – outburst in defiance of all – all right now – *(She is straight, still.)* Still as, and level as, the strand of sand when tides have all receded… there… *(She smiles, coolly.)* Euphoric Gay. *(She goes out.)*

HOGBIN: *(Going to HELEN.)* Be arms for you. Brush teeth. Rub eyes. And scratch you where you itch. Anticipate every move your invisible limbs would make… *(He encloses her.)*

Interlude

TWO MUSLIMS enter, with a hamper carried by a EUROPEAN SERVANT. They gaze over the country.

ASAFIR: John, flag please.

YORAKIM: Or someone will take a shot.

ASAFIR: Will pot away.

YORAKIM: And make a shambles of the lunch. *(THE SERVANT erects a white flag.)*

ASAFIR: Thank you, now dish away, I famish, I absolutely famish, oh, look, a skull.

YORAKIM: Trojan.

ASAFIR: Greek.

YORAKIM: The unmistakable long jaw of all –

ASAFIR: The instantly recognizable short forehead of the –

TOGETHER: WE JOKE LIKE THIS TO KEEP THE HORROR DOWN.

YORAKIM: Another flag there, John –

ASAFIR: He's serving lunch –

YORAKIM: Yes –

ASAFIR: He's only got two –

YORAKIM: So he has. Two only. I was thinking, however, is it visible from all the promontories?

ASAFIR: Get a flag yourself. *(YORAKIM stares at ASAFIR.)* All right, I will –

YORAKIM: No, John will. *(Pause.)* I do not think myself better than the servant. That is not the issue. The issue is that in showing myself willing to perform his functions, we –

ASAFIR: I can perfectly well –

YORAKIM: ERODE THE BASIS OF SERVICE. *(Pause.)* It would. Erode it.

ASAFIR: Yes, but if, in this instance, a flag of truce would make the crucial difference between life and death –

YORAKIM: IT'S FALSE! IT'S FALSE!

TOGETHER: WE GET LIKE THIS WHEN DRAWING LINES ACROSS THE WORLD.

JOHN: *(Pointing.)* TERRORISTS!

YORAKIM: *(Spilling his tray.)* Fuck…!

JOHN: Hundreds of –

YORAKIM: Oh, fuck…!

ASAFIR: *(To JOHN.)* The pilchards, please…! *(They sit rigidly on the stools. JOHN serves.)* Ah, pilchards…!

YORAKIM: Oh, Allah –

ASAFIR: Pilchards, I remark –

YORAKIM: *(In control.)* Yes.

ASAFIR: Pilchards, etcetera.

YORAKIM: *(Seeing THE TERRORISTS.)* With knives…!

ASAFIR: The pilchards have knives…?

YORAKIM: WE ARE IN MORTAL –

ASAFIR: *(To JOHN.)* Show them the maps. Shake out the maps. *(JOHN indicates maps. They fall into sheets. He exhibits them.)* Good. Tell them we are of the neutral powers. Tell them we are mappers of the frontier, accredited by the armistice commission, cartographers with no axe to grind. Show them the seals and *laissez passers* of all parties –

YORAKIM: Fuck and fuck –

ASAFIR: We have no weapons but – *(JOHN is demonstrating certificates.)* SHOULD HANDS BE RAISED AGAINST US WE WILL CALL DOWN STRIKES –

JOHN: *(Demonstrating.)* Crops – WOOF!

ASAFIR: And terrible vengeance will be –

JOHN: *(Miming.)* Huts – WOOF!

ASAFIR: *(To YORAKIM.)* Pilchard?

YORAKIM: I think we are going to be killed.

ASAFIR: Not for the first time.

YORAKIM: Not killed for the first time…?

ASAFIR: Not the first time you have –

YORAKIM: I dreamed this.

ASAFIR: I know.

YORAKIM: When I was a child I dreamed this moment –

ASAFIR: We should have asked for guards. In retrospect we obviously should have asked for guards. I thought the flag would speak but clearly it does not. At least not adequately. I do apologize.

YORAKIM: *(Describing the dream.)* I fall to the ground –

ASAFIR: I don't think John is getting anywhere –

YORAKIM: My head is separated from my body by a single blow –

ASAFIR: Are you, John? Getting anywhere?

YORAKIM: Bounce it goes, and bounce –

ASAFIR: *(Standing now.)* Thank you, anyway –

YORAKIM: *(As GAY and OTHERS enter, armed.)* The unusual perspective of a severed head… *(Pause.)*

GAY: I am going to cut your throats. *(Pause.)*

ASAFIR: Why, for goodness' sake?

GAY: *(To JOHN.)* And you, collaborator, you will be burned in a dustbin.

ASAFIR: Make the following points, please –

JOHN: *(To GAY.)* I WANTED A JOB, MATE.

ASAFIR: One.

YORAKIM: Get a move on, she –

ASAFIR: One. *(He pauses, wearily.)*

YORAKIM: GO ON, THEN...! *(Pause.)*

ASAFIR: No, I don't think there is any point...

GAY: You arrogant and half-dead mannikins.

YORAKIM: You have offended her, and now we shall be most cruelly used.

GAY: In your imperialist silks and turbans spun of slavery.

ASAFIR: I have no political opinions, I am a simple administrator of a frontier line but I will not stoop to plead to a European bitch. There! I have given away my feelings and please do it quickly.

JOHN: *(Desperately.)* I WANTED A JOB FOR MY MUM WHOSE SPINE HAS TURNED TO BISCUIT – ALL DAY SHE CRIES IN BED –

GAY: Extenuating gibberish. Many of us suffer but how few of us betray.

JOHN: Many of us don't love our mothers –

GAY: OH, BURN HIM QUICK! *(They drag him away.)* I think, if we heard all the excuses in the world, no action would occur, and justice would attenuate, an incomprehensible word.

ASAFIR: Not a bad thing, surely?

GAY: YOU WOULD SAY THAT BECAUSE YOU ARE ON TOP.

ASAFIR: Admittedly. Such is the yawning gulf between our cultures, nothing I say can possibly affect you –

YORAKIM: No –

ASAFIR: Were I possessed of all the wisdom of my race it could not –

YORAKIM: *(In despair.)* No, no, WRONG ARGUMENT!

ASAFIR: *(To YORAKIM.)* I am not concerned with survival, I am concerned with truth.

GAY: Excellent! Because I shall cut your throats whatever you say. You could be utterly persuasive, logically coherent and morally supreme, and I would still act. KNIFE! *(She holds out her hand to A FOLLOWER.)* Does that fill you with despair?

YORAKIM: Yes…

ASAFIR: No…

YORAKIM: IT FILLS ME WITH DESPAIR.

ASAFIR: I regard it as the essence of the human condition.

GAY: *(Triumphantly.)* In which case it would be a disappointment if you were spared!

ASAFIR: *(Conceding.)* I am hoist with my own philosophy.

GAY: You are! Now take off your funny clothes, you are dying naked.

ASAFIR: Are we not sufficiently within your power but you –

GAY: NEVER SUFFICIENT. *(Pause.)* Do you think I'll let you die with dignity? Your dignity affronts me. STRIP THEM IF THEY – *(They let fall their clothes.)* Take this one away and cut his throat.

ASAFIR: Don't kill my colleague. He is terribly in love with life and –

GAY: THAT'S WHY I WANT TO ROB HIM OF IT. *(They take him out.)* You really do not understand the nature of revenge. Its satisfactions. Do you?

ASAFIR: No. I just draw maps.

GAY: Your false neutrality.

ASAFIR: I make lines on cartridge paper.

GAY: Your spurious privilege.

ASAFIR: And even as I draw the line I think, this line can't last. Sometimes we draw the line down the middle of a church, and sometimes through a mosque. A dozing drunkard with a reed could mark the frontiers just as well.

GAY: Then why –

ASAFIR: It brings me near the essence of all life. *(Pause. She looks at him for a long time. Then extends the knife to another.)*

GAY: Execute him. Because what he tells me I don't wish to know. *(They lead ASAFIR out.)*

ACT TWO

PROLOGUE

MACLUBY: In the ribbon of green a man is hoeing
Refugees

This one tried wit on thieves
This one tried pity on the police
This one wasted irony on the fanatic

In the ribbon of fertility rich horticulturalists
Dispute the skills of sportsmen

The hours are dying like wasps in the jam
Even blood
Would creep out of an artery
With the stray cat's indolence

And the murdered mistress makes no special noise
She does not beat
She does not hammer with her heels
The hanging gong of the afternoon

The silence of the valley is held breath
The outbreak
Lives in the contingency
The effect of the day's taste in the mouth
Not just the act
But the choice the act induced

Sarajevo did not cause the death of fifteen
Million

The theft of Helen did not cause the Siege of Troy

Or Japan's atrocity Hiroshima

No more causes of wars will do

NOT JUST THE ACT

But the choice the act induced

Shh

All peace is stopped breath
Shh
All love's suspension of returning solitude

At night the temple trembles
And the park is tense

Its false orders
Its unearthly symmetry

It knows its chance is brief

We inscribed the fountain as if we believed
This dispensation was eternal
The empire was unshakable
And at the spectacle of culture
Dirty tribesmen would not
                    could not
                    but kneel

Oh, the tomb's false request for exemption
                    This at least
                    This surely must
                    This cannot but command
Your temperance
You yet unborn
You yet to conquer

The cynicism of the generations
Is no less atomizing than the swipe of weapons
Wielded by the hour's enemy

                    That was my only
                    What is that trivial thing to
you
                    Your passion for destruction
might at
                    least

The litter of unavailing arguments
A cloud of disbelief in every tongue

Drifts out of cities
Giving earth her rings

More terrible than Saturn

WE ENTER AFTER THE SIEGE
WE DO A LITTLE KILLING

WE ARE NOT OLD FASHIONED
WE DO NOT SPARE THE WOMEN

WE STRING UP THE RESISTERS
AS WE ARE PERMITTED

WE TICKLE THE INFANT'S CHIN
AND WATCH ITS SISTER SPITTED

And with the draining out of this joyful
Malevolence experience depression such as the
Act of an equal love induces

We played cards with the survivors
Whose grins were false
I was sorry to detect…

SCENE ONE

SAVAGE is seated and with authority.

SAVAGE: My great peace. WHO COULD LIKE ME NOW? My restoration. WHO COULD SEE ME WITHOUT HATRED? I no longer sit on the edge of my chair. My arse spreads. My arse occupies! DR SAVAGE SUPREMELY VILE, ENTER ALL SUPPLIANTS! *(He leaps up as a crowd surrounds him.)* Not there! Don't come any nearer! Not there, there! SILENCE! Speak when I indicate you thus – a finger pointed – no shoving – MY WISDOM IS AVAILABLE TO ALL – I said no shoving – thus far and no further – SHUT UP AND STILL AS GARGOYLES – *(He points.)* You! *(He feigns attention.)* Mm. *(Pause.)* Mm. *(Pause.)* Mm. *(Pause.)* Enough. The details are – you go on – like an old woman who has the doctor's ear – STOP. *(Pause.)* I meditate. *(Pause.)* I pass judgement. Of course the verdict's the source of future quarrel! NEXT! You! Not you! The one with the bulbous nose – HAVE YOU GOT A BULBOUS NOSE? You have? The physiognomy of Trojan archetypes! The wall-eyed, then. *(Pause.)* Mm. *(Pause.)* Mm. *(Pause.)* Mm. *(As he performs this, HELEN enters, watches unseen.)* Mm. *(Pause.)* STOP! I meditate. *(Pause.)* I pass judgement. Of course the wrong man suffers! NEXT! You! Not you! The one with the jug ears – not you – HAVE YOU GOT JUG EARS? You have? The classic feature of the Trojan race! The hare-lipped then. *(Pause.)* Mm. *(Pause.)* Mm. *(Pause.)* Mm. *(Pause.)* I tire of – the plethora of ramification – PRECIS IS THE KEY TO JUSTICE, STOP! *(He rolls on his knees, laughing, sees HELEN, is still. He holds up his hands.)* No bin. *(He stares at her. He claps his hands. THE SUPPLIANTS depart.)* The political arrangements of Laughing Troy leave much to be desired but – *(Pause.)* Always we talk of making a new man but the old man will insist–*(Pause.)* His servile habits – his melancholy aspect – *(Pause.)* And the tendency of poets to crop up like weeds and spread dissent but only for dissension's sake, why? Why? *(Pause.)* Someone is chalking walls with very long words, who? *(Pause.)* And laughter…! You would think sometimes they were pissing milk crates, judging by their rictus jaws. *(Pause.)* There is a medical disorder called Iron Cheek, have you heard? The oiling of the jawbone with whalefat offers some relief but laughter seems to hurt the face as I imagine endless weeping would, it's epidemic and some have died, no one predicted this but – *(He stares at her.)* When you were whole I did not feel for you what – *(HOGBIN appears, skips behind HELEN.)* WHO SAID YOU COULD COME IN…! This retinue, this circus of the maimed and callow – it spoils your –

HOGBIN: 'ho says I'm callow? I say you're 'ollow.

SAVAGE: Dignity in suffering!

HOGBIN: You say callow, I say hollow, you say shallow, and I say –

SAVAGE: DOES HE HAVE TO ACCOMPANY YOU AT ALL TIMES OF –

HELEN: Yes. *(Pause.)*

HOGBIN: I say you could 'ave more limbs than an octopus and still not grasp a simple truth, such as –

SAVAGE: SHUT UP, YOU –

HOGBIN: Pity makes your cock big, so pity's only power – OI!

SAVAGE: I DO NOT SEE YOU. *(Pause.)*

HOGBIN: 'e doesn't see me…

SAVAGE: He does not exist, however present he may be.

HOGBIN: I don't exist…

SAVAGE: Like the butler in the bedroom, or the skivvy at the hearth, to the master you're invisible.

HOGBIN: *(Screwing himself into a combination of the three monkeys.)* I'm invisible… *(Pause. SAVAGE grapples with speech.)*

SAVAGE: I have followed you down streets…and where I saw you once…returned…at the same hour…fruitlessly, of course…what is your itinerary…you do presumably go… I WILL PERSIST WITH THIS…you have your place but I obviously *(Pause.)* My lungs, my stomach have all gone void and howling with – *(In desperation he extends a hand to her.)* Helen – *(Suddenly HOGBIN slaps his face.)*

HOGBIN: There!

SAVAGE: *(Reeling.)* What –

HOGBIN: *(Darting behind HELEN.)* Her arms, not mine! *(SAVAGE makes to grab him.)* HER ARMS...! *(He pretends to scratch HELEN's neck.)*

HELEN: What?

SAVAGE: How can I when –

HELEN: What? *(Pause.)*

SAVAGE: I have to be your lover. I who invented your condition MUST. *(Pause.)*

HELEN: To be my lover? And what is that? *(Pause.)*

SAVAGE: What is it…?

HELEN: WHAT IS IT, YES!

HOGBIN: *(To SAVAGE.)* Are you deaf or something? You talk about the beginning and she wants to know the end. *(SAVAGE reaches out. Again HOGBIN beats his hand away. SAVAGE reels.)* Thinks to finger me. Thinks to touch specific parts will weaken all resistance. He's read a book on the erogenous zones which says the touch kills argument.

SAVAGE: Help me.

HOGBIN: HELP YOU? HELP YOU?

SAVAGE: I twist. I writhe. I'm poisoned. Mind of slab of concrete and the minutes hang off me like crankshafts, I could snap the hands off clocks they move so sullenly. THE LENGTH OF A NIGHT, do you know THE IMPOSSIBLE DURATION OF A SINGLE NIGHT, I lick the clouds for dawn, and cats, I know their tracks and habits, the wriggle of the tomcat's arse and all the lashing of dawn choruses, IT HURTS TO LOOK AT YOU, I would chuck imagination in the ditch and bury it for one moment of your sad mouth against my sad mouth. *(He sees HOGBIN's expression.)* WHAT'S HE TO YOU, THE GRINNING BASTARD? *(He bites his lip. Pause.)*

HELEN: Nothing new. *(Pause.)*

SAVAGE: No…

HELEN: In your message. *(Pause.)*

SAVAGE: Well no…

HELEN: Is there?

SAVAGE: I suppose there wouldn't be –

HELEN: Nothing new in that. *(Pause.)* Why maim me? *(Pause.)* I WAS ALREADY A SPECTACLE OF PAIN, WHY ELSE DID THEY WANT ME? *(SAVAGE stares at her.)* Beauty did you say? No, it's pain they loved… *(HOGBIN's hands reach up to SAVAGE's face, and hold him.)* My kiss is stiff as brick, and my womb full of straw, but he won't mind… *(He draws SAVAGE to HELEN's breast.)* Arid Helen… But he won't mind… *(SAVAGE shudders.)* Listen, his male murmur, his male thirst… *(CREUSA enters, looks.)*

CREUSA: Who needs arms to fasten in their buttocks? *(Pause.)*

HOGBIN: I can't see you today…

CREUSA: I'LL THRUST MY ARMS IN A REAPING MACHINE, WILL THAT MAKE ME POPULAR? *(Pause.)*

HOGBIN: I can't see you today…

CREUSA: Well, no, you've got work to do. SHOULD I STUFF MY ARSE IN A SHREDDER?

SAVAGE: *(Catching a sound.)* Shh! *(Pause.)*

CREUSA: I plant it like a seed. Mum's Troy. It sprouts. It blooms. It sends out runners.

SAVAGE: *(Getting to his feet.)* Listen! *(Pause. He cups his ear.)* No laughter…

HOGBIN: *(Straining his ear.)* No drums.

SAVAGE: Or rattles. THE TAMBOURINE HAS CEASED, HEY!

SHADE: *(Running in.)* SILENCE…! WHERE'S IT COMING FROM?

HOGBIN: *(Pointing arbitrarily.)* There… *(EPSOM and GUMMERY hurry in.)*

SHADE: *(Indicating.)* There! *(EPSOM rushes in the direction.)*

HOGBIN: No, there! *(GUMMERY looks in bewilderment, and EPSOM returns, blankly.)*

EPSOM: Hold it…

SHADE: Noises are starting in my head. The whispering of shared and subtle sacraments. Start a carnival! *(No one moves. Pause.)* I hear the little stirring of the private act. Make the bands play! *(Still no one moves. Realisation dawns on SHADE. He walks slowly across the stage, stops.)* The word today is – *(Suddenly, as if impulsively, GUMMERY seizes SHADE in his arms, pinioning him and lifting him off the ground.)*

GUMMERY: No word!

SHADE: Oh, Brian, you – Oh, Brian, you magnificent specimen, I twitch in your embrace as the helpless hamster in the infant's fingers. BUT TO WHAT EFFECT! *(Pause.)* All right, I'll have a tantrum. *(He kicks his legs like a baby.)*

Tantrum, all right? Now, can we get back to politics, we have a state to govern. *(Pause.)*

GUMMERY: What shall I do? *(He turns to anyone who will listen.)* What shall I do? *(Pause.)*

SHADE: Come on, Brian, they will be missing you in the gymnasium. Put me down, will you. *(Pause.)*

GUMMERY: I can't put you down.

SHADE: You can't? Why not?

GUMMERY: Because I picked you up.

SHADE: What? Logic! Logic! Can't put me down because you – Logic! Logic!

GUMMERY: I picked you up to stop you, and if I put you down you'll start again. So I can't put you down. *(Pause.)*

SHADE: Well, Brian, you have a problem. It comes to making gestures that you can't complete.

EPSOM: Put him down if he promises to –

SHADE: NO DEALS.

EPSOM: Barry, you ain't in much of a position to –

SHADE: I AM IN THE BEST POSITION. I HAVE THE BRAIN. *(Pause.)* Really, who would credit this? People don't know how they're governed.

GUMMERY: *(To EPSOM.)* I don't know what to do…

SHADE: You don't, do you? You really don't?

GUMMERY: Les? *(EPSOM shrugs.)*

SHADE: No luck with Les.

GUMMERY: SHUDDUP WILL YER! *(Pause.)*

SHADE: I won't ask if your arms are aching because you are in such wonderful condition no doubt you could keep this up for weeks,

I only ask you, in all humbleness, do you know what you're doing? *(Pause.)*

GUMMERY: No.

SHADE: Excellent. Point of departure. Now, put me on the ground and we –

CREUSA: No –

SHADE: What?

CREUSA: No –

SHADE: Come again –

CREUSA: Don't –

SHADE: Brian, this is a Trojan bitch –

CREUSA: Put him down and they'll hate you in every bar between the dockyards and the allotments –

SHADE: Brian –

CREUSA: Women will knit your shape in wool and throw darts at it –

SHADE: Listen, we fought ten years for one whore, don't let another –

CREUSA: KEEP HIM UP, I SAID.

SHADE: COME ON, DOCTOR, IT'S YOUR GOVERNMENT! *(Pause.)* Oh doctor… I think you wear silence like a tart wears frocks, half off the shoulder…to make more appetizing the hagflesh underneath…ANYTHING UNDERNEATH? *(Pause.)*

SAVAGE: I must betray you, do you mind? *(Pause.)* I am a traitor by instinct, because to doubt is treason, and I doubt commitment even as I utter it, whether to women or the state. Have you noticed, I write constitutions as boys make planes from glue and balsa? *(Pause.)* And now you ache to punish me. I do understand that, the thirst for punishment, I do know disloyalty burns the stomach to a cinder. *(Pause.)* Don't put him down, he'll only ram sharp things in our eyes…

SCENE TWO

FLADDER, seated, weaves a massive basket.

HELEN: When you lost your tongue, did you stop thinking? *(He looks at her.)* The contrary, of course. *(Pause.)* And so with me. *(Pause.)* ARMLESS I REACH OUT, WHY? *(Pause. He works.)* I tell you this because you are my husband. Come what may, this fuck or that, this famine or this riot, you are my husband. *(Pause.)* Funny word. I think it most mean, like old domestic dog, or cat, HAD TEETH ONCE. WAS WILD IN CERTAIN STATES. *(He stops.)* Oh, don't weep. DON'T WEEP I HONOUR YOU. *(Pause.)* All right, not honour, I don't honour you, I retail my life. *(Pause.)* WHO ELSE SHOULD I TELL? I am carrying the doctor's child. *(Pause.)* I think. *(Pause.)* Do do the raffia. Weave on. *(Pause. She spontaneously goes to him, nuzzles his head.)* Oh, you must have developed so much in your silence, I think if your late wisdom was inscribed I'd say, BRILLIANT BUT UTTERLY INCOMPREHENSIBLE! So remote you are, so distant from our – *(CREUSA appears. HELEN turns to face her.)* Don't pester me, I can still kick.

CREUSA: Answer –

HELEN: You bother like a barmy wasp – you cling –

CREUSA: Answer –

HELEN: WHAT IS IT, JAM ON MY LIP?

CREUSA: WHY AREN'T YOU ASHAMED OF YOUR LIFE? I INSIST YOU'RE ASHAMED OF YOUR LIFE. *(Pause.)* I think my cunt drips acid and if he were to enter me I'd scald the seven skins off him, WHOSE CHILD IS IT, I make a fool of myself, obviously, an utter fool, they say the ex-queen's cracked, half her head's turned biscuit, and then I think, a fool, so what, a fool to who? I won't stuff hatred down, a little wire sawing away inside my gut and grin all rights, I wont! *(Pause.)*

HELEN: He stands beside me.

CREUSA: Yes.

HELEN: And close.

CREUSA: Go on.

HELEN: His belly – you want to know this, do you –

CREUSA: Yes –

HELEN: To my arse and so – *(Pause.)*

CREUSA: Go on – please – *(Pause.)*

HELEN: No more.

CREUSA: MORE. YES!

HELEN: You want the pain. You want it…how you want… *(Pause.)*

CREUSA: The hate grows on my gums at night. Thick paste of loathing. I spit it in the sink. *(HOGBIN enters gaily.)*

HOGBIN: *(Holding them out.)* Washed our hands! *(He sees CREUSA, stops. She goes out.)*

HELEN: Twelve Troys! *(He goes to feed her from a bowl.)* Twelve Troys and then –

HOGBIN: Egg mayonnaise!

HELEN: Twelve Troys and then what?

HOGBIN: Twelve?

HELEN: Twelve, yes. And me to suffer under every one! *(Pause. He stares at her.)*

HOGBIN: *(Thrusting it to her lips.)* Brown bread –

HELEN: NO BREAD!

HOGBIN: Egg, then –

HELEN: NO EGG!

HOGBIN: Must eat!

HELEN: Why eat? To live? For what? For love? Whose love?

HOGBIN: Yer going on –

HELEN: Your love? I HAVE NO ARMS! I WATCH, I LISTEN. HELEN HAS NINE TROYS TO SUFFER, ALL RIGHT, I EAT, ALL RIGHT, THE BREAD, THE EGG, I PERSEVERE, SHH! *(He feeds her.)*

GAY: *(Entering.)* MUM'S TROY. The first lesson. *(Pause.)* I am not a mum. But I did write the lesson. *(Pause.)* In the first place was the ARISTOCRACY, and they were so idle they gave away their infants to others to suckle, so the infants grew up most confused regarding love, not distinguishing their mothers from their nurses or their arses from their lips, and consequently PLUNDERED THE WORLD WITH ICY HARDNESS. And after them came the DEMOCRATS, who believed life was too short for privilege, so they sent their infants into SCHOOLS to learn the way of the world, and they emerged from schools like tigers, intent on butchering the WEAK. And finally there came the LOVING MOTHERS, who kept their infants close, breathing the breath of the child and sleeping its sleep, so each single child grew up full of certainty the world loved her, which it did, to some extent. But so did all the others, LOVE'S A DRUG, YOU

SEE, and they tore each other to ribbons in their jealousy! *(Pause.)* Unofficial verson. *(A thunderous noise.)*

SCENE THREE

SHADE, imprisoned in the woven basket, is raised by pulleys drawn by EPSOM and GUMMERY. SAVAGE watches.

SHADE: Oh, dear, I shall get wet…! The piss of Zeus will shrink me like a garment, sodden one minute and bleached the next I LIKE IT HERE INCIDENTALLY I'll shrivel until this little floor is vast as plains which take me days to scuttle over I ALWAYS WANTED THIS, DIDN'T YOU KNOW? My longing to be stopped – *(He touches the sides.)* Edge! Edge! OH, LOVELY LIMIT TO MY DREAM! Goodbye, Brian, and goodbye, Les, I shrink, you great empire builders, *au revoir,* I have my provinces as well, WHAT'S ROME TO A GALAXY? WHAT'S RUSSIA IN THE SUN? SPECK, BRIAN, SPECK! *(He is still. GUMMERY and EPSOM leave. SAVAGE watches the basket.)*

SAVAGE: Because I was an intellectual I chose to follow thought, thought to the finish, that is the duty of one, isn't it? The finger of thought beckoned me past the frontier post where others who had been my equals stood or waved me through, YES, YOU STAY BEHIND AND COURT YOUR ADMIRERS, oh, the teachers with their followings, the gifted with their cliques, they carve their names in wet cement to the sound of the acolyte's giggles. DANCE ON THE SKIN OF KNOWLEDGE but don't fall through, you'll drop forever. *(Pause.)* HELEN! *(Pause.)* It howls here and no cunning girls of seventeen think I am fascinating, no youths can be seduced in my dim study or learn the trivial habits of depravity over set texts, KNICKERS AND KAFKA, SALIVA AND THE GREEKS! HELEN! *(She enters, with HOGBIN, looks at him.)*

HELEN: Oh, my ugly lover…

SAVAGE: Yes…

HELEN: Oh, my shapeless adorer, would you hack my legs off also? Legless, would you desire me more?

SAVAGE: I don't…

HELEN: You do know, yes, you do…

SAVAGE: I don't…

HELEN: WHAT PART, THEN…! *(He hides his face.)* What joint or knuckle, what pared-down, shredded, particle would serve to be the point at which your love would stop, ESSENTIAL HELEN? Slithering over rocks, some slither of cheek or gum, there! Saw her! Flap of appendix in the rock pool! *(He goes to reach for her.)* Don't come near me. The greater the space between us, the more I suffer. It conducts my heat. She tells me I must be ashamed. I'm unashamed. And so are you, twice the dead of Troy and I would not apologize. I have your child or maybe not, all this and unashamed. *(He goes out to reach for her.)* Don't come nearer…! You will kill my ecstasy. *(He stops.)* They hate me in Mums' Troy, they hate me worse than ever Shade or Fladder did, can it be true that every life is precious, can it? Mums' Troy is babies, all the kerbs are padded and the rivers hung with nets, breasts out in the market and the endless music of their gurgles, the PREPOSTEROUS CLAIM OF LIFE –

SAVAGE: Kiss me –

HELEN: Your squirt, my fluid, look out, CLAIMS FROM THE MUDDY WATER! They all want their ninety years and I brought whole regiments to earth like swatted flies on wallpaper…

SAVAGE: Kiss me –

HELEN: THE SNAIL'S INSISTENCE ON ITS RIGHTS! *(She halts him.)* If I saw a baby drift by on a raft of rushes I would not lift a finger for it, though the river bubbled it to sharks or iceflows, pity, the great unending ribbon of pity, it has no end except exhaustion, I have a child in me and yet I hacked the features off dying boys, and I have watched priests visit the starving whilst eating sandwiches, but listen, the doctor must be fed! The doctor must eat even if the patient starves, that's logical! All this logic! All this pity! Kiss me, now. Kiss me…! *(He kisses her.)* Your mouth would draw me in and make me vanish, a sweet in your jaw, sucked to oblivion… *(They kiss.)*

HOGBIN: *(Withdrawing from their embrace.)* Nine Troys to go…!

GAY: *(Off.)* Psst!

HOGBIN: Wha'?

GAY: Psst!

HOGBIN: Where! *(He stares in the dark.)* Can't see yer, here –

GAY: *(Emerging.)* Got to have a baby.

HOGBIN: Got to 'ave a –

GAY: You'll do.

HOGBIN: Me? What 'ave you –

GAY: *(Jerking her skirt up.)* Like this –

HOGBIN: Hold on –

GAY: WHAT FOR. *(She glares at him.)* New Troy's for babies. So. *(Pause.)*

HOGBIN: Look I –

GAY: WHAT! *(Pause.)*

HOGBIN: No will. And no desire. Sorry.

GAY: Look, pregnant women get three ration books. That's will. I got my legs open. That's desire. Now do it.

HOGBIN: I can't just –

GAY: YOU ARE INTERFERING WITH MY HAPPINESS. *(Pause.)* The happiness I'm entitled to, you are frustrating it.

HOGBIN: Ask someone else.

GAY: I have done. I just asked Homer. Homer can't.

HOGBIN: He can't!

GAY: Apparently he can't. He wept. Absurd. And he's been pestering me for years. *(Pause. He looks away.)* Really, if you were a dog, you would. Have you seen dogs? *(He shakes his head.)* If you don't, I'm down the harbour. *(Pause. She turns swiftly.)*

HOGBIN: Don't do that.

GAY: Why not? Lots of dogs down there, in sailors' outfits, woof! *(She laughs. Then she puts her arms round his neck. Sound of infantile wailing.)*

SCENE FOUR

GUMMERY, EPSOM enter with babies under each arm, which they place on the ground. MACLUBY enters, passing HOGBIN, OTHERS also carrying babies. The stage rapidly fills with babies, as the carriers come and go.

MACLUBY: The land restocked. *(They gurgle. CREUSA brings two further armfuls.)* The terrible regime of innocence. *(And others.)* Its jurisprudence.

CREUSA: WHY FUCKING NOT.

MACLUBY: *(Shrugs.)* No reason.

CREUSA: No reason. And who wants it? Reason brought us to extinction's edge. NO REASON IN MUMS' TROY. *(Babies are filling the stage.)* We found a scientist and made him sweep the street. He swept the street but chalked formulae on kerbs. So we gave him lavatories to swab. He swabbed the lavatories but made secret drawings on the underside of seats. So we executed him. It is a sickness, curiosity.

EPSOM: *(Putting down A BABY.)* 'oo's a little baby, then, 'oo's a little –

CREUSA: You are mocking that child.

EPSOM: Am I? Sorry.

CREUSA: The child is your superior.

EPSOM: Yup.

CREUSA: A moral genius compared to you.

EPSOM: Yup.

CREUSA: *(To GAY.)* Gay, please.

GAY: The Second Lesson of Mums' Troy.

CREUSA: Louder. They will be silent if you interest them. They will be attentive if you win their respect.

GAY: Yes… *(She clears her throat.)* THE SECOND LESSON OF MUMS' TROY.

CREUSA: A baby is not a baby.

GAY: No.

CREUSA: It is an adult in a state of moral excitement.

GAY: Yes.

CREUSA: Go on.

GAY: Innocence is not without authority! Nor does purity go unarmed! The meaningless violence of Old Troys is replaced by the liberating force of pre-articulacy – *(To CREUSA.)* They aren't listening –

CREUSA: Oh yes, they are –

GAY: Are they?

CREUSA: Go on –

GAY: *(Louder.)* Spared language but also spared – *(She turns to CREUSA in despair.)* I can't seem to make them –

CREUSA: You are imposing oppressive notions of silence and discipline on them. They are engrossed –

GAY: *(Puzzled.)* They're –

CREUSA: ENGROSSED. *(She stamps her foot on the ground.)* SHHH. *(Silence. Pause.)* Where's Helen? *(EPSOM looks at GUMMERY.)* Fetch Helen, please. *(They go out. Gurgles of contentment fill the stage. CREUSA walks up and down between THE BABIES. HELEN appears, with SAVAGE. Pause.)* Helen, where's your baby? *(Pause.)* Ask you again. *(Pause.)* Where's your baby? *(Pause. THE BABIES begin to fret.)* Oh, God, they sense catastrophe… *(She stamps her foot. Silence.)* Helen, is your baby still alive? *(Pause. THE BABIES start to cry.)* Oh, they cry with horrible anticipation…!

SAVAGE: She –

CREUSA: SHUT UP, YOU. Helen, have you…terrible to speak this but…have you…awful but we must endure…

SAVAGE: She is the –

CREUSA: SHUT UP, YOU! *(Pause.)* Betrayed the sacred trust of motherhood…? *(Pause.)* Have you, my dear? *(She stamps her foot. THE BABIES are still.)*

HELEN: It died.

CREUSA: Of what?

HELEN: Insignificance. *(THE BABIES screech.)*

GUMMERY: MUR – DER!

HELEN: You should know.

CREUSA: You stifled innocence. You hung a cloth over its face.

HELEN: Innocence? No, it was guilty. They all are.

CREUSA: Of what?

HELEN: Aborting love.

CREUSA: *(To a rage of BABIES.)* They accuse! They prosecute!

GAY: *(Ignoring THE COURT, to HOGBIN.)* Love you.

HOGBIN: Wha'?

GAY: Love you!

HELEN: The more you sin yourselves, the more you must insist on innocence, you impose it on your infants.

CREUSA: TO KILL YOUR OWN CHILD…

HELEN: It would have been a killer, too, of the love I suffer for its father. I never let a child come in the way of love. You know the appetite of babies. And this one was voracious. *(THE BABIES strike new notes.)* Half my sons slew men they never knew, and half my daughters slept with murderers…!

CREUSA: You stuffed a pillow on its face!

HELEN: I was more charitable than that.

CREUSA: How, then?

HELEN: I did it with my breast. *(THE BABIES are stunned with horror.)* A breast is milk, but also, pillow…

EPSOM: Brian, I think I will be sick…

GUMMERY: A mother kills her – I can't say it – with 'er – I can't say it –

GAY: *(To HOGBIN.)* We'll grow old together! I'll be an old apple, and you'll be an old pear!

EPSOM: We should 'ave murdered 'er! *(He comforts a nearby BABY.)* Oochie, coochie, coochie… When she stood in the ruins of Old Troy – oochie, coochie! Murdered her!

CREUSA: *(Walking among THE BABIES.)* Some want revenge…but others…call for clemency…

HELEN: They hate…

CREUSA: Not hate…

HELEN: Hate, wordlessly. What they would not give for a word! And we, who have words, scream…

CREUSA: Call for clemency, from there… *(She indicates A BABY.)* He argues…

EPSOM: It's a she.

CREUSA: She persuades. She is most effective. And they *(She indicates all THE OTHERS.)* agree! Your plea –

HELEN: I made no plea –

CREUSA: Your plea finds sympathy! I am so happy for you! *(Pause.)* But at the same time – our disapproval must be registered. The act may be forgiven, but it must be marked… *(Pause. She walks among THE BABIES.)* How quiet they are, not vindictive, but melancholy, philosophical…

HELEN: Oh, listen…the prelude to my pain…

SAVAGE: Helen!

HELEN: The gulf of imagination yawns…

SAVAGE: Helen! *(Pause. CREUSA moves silently among THE BABIES. Stops. Pause.)*

CREUSA: They ask…in all humility…for him who suffers most…to choose… *(She looks at SAVAGE. HELEN lets out a terrible laugh. Pause.)*

HOGBIN: Hold it…

CREUSA: Shut up…

HOGBIN: Not 'im, not 'im, 'e's –

HELEN: *(To HOGBIN.)* YOU STIFLE HIM. HIS MIND. ITS DREAM. YOU TRAMPLE HIM. *(Pause.)*

SAVAGE: They say… *(Pause.)* If I interpret them… *(Pause.)* You have failed to be a mother, and therefore should not look like one… *(THE BABIES screech.)* I SAID IT! I SAID IT!

CREUSA: *(To EPSOM, GUMMERY.)* Out – quick – and do it!

HELEN: Oh, I'll be good! Oh, this time, promise! I'll be good!

HOGBIN: *(To SAVAGE.)* MANIAC!

SAVAGE: Don't you want to know! Oh, don't you WANT!

HOGBIN: Helen! *(EPSOM and GUMMERY lead HELEN away.)*

SAVAGE: You want to save her. But she can't be saved. I KNOW WHAT HELEN IS. *(HOGBIN hurries after.)* She could have reared the child in a garden. She could have stayed in Greece. ALWAYS THE POSSIBILITY OF SILENT LIFE BUT… *(He walks through THE BABIES.)* And he throws his pity at her, like confetti in a hurricane…

CREUSA: You know too much.

SAVAGE: Yes.

CREUSA: DO YOU KNOW YOU CAN KNOW TOO MUCH.

SAVAGE: Yes. I know even that. *(Pause. THE BABIES begin complaining.)*

CREUSA: *(To THE ADULTS.)* Clear them out. *(THE ADULTS collect up the bundles and carry them away. SAVAGE sees MACLUBY.)*

SAVAGE: How many selves have we got, MacLuby? *(MACLUBY looks at him.)* Old self, grab it, can we? Old self off the shelf? *(He stops.)* Show us an old self, MacLuby!

MACLUBY: Trembling…

SAVAGE: Yes…

MACLUBY: Shuddering…

SAVAGE: Yes, but not with horror! How you would love that!

MACLUBY: Me? No.

SAVAGE: How philistine and trite! My grappling with conscience, my submission and supine apology, suicide from a borrowed rope, no. *(MACLUBY shrugs, sets off.)* Show us an old self. *(He stops.)*

MACLUBY: Wants to reach into the wardrobe –

SAVAGE: Yes –

MACLUBY: Take an old self off the hanger –

SAVAGE: Yes –

MACLUBY: Blow the dust off and –

SAVAGE: Why not? How else can I see if I've travelled? *(Pause. SAVAGE's SON enters. They stare at one another.)*

BOY: *(Tossing a bar of soap.)* Ashes of roses... *(Pause.)*

SAVAGE: What...?

BOY: Ashes of roses... *(Pause.)*

SAVAGE: Good... *(CREUSA enters, gesticulating wildly to EPSOM and GUMMERY.)*

CREUSA: He said –

EPSOM: We 'eard what he said –

CREUSA: HE SAID – SHE WAS NOT A MOTHER –

GUMMERY: We –

CREUSA: LISTEN – EXACT WORDS – THEREFORE SHE SHOULD NOT LOOK LIKE ONE –

EPSOM: She doesn't –

CREUSA: WHAT!

EPSOM: She doesn't look like one. *(Pause of exasperated disbelief. To GUMMERY.)* Does she? *(GUMMERY shakes his head.)*

CREUSA: What's a mother got?

EPSOM: What's a –

CREUSA: YES, WHAT? *(They stare at one another in bewilderment. CREUSA tears open her garment.)* IT'S BREASTS SHE'S GOT! *(Pause.)*

EPSOM: *(At the point.)* We'll go back and – *(CREUSA catches sight of THE BOY, standing. She stares at him. Pause.)* Shall we? *(She goes to him, smells his hair, his skin. Pause. She sits on the ground.)* Go back and – *(She does not reply. A wind grows from a whisper.)*

SCENE FIVE

HOGBIN enters with a dish on a pole, which he extends to the cage. He waits. He grows impatient.

HOGBIN: Dinn – er! *(The wind. Pause.)* Dinn – er! *(Pause. He puts down the pole, flashes his torch at the cage. It is empty. He turns the torch off, then on again. He falls heavily to the floor.)* ED – U – CAT – TION! *(He seizes the pole. Wields it.)* Against irrationality the pole of knowledge! OFF! *(He prods at the air. Pause. He approaches the cage.)* Are you in there? *(Pause.)* Are you, though…? *(Pause.)* Come again…? *(Pause. HOGBIN emits a cry of horror. A tiny laugh from the cage. He sinks to the floor. Daylight. HELEN enters, armless, legless, pushed by HOMER in a chair.)*

HELEN: I've missed you! I really have! I went to brush my hair, and where were my arms? I went to get out of bed, and where were my legs? Fortunately my creator appeared and lent me limbs, but he can't do a woman justice as you can, look, he's got my blouse on back to front. I didn't criticise. He is at least a hundred, aren't you. One hundred at least. Gay says you love each other, but how can you, there is nothing to love, or do you love that? Do you love her vacancy and plan to write your signature across her void? My stumps hurt when the wind is in the East, which is the prevailing angle THE MORE THEY INJURE ME THE MORE THEY HATE, can you explain that? You're educated. *(He looks at her.)* They want to pity me, it is there only hope, but I am not pitiful, am I? I cannot think why they neglect my face, it is the obvious starting point, but perhaps they need to see me weep. I do weep. Or shout an accusation. They long to be accused. I WON'T SATISFY THEM. *(Pause.)* My clothes are so exquisite, I found a woman who understands the trunk, as form, its own aesthetic, and her hemming is magnificent. I think in future we shall all be mutants, we shall be born so, and all limbs will be knobs, and some will have more, and some will have less, and there will be such a wonderful variety! It will happen in the womb, how I don't know, some fine powder will fall from the sky, or something in the water, and we will be such a fascinating menagerie! I set this fashion, as I did in Attica, I was slavishly copied there, but now I am rather too progressive. Do you know what Doctor Savage says, he says I am two mouths, that's all. TWO MOUTHS! And I ran every morning in Old Troy. While Paris kipped his coital kip I was up and tearing through the market, the porters' bawdy in the slipstream of my arse! They pelted me with fruit and once I let them cluster me, on sacks. But only once. Royalty is loved for its transgressions but not habitually. *(Pause.)* Are you deserting me? *(Pause.)*

HOGBIN: I am losing my mind…

HELEN: Which mind? The one you brought to Troy with you?

HOGBIN: WHICH MIND?

HELEN: Yes. Which? Do you think you lose your mind? You find others. Do you think you lose your sight? You see by other channels. And the legless also manoeuvre! I once saw a fingerless woman with twelve inch thumbs. OF COURSE I SAY THIS TO CONSOLE MYSELF. *(Pause.)* You want your mind, but why? To document your pain? To put order in it?

To fix its mayhem, why? WELCOME PAIN I ALWAYS WAS EXPECTING YOU. Even in copulation, even in the madness of torrential fuck I knew my agony awaited me. Is Gay delivered of her monster yet?

HOGBIN: It's not a monster.

HELEN: How do you know?

HOGBIN: Because we're healthy.

HELEN: Healthy? What's health to do with it? Of course it is a monster but it merely lacks the strength SHH! I WAS PUNISHED FOR SAYING THIS LAST MONTH, SHH! *(She looks at HOMER.)* This man is a monster, aren't you?

HOMER: Yes.

HELEN: I believe he would torture the world to death, for disappointment.

HOMER: Yes.

HELEN: Poet's Troy will be the worst yet. POETS' TROY, DUCK YOU INNOCENTS! *(Pause. To HOGBIN.)* Hold me, and tell me what I feel like. I cannot hold myself.

HOGBIN: I can't.

HELEN: Why ever not?

HOGBIN: I'll only – I'll get all – start to –

HELEN: Go on, then –

HOGBIN: No.

HELEN: HOLD ME…! *(He goes to her, puts his arms round her. Pause.)*

HOGBIN: I want –

HELEN: What? What do you want?

HOGBIN: A clean, white shirt… *(Pause.)* A tie… *(Pause.)* And trousers, with a perfect crease… *(Pause.)*

HOMER: When Troy fell I followed Odysseus. I followed him because I could not bring myself to look into the ruins. We all knew, there was a history in the ruins. But I thought, there will be no public for a song about the ruins.

HOGBIN: IT'S YOUR JOB, YOU BASTARD. *(Pause. CREUSA enters.)*

CREUSA: You wife's in labour. *(HOGBIN detaches himself from HELEN, starts to go.)* The Mums are in attendance. But you may wait. You wait, and pace. Up and down, you pace. Your painless hours. Pitiable thing. *(He goes out. To HELEN with joy.)* Another baby! *(Pause.)* My son appeared.

HELEN: Did he?

CREUSA: As if to cleanse me. My lost son. As if to make the juice of kindness flow from my dry and withered ducts. Tears from the baked kernels of my eyes. As if, flinging our arms about each other we would cry, 'Forgive…!'

HELEN: And…?

CREUSA: And I would be washed in pity and walk with a serenity I never found in all my kicked-up life…

HELEN: But…?

CREUSA: It isn't like that. *(Pause. Then HELEN laughs.)* Yes, do laugh. You know, don't you, it isn't like that? The redemption? The reunion? All lies? *(HELEN laughs.)* She knows, she knows better than you! *(She looks at HOMER.)* REDEMPTION FUCK. *(Pause.)* No, we change, we do change. There's the misery. Except for you. *(Pause.)* He told them, tear your breasts off. But they made a torso out of you instead. Men don't grasp metaphors, do they? Not swift to connect. Under the circumstances the babies recommend you may keep the rest –

HELEN: I thank the babies –

CREUSA: Do you?

HELEN: Profusely. *(Pause.)*

CREUSA: I think even as you say a thing, you know it to be false. You know it, and yet you say it. I think you are the enemy of all Troys no matter whose. I think you believe nothing and therefore ought to suffer everything imagination might conceive. I AM A BETTER PERSON THAN YOU.

HELEN: Yes.

CREUSA: However cruel.

HELEN: Yes.

CREUSA: For all the rotting of my kindness and the crumbling of my soul –

HELEN: Yes –

CREUSA: I AM. I AM. *(Pause. She runs to HELEN, holds her.)* Oh, you sliced thing you make me SHUDDER. *(To HOMER.)* Doesn't she? Make you SHUDDER? *(She caresses HELEN.)* Say you deserved it, say you earned it, say it, say…

HELEN: Yes…

CREUSA: I cannot resist you. I, the better person, cannot resist you, why? When you are so incorrigible, why? This terrible but honest place. This island of confessions. I long for you, and my son is earth, is pebble. *(To HOMER.)* Can you explain that? *(He shakes his head.)* HE DOESN'T WANT TO KNOW ANY MORE… *(She lovingly undoes HELEN's buttons.)* And he puts her blouse on back to front…

SCENE SIX

SAVAGE is sitting under the cage.

SAVAGE: So Alexander the Great came to the barrel where Diogenes was living FUCK KNOWS WHY HE LIVED IN A BARREL THE POSEUR and said I am the most powerful man in the world, come to listen to you, the wisest man in the world, speak. And the yob waited. The yob waited for the poseur. And Diogenes said, timing this exquisitely, and WITH ALL THE CALCULATION OF A MAN WHO KNEW NO AUTOCRAT WOULD STOOP TO TEAR HIS BOWELS OUT, the poseur said, BELIEVING HIMSELF SECURE IN HIS REPUTATION AS FIVE PERSIAN ARMIES BEHIND THEIR STAKES, said, YOU HAVE TO ADMIRE THE PREDICTABILITY, YOU REALLY DO, you are standing in my sunlight. *(Pause.)* DO YOU CALL THAT WIT! DO YOU CALL THAT INSOLENCE? *(Pause. A tiny laugh from the cage.)* The intellectual Bajcsy-Zsilinsky had been a racist murderer, an anti-semite, a killer of trade unionists, a scrawler of slogans, a publisher of slanders, an editor of intimidating magazines, anti-pity, anti-intellect, but when the Nazis came he met them with a gun. HE HAD TRULY TRAVELLED. And they shot him in a cellar. BANG. The futility of acquiescence versus the futility of resistance. BANG. Why are you dressed like an accountant? *(HOGBIN has entered, and waits.)* Are there accountants in Mum's Troy? How can there be when there's no money? But no, that's logical, that's symmetry, the increase in the level of poverty will be matched by the rise in students of accountancy, and as for poverty we recommend more barrels! *(Pause.)* No, you're worried, I can see you are. I go on, and you're worried. I humour myself and you fret. THAT'S HOW WE ARE, JOHN! I pretend. I act sympathy. *(He pretends to listen.)* The ear – extended. *(Pause.)*

HOGBIN: It ain't normal. *(Pause.)*

SAVAGE: Ah.

HOGBIN: IT AIN'T NORMAL.

SAVAGE: Pity…perhaps…

HOGBIN: They say it's me.

SAVAGE: Who does?

HOGBIN: The Babies.

SAVAGE: Say it's you…?

HOGBIN: I said why don't yer let me see it, they said just stand there, I said you're hiding something they said wait, I said it's my kid too, you – and I released a torrent of abuse –

SAVAGE: Well, naturally –

HOGBIN: I was that tense –

SAVAGE: Inevitably –

HOGBIN: And I saw it, and it was – *(Pause.)* They say I am a genetic criminal. *(Pause.)* What's that? *(GAY enters, sits. Long pause.)*

GAY: I do not love it. *(Pause.)* How I wanted to… *(Pause.)* And how absurd to want.

HOGBIN: A GENETIC CRIMINAL, WHAT'S THAT! Gay, you testify –

GAY: The testicles can testify.

HOGBIN: Gay –

GAY: SHH, I AM THE TEACHER! *(Pause.)* Because I know, and always knew, to be born was absurd. So absurd that to be angry was equally absurd. And just as being angry was absurd, so caring was absurd. Quite as absurd. Which left me only – ecstasy. Not my mother's ecstasy, not the fucking-out of consciousness – but the different ecstasy of perpetuating absurdity because what else can you do when you are the victim of a joke but participate in the joke and so outjoke the joker? LAUGH LOUDER, ALWAYS LOUDER STILL. So birth was ecstasy. Through the red blankets of pain I applauded all the blind and inexorable circumstances that brought life into this sticky planet. MORE LIFE! AND MORE LIFE YET! *(Pause.)*

HOGBIN: We'll find a shack. I'll put some flowers round the –

GAY: If only it were malice! The surge of mud that – the earthquakes that – the flood which suffocates the infant and the murderer. If only it were malice…but it isn't…how intolerable…How impossible to assimilate… *(Pause.)* So of course you're guilty. You have to be. And I have to hate. *(She extends a hand to him.)* What's your innocence got to do with it? *(He takes her hand.)* Hide, then. *(She shouts.)* THE CRIMINAL IS TOUCHING ME! Hide…!

HOGBIN: Gay –

GAY: POL – ICE!

HOGBIN: HIDE WHERE?

SAVAGE: And so, to hide him from his enemies, Athene wrapped him in a mist…

HOGBIN: Give us a mist, then!

GAY: POL – ICE!

HOGBIN: *(Running one way, then back again.)* Mist…! Mist…? No mist!

SAVAGE: Opinion.

HOGBIN: Wha'?

GAY: *(Hurrying out.)* THE CRIMINAL ENEMY OF MUM'S TROY! *(She points to HOGBIN.)*

SAVAGE: OPINION – *(Men rush in with sticks.)* IS – THE – MIST. *(HOGBIN turns to face them. A fraction of calculation elapses.)*

HOGBIN: Helen did it. *(They stop.)*
I mean.
I mean, the misery that woman's.
I mean, her life continues in the same old.
I mean, the very sight of her.
I ask you. *(Pause.)* I am the Accountant and therefore the disposer of all life and death, all marriage, surgery and literacy any of my calculation, yes, even the colour of the woman's pants and the baby's rash. *(Pause.)* She is guilty, you know that as well as me –

EPSOM: I 'ave chopped 'er twice, son –

HOGBIN: And is that sufficient? Two?

GUMMERY: Stood in her blood –

HOGBIN: I ask you. I don't seek to persuade, I merely ask –

GUMMERY: Her blood stopped round my ankles –

HOGBIN: Sufficient, was it? Two? I ask, that's all –

EPSOM: WHAT MORE IS THERE? *(Pause.)*

HOGBIN: What more? What more? Is imagination suffocated then? Is anger drained? Is all possibility exhausted by four strokes?

EPSOM: We ain't sophisticated –

HOGBIN: No, but dream a little, you have dark yards of unthought thought –

GUMMERY: Common soldiers, of the wars –

HOGBIN: Common, no! It is the likes of her have taught you commonness! You have in you the seeds of every genius who ever walked, but unwatered, no, don't, don't, it hurts to hear your nature stamped on, and by you… *(Pause.)*

GUMMERY: I have axed seven Troys. What are you after?

HOGBIN: After?

GUMMERY: YER CAN'T MANIPULATE THE PEOPLE.

HOGBIN: And would I try? Would I? I, scarcely shot of his virginity, new to the razor, gauche, louche, cunt-mad, cunt-terrorized, swallower of substances and kicker of cans, would I aspire to work one over you? You, whose faces are bibles of experience, would I have the neck? *(Pause. They admire him.)* Educated I may be, for all that means, and perceptive, yes, gifted, I grant you, and with skills of certain sorts, Accountancy and the European Mind, but arrogance, I'm spared, as you can see. *(He bows.)* All my wits are fagends, chip bags, and gutter dross beneath your boots… *(Pause.)*

EPSOM: Thank you.

HOGBIN: No more than your due.

EPSOM: He says so.

HOGBIN: I say so, and repeat as often as you fancy –

EPSOM: AND AGAIN!

HOGBIN: I praise, I praise, but listen to what little judgment I have assembled, Helen's limbs are neither here nor there –

EPSOM: No, neither. Here nor there.

HOGBIN: *(Acknowledging.)* You have the sticks, to you the wit – But Helen still rules Troy, the explanation for your unhappiness. *(Pause.)*

GUMMERY: What unhappiness?

EPSOM: 'HO ARE YOU CALLING UN'APPY? *(HOGBIN permits himself a smile.)*

HOGBIN: The unhappy, how slow they are to recognize themselves…! I say instead, unfulfilled. *(Pause.)* A jug half empty. An engine at low revs. An athlete with bound feet. I ask you, have you never thought you could do more?

EPSOM: You 'ave the echoing tones of an advert for mother's tonic –

HOGBIN: WELL, YES, BECAUSE GREAT TRUTH SHARES LANGUAGE WITH GREAT ERROR, and luscious sunsets are reflected in slum windows… *(Pause. HOGBIN waits.)*

GUMMERY: *(At last.)* Yes…

EPSOM: Brian –

GUMMERY: Yes, I said. *(Pause.)* Because yes, who's happy? Don't say you are, Les, don't please, your fifteen pints are testimony to a desperate life. –

EPSOM: AND YOUR BODY. *(Pause.)*

GUMMERY: My body? What of my body?

EPSOM: I've often thought, why is Brian so very – infatuated – with 'is body? A woman's, yes, that I cop, but to lavish such attention of yer own –

GUMMERY: WHAT IN FUCK'S –

EPSOM: Evidence of something, Brian –

GUMMERY: WHAT! WHAT!

HOGBIN: You see! You see, how once we look, we see! All points to our restlessness, and why? Because we know, we know, in every area, we are not whole… *(A profound pause.)*

GUMMERY: *(Looking around.)* We'll say we couldn't find you… *(To SAVAGE.)* Could we? Couldn't find him? *(They go out. HOGBIN sinks to his knees, exhausted, ecstatic.)*

HOGBIN: Oh, wonderful, oh, luscious, GIFT OF THE GAB.

SAVAGE: I see your education was not wasted…

HOGBIN: All your seminars – SHIT ON THEM – all your criticism – PISS ON IT –

SAVAGE: Yes, yes –

HOGBIN: The Speak. The Speak! THE – WORD – SAVES – LIFE! *(EPSOM comes back.)*

EPSOM: You do it.

HOGBIN: *(Horrified.)* What?

EPSOM: *(Flinging a sickle, which slides over the floor.)* What Helen needs. *(He goes out again. HOGBIN looks in horror at SAVAGE. SAVAGE lets out a laugh.)*

HOGBIN: Laugh. I love laughter. *(He laughs again.)* No, I love it. I do. Laugh. In the death camp. In the execution chamber. Balls to giggling, no, real laughter, please, the cosmic stuff, YER THINK I CAN'T DO IT, CUNT? *(SAVAGE stops.)*

SAVAGE: I think it's easy. I think there is nothing easier in the world.

HOGBIN: FLESH, WHAT'S THAT?

SAVAGE: Quite.

HOGBIN: The jets come down, maim, maim! The rattle of the bofors, FLESH, WHAT'S THAT?

SAVAGE: You tell me.

HOGBIN: The stabbing on the Number 3. The wife carved in the basement. FLESH, WHAT'S THAT?

SAVAGE: Indeed…

HOGBIN: Two 'undred pounds of murder in the Mercedes boot, FLESH, WHAT'S THAT! *(Pause. He is kneeling on the floor with the weapon.)* Shove off, I 'ave to prepare myself… *(Pause.)*

SAVAGE: Will you tell Helen, or will I? *(Pause.)*

HOGBIN: Me.

SAVAGE: I'll send her, then?

HOGBIN: Yes. *(SAVAGE looks at him.)* Go on, then. *(SAVAGE withdraws. A great silence, attended by a movement of sky and light. At last HOMER appears, pushing HELEN. They stop.)*

HELEN: My boy. My only one. *(HOGBIN doesn't move. SAVAGE enters. HOMER goes to HOGBIN, who is dead. He looks at SAVAGE.)*

SAVAGE: HE REFUTES THE ARGUMENT. And how? By counter-argument? Not Hogbin. No, Hogbin chooses to ignore. NO MORE QUOTATION OF THE EMACIATED TEXTS! The testimony of experts, the beautifully laid bricks of theory, the towering cathedrals of logic, NOT FOR HIM! *(Pause.)* I wrote on his report, this student follows arguments, but lives by instinct, but which instinct, SHAME? *(Pause.)* They'll put this down to love. But is it? *(He grabs HOMER.)* Is it? Is it love? *(GAY enters. SAVAGE releases HOMER.)*

GAY: Is my husband dead? *(They look at her.)* We were going to grow old together…! *(Pause.)* We were. When he had done his sentence. I would have waited at the prison door, holding the unloved blob. I would and he – *(To SAVAGE.)* Unforgivable, isn't it? UNFORGIVABLE PESSIMISM! *(Pause.)* Which I have never suffered from and cannot for the life of me comprehend. *(She looks at him, feigning objectivity.)* Of course the only man I ever loved would choose to kill himself, that was as certain as night follows day, water runs downhill, etcetera, so why I, heaven knows why I – *(She begins caressing his body, kissing him, undressing him.)* should be like this – at all – I can't – think – what – *(She moans.)*

HELEN: Gay.

GAY: When I – and – obviously – *(She sobs.)*

HELEN: Gay.

SAVAGE: Let her.

HELEN: Let her, why?

SAVAGE: Mourn –

HELEN: Mourn, why?

SAVAGE: WHEN PARIS DIED YOU FILLED ALL TROY WITH MAD WOMAN'S HOLLERING! *(She looks at him.)* And pints of your spit ran down the lintels, and your legs were bruised with kicking the inanimate, and servants ran from your flying pans of piss! *(To HOMER.)* He knows! He heard it!

HELEN: In those days I swept over every kind of trivia. *(SAVAGE stares at her.)* How you hate that. How you hate me to pulp the past and look on old fevers with contempt. What are you afraid of? Your coming neglect?

GAY: *(Rising to her feet.)* Better now! *(She straightens her dress. To HOMER.)* Was he a hero? You know what heroes are.

SAVAGE: Coming neglect?

GAY: Heroes have reputations, and these reputations matter more than life itself. Is that correct?

SAVAGE: WHAT NEGLECT?

GAY: At crucial points the hero must choose between the death of reputation or death itself. Invariably he chooses –

SAVAGE: I DENY NEGLECT'S THE CONSEQUENCE OF PASSION –

HELEN: Why? It happens.

SAVAGE: I STILL DENY.

HELEN: Deny by all means –

GAY: WILL YOU BE SILENT. I'M BEREAVED! *(Pause.)*

HOMER: Helen, they will make you smaller still…

HELEN: *(Horrified.)* Will they…? Oh, will they…? Have you seen…? *(GUMMERY, EPSOM, OTHERS, rush in.)*

GUMMERY: New Troy! Don't move, you unfulfilled!

EPSOM: *(Seeing the body.)* Oi! *(He points.)* Accountant. Dead.

GUMMERY: *(Appalled.)* Wholeness he promised me…

SAVAGE: Yes, but he was in a state of horror. Terror lent him speech.

GUMMERY: Wholeness…

SAVAGE: Speech of a reckless order –

GUMMERY: I long to be whole! *(SAVAGE is silent.)*

HELEN: Whole, yes, but whole for what? Health yes, but health for what? I am neither whole nor healthy and I am in torment if the wind blows from the East but have I ever asked for peace?

GUMMERY: Shut up.

HELEN: I ask you, peace for what? You must ask better questions –

GUMMERY: Shut up!

HELEN: Shh! Helen, not queen now, shh!

GUMMERY: How did he die?

SAVAGE: By choosing not to live.

GUMMERY: What was his name? Accountant, was it?

SAVAGE: He seemed content to be called Hogbin. I never heard him shun it.

GUMMERY: *(Hurt.)* Hogbin? We can't have that. I prefer he be called – *(He is inspired.)* Hyacinth. *(He looks at him.)* I give up arms today. And punch nobody.

EPSOM: Brian –

GUMMERY: I give up knackering. And bruisery. I preach Hyacinth.

EPSOM: Brian –

GUMMERY: There are hyacinths all along the seashore. We waded through them, coming off the boats.

EPSOM: Remember it…

GUMMERY: I PREACH HIM, THEN. I, utterly illiterate, will preach, and where I falter, PRAISE MY EFFORT. *(He braces himself.)* How much easier it was down the gym… *(Pause.)* Hyacinth says, great sunsets are reflected in slum windows. I WAS SUCH A WINDOW.

EPSOM: Oh, fuck it, Brian –

GUMMERY: I WON'T DESIST THOUGH SPEAKING COSTS ME BLOOD.

EPSOM: Daft bugger –

GUMMERY: Or grow wild with you, Les, however ill your criticism. Hyacinth would have me hear!

EPSOM: *(Indicating HOGBIN's body.)* Corpse of a yob!

GUMMERY: Throw away your liquor!

EPSOM: Bollocks.

GUMMERY: Tip away your beer!

EPSOM: Twice bollocks!

GUMMERY: I forgive this, Les –

EPSOM: *(Turning.)* YOU ARE A MURDERER.

GUMMERY: Was, Les, was –

EPSOM: AND A WOMAN BUTCHER.

GUMMERY: Was, was –

EPSOM: AND A CHILD SPITTER.

GUMMERY: Add to my list! Record not one, but every act of unfulfilment!

EPSOM: Unfulfilment? It was your finest hour!

GUMMERY: A slum window, reflecting every kind of filth, and you, on your rotting hinges, also reflect –

EPSOM: Don't call me a slum window –

GUMMERY: Oh, you catcher of bad lights! PRAISE MY POWERS AND THE BODY, SHRIVEL!

EPSOM: Goodbye, biceps…

GUMMERY: SHRINK!

EPSOM: Pectorals, ta-ta…

GUMMERY: Yes, muscles waste, because they flexed for evil. *(He waves his hand.)* That's it for today! *(He is breathless from exertion.)* I am tireder than I was from ninety press-ups, but I find myself, my unborn self…coming through the dark..

EPSOM: I shall miss you, my ol' mate…

GUMMERY: *(Wiping the perspiration off his face.)* No, we shall –

EPSOM: No, we shan't –

GUMMERY: Seek you out and –

EPSOM: One day…one day… *(He goes out.)*

GUMMERY: *(Going to the cage.)* Listen to me, did you? *(He laughs, shakes his head.)* No, we do change, we do… Make you a new cage…promise! *(He stretches wearily on the floor.)* To lie down… and know…what comes up behind me finds me…vulnerable…since I was a boy soldier, I always stood with my back to walls… *(He sleeps, vulnerably.)*

GAY: He's asleep.

HELEN: Oh, his little freedom… I could put his whole consciousness into my ear, and it would fit. Or up a fingernail…his entire knowledge would lie like greasy dirt between my toes…

GAY: Her arrogance… I do admire her arrogance, without admiring her at all…

HOMER: No one admires Helen. It is not admiration Helen wants. If I had made her admirable, who would know her name? *(He goes out.)*

SAVAGE: She is worn down. She is a butt. A scrag. She rubs out virtue BUT THE RUBBER ALSO SHRINKS...

GAY: How I detest you. The things you say to make your smoked-out lives seem purposeful!

SAVAGE: MY LIFE IS PURPOSEFUL. *(HELEN shrieks with a shrill laugh.)* Shriek, yes.

GAY: *(Goes to HELEN.)* Oh, your dirty furrows…! I think of you two as fields deep in unrotted litter, ploughed and ploughed again and yielding less with every harvest I am a perfectly beautiful and fertile woman and I would not exchange one fallen hair for all your consciousness. *(Pause. She looks up.)*

HELEN: How you hate us.

GAY: Yes. Now someone cart my husband to the beach and let crabs chew his bits, this ten-day funeral nonsense was only an excuse for fucking, the widow got the males erect, I saw it, child between the laden tables, bewildered child, I saw it all –

HELEN: That's as it should be –

GAY: IS IT!

HELEN: Yes, fuck the widow out of grief.

GAY: YOU WON'T DO ANYTHING PROPER. *(Pause.)*

HELEN: I don't think we ever shall be reconciled. Neither time nor pain will bring us close.

GAY: Never. Your misdemeanours in Old Sparta were bad enough, but wickedness was fashion as long as there was order. There is no order any more. You're fifty and ridiculous.

HELEN: Oh, Helen, out of date!

GAY: Habitual NAUGHTINESS.

HELEN: What's worse than being out of date?

GAY: Fatuous MISCHIEF.

HELEN: Armless and outmoded, god help me.

GAY: Where is the truth in you? Everything is gesture! *(Pause.)*

HELEN: Now, that's unfair –

GAY: Good, unfairness is our atmosphere! I hear my child calling, and though I hate it, I will give it milk. Obligation. Do you know the word?

HELEN: Yes. It's what we owe our feelings. *(GAY rushes to HELEN, seizing her head in her hands.)*

GAY: TRUNCATED AND PONTIFICATING –

HELEN: You are strangling me –

GAY: SLUT. *(She detaches herself.)* You do – you really do – bring the violence out…in us… *(She goes out as MACLUBY and FLADDER enter with a cart.)*

SAVAGE: My student's dead.

MACLUBY: But not without his uses…

SAVAGE: I thought he'd learned a trick or two, but no, he's dead…

MACLUBY: *(Lifting the body onto the cart.)* Dead in one sense.

SAVAGE: *(Looking at the body.)* And once he jolted to cheap music…

MACLUBY: Persistent in another…

SAVAGE: *(Holding the dead youth's ankle.)* His foot could not keep still – *(He shakes it.)* JIVE NOW! Still now. THROB NOW! Still now. *(They begin to move away.)* Regret his death? No, a teacher must, a teacher worthy of the name, must welcome all the horror, such as – DEATH CALLS IN ALL OUR CAVITIES – and one he drummed his fingers in tutorials – *(He seizes HOGBIN's hand.)* DRUM NOW! Still now. TWITCH NOW! Still now. But he emerged, he crawled from underneath the ruins of the rhythm, to know such things as – DEATH CALLS IN ALL OUR PASSAGES. *(They start to move.)* Don't go, don't go, let a man converse, eh? *(To MACLUBY.)* Regret his death, did you say, no, no, you see, he wanted through his fog, his pulsing fog, not knowledge but MORALITY, which I don't reach… *(They push the cart out.)* WHERE ARE YOU TAKING HIM?

BOY: *(Entering.)* Hyacinth… *(He tosses a bar of soap to SAVAGE. SAVAGE catches it. Pause.)* New Troy of Cleanliness. *(THE BOY looks at his FATHER, then turns and follows the cart.)*

HELEN: *(A sudden access of horror.)* Do you love me?

SAVAGE: Are you afraid?

HELEN: I SAID DO YOU LOVE ME?

SAVAGE: You are, you are afraid…!

HELEN: Say, then!

SAVAGE: Love? We have burst the word… *(He looks after the departing cart.)* He looked at me and thought – I'm sure he thought – I could boil that… *(He smells the soap. Pause. He smells again. An expression of horror.)* HOGBIN! HIS VERY ODOUR! HOGBIN! HIS VEST AND SOCKS!

Interlude

A German archaeologist, circa 1902.

SCHLIEMANN: I came in search of Troy. I came in search of Helen's bed. Why? Because I am a European, and Europe begins in Helen's bed. But could I find Troy? I found Troy upon Troy upon Troy.

ASAFIR: *(Off.)* Effendi! Effendi!

SCHLIEMANN: I hired labourers. I hired Anatolians, the finest diggers in the world. To see him dig! They talk of the coolie, but see the Turk!

ASAFIR: Effendi!

SCHLIEMANN: The Asiatics took Helen into Asia. The Europeans took Helen back again. At that moment they became a culture!

ASAFIR: *(Entering with an object.)* Effendi… *(THE LABOURER thrusts the object at SCHLIEMANN.)*

SCHLIEMANN: Oh, Johnny, will you never learn? Dig, Johnny! *(THE LABOURER is disconsolate.)* The peasant does not discriminate between the spewings of industrial society and the most precious artefacts of the ancient world. THIS IS A BAR OF SOAP! *(He hands it back to him.)* Please, bring me only good. *Nein gut, ja? (ASAFIR tosses the soap away.)* You could wash with that! Don't you want to wash? *(He goes out.)* These Troys, clustering upon real Troy, called themselves Trojans, but were they Trojan? Was Troy not dead?

YORAKIM: Effendi!

SCHLIEMANN: Desperate and ever-less viable imitations of a cultural entity expunged by history –

YORAKIM: Effendi!

SCHLIEMANN: *(Patiently.)* The Turk, avaricious and notoriously cruel, is also a natural gentleman. In this, he astonishes us, who think of cruelty as alien to manners, what have we here? *(YORAKIM holds out a BABY in a cloth. Pause.)* Are you trying to be funny? *(YORAKIM thrusts it at SCHLIEMANN.)* No, I do not wish to handle it. *(And again.)* Thank you, take it to its mother.

YORAKIM: No mother.

SCHLIEMANN: Well, that's unfortunate. Did its mother die?

YORAKIM: *(Thrusting again.)* NO MOTHER.

SCHLIEMANN: Then it must be taken to the Ottoman authorities. We are not an orphanage, we are an expedition.

YORAKIM: *(Pointing to the ground.)* Dig! Dig!

SCHLIEMANN: Yes, good, dig until the light fails.

YORAKIM: IN DIG. *(Pause.)*

SCHLIEMANN: The child was in the dig? *(YORAKIM nods emphatically.)* Now, this is silly, how could it have been in – IT DOESN'T HELP FOR YOU TO SHOUT AND WAVE, IT DOES NOT HELP. *(He uncovers THE CHILD, then sways with horror.)* Its arms are missing…! *(He thrusts it back at YORAKIM.)* What are you – what the – YOU ARE TRYING TO SABOTAGE MY MENTAL STABILITY – it is hard enough to work in climates of this kind without – I HAVE NEVER LIKED YOUR FACE IT IS A SCREEN OF CUNNING –

YORAKIM: *(Indignantly.)* IN – DIG.

SCHLIEMANN: Liar! Asiatic liar!

YORAKIM: NO LIAR! *(Pause.)*

SCHLIEMANN: What is a lie to you in any case? Scarcely a stain upon your soul, deceit is the weapon of the underdog, nothing can be credited where race rules race, but I AM AN ACADEMIC AND TRUTH IS MY – *(Pause. He sways.)* All right, very well, thank you, this was bound to be a testing time, one cannot expect, seeking the bed, the seed and womb of Europe, can't expect, the womb of Helen being, no, you can't, and I certainly do not expect, so – *(Pause.)* Listen, my friend – *(Pause.)* No – you are not my friend, I apologize – listen, whoever you are, no baksheesh for baby, *nein. (He waves his hand. YORAKIM starts to leave, then suddenly stops, shouts.)*

YORAKIM: Effendi! *(SCHLIEMANN turns, alarmed. YORAKIM chucks the baby at him. SCHLIEMANN catches it, instinctively, as YORAKIM runs off.)*

SCHLIEMANN: AAAAH! *(He holds it at arm's length, in disgust. Darkness is falling. The sound of the evening prayer fills the stage as THE LABOURERS kneel towards Mecca.)* Your imperfection horrifies me…creeps along my wrists… *(Pause.)* Soon, so soon, the birth of monsters will be an impossibility, such will be the sprint of science…and all pain abolished…YOU WERE BORN TOO SOON. *(He puts it on the ground.)* Even if my wife fell ill I could not sponge her face all day, I could not change her linen and remain a genius, it is a full time occupation, YOU ONLY COME TO ME BECAUSE I AM A CHRISTIAN, but I also owe a duty to my soul. I REFUSE TO HAVE MY MORALITY EXPLOITED! *(He kicks the baby.)* YOU EXPLOIT ME! *(Pause.)* Oh, God, am I one of your flock? *(ASAFIR appears, holding a sickle.)*

ASAFIR: Effendi!

SCHLIEMANN: The responsibilities of this ethic are too onerous, as Christ knew, and incompatible with freedom, AS CHRIST KNEW.

ASAFIR: Effendi?

SCHLIEMANN: *(Looking at it.)* I don't think, I really do not think this is of the least… *(ASAFIR jerks his head towards THE CHILD.)* archaeological… *(He does the movement again. SCHLIEMANN sees.)* Oh, God, I do think the Turkish mind is of such extraordinary and shuddering cruelty… *(ASAFIR goes to THE CHILD.)* HOW CAN YOU MAKE CARPETS LIKE YOU DO? *(SCHLIEMANN turns his back, resumes his lecture.)* These later Troys, clustering like – *(He hears the blow, lets out a stifled cry.)* like – THERE WOULD BE NO KNOWLEDGE IF PITY GOVERNED, WOULD THERE, ASAFIR? YOU KNOW.

ASAFIR: Effendi?

SCHLIEMANN: You know. Look me in the eyes and say you know. Look me in the eyes, then… *(He takes him by the shoulder.)*…stare in my European eyes with your Asiatic eyes, go on, stare, STARE…! *(ASAFIR stares at the ground.)* Off now, Asafir, you casual murderer, you are already late for prayers…

ASAFIR: Baksheesh?

SCHLIEMANN: Baksheesh… *(Pause. He dips in his pocket.)* Baksheesh…

Act Three

PROLOGUE

MACLUBY: The exhibitionists!

No, they are though, to wreck our peace.

REFUSE TO BE WRECKED

I do

I say

Listen

Copy me

I say

This is just another death I am singularly

Unimpressed I look you in the eye whilst not

Reducing one iota my walking pace

Oh, you are cutting your throat

Oh, you are dying on the steps

Oh, I go,

Fancy,

And if the blood goes surging

If it gushes down the cracks

I lift my leg

With

Such

Exquisite

Grace

No, you have to or they will GET OUR PEACE AND

BITE IT

This suicide epidemic
This madness epidemic
And the beggars are a lake
A lake of beggars
A pond of suicides
The rapids of the mad
IT TAKES SOME NAVIGATING THE CONTEMPORARY STREET
But this is a revolution
WHO SAID
This is a revolution
NOBODY TOLD ME
I am a revolutionary also
Says the millionaire in the two-piece suit
And truth dripped through their jeers
In bloody clots

The weak brains pop
The frail imaginations pop
Like skulls in the boiler
Stalin
Who grew in wit as he grew in cruelty
Lenin
Who later on was rarely seen to smile
Robespierre
Gorky
Brecht
AND ALL THE STRATA SMASHERS
ALL THE RIPPERS OF THE ROOTS

They knew
That under pressure
They called it
THE INTENSIFICATION OF THE STRUGGLE
Excellent
They called it
THE GROWING STRAINS OF
CONTRADICTION
I do love that
Under pressure
OUR BRAINS WOULD POP
I hear it, shh!
I hear it, shh!
This also is a revolution, then
NOBODY SAID
Oh, yes, a proper
I NEVER KNEW
Shh!
The youth are popping
But they are always to the fore
Chucking bottles
Waving bayonets
Throwing matches at the poor
They are such ruthless imperialists of the soul
No
Let youth go
Bid youth farewell
Paris
Petrograd

Budapest
Warsaw
Europe's youth to the fore
To the workshops
Let us batter out a modern laugh
A laugh for the era
Not a boring howl
But something growing from the bowel
HAAAAA!
It's only the madwoman skating
Exquisitely skating on the suicide's gore

SCENE ONE

The gaol in Fragrant Troy. A place of baths and faucets.

HELEN: Where was the fat on him? Even his buttocks would have earned a greyhound's pity…

SAVAGE: No fat…

HELEN: No fat, and yet boiled down he make a million bars to perfume Troy with…

GAOLER: *(To SAVAGE.)* Wash, you!

SAVAGE: I'm clean.

GAOLER: No one is clean.

SAVAGE: All right, but washed –

GAOLER: Wash again –

SAVAGE: It hurts my skin to wash it hourly –

GAOLER: The lather of Hyacinth brings only comfort to the sore –

SAVAGE: Yet, but –

GAOLER: Wash, then –

SAVAGE: Again?

GAOLER: Again. *(Pause. SAVAGE goes to the basin.)*

SAVAGE: I could go joyfully to a tramp's groin now –

GAOLER: And do it thoroughly.

SAVAGE: Or suck great lungfuls from whores' cavities –

GAOLER: Front –

SAVAGE: Every crack would be a garden –

GAOLER: Back –

SAVAGE: The rank old human odour flooding the tortured nostril –

GAOLER: Now do her –

SAVAGE: Fart's paradise and sweat's apotheosis!

MACLUBY: *(Entering.)* Today, you are fifty! *(He drapes a garland on him.)*

SAVAGE: Fifty…?

MACLUBY: And Helen fifty-five!

SAVAGE: But I was born in August!

MACLUBY: Why shouldn't dates be flexible! What's wisdom if it can't burst calendars? What's a system if it can't call this the New Year One and abolish stacks of squalid centuries?

SAVAGE: Let us out of here, we die of disinfectant…

MACLUBY: Fifty! An age without distinction! Fifty, and no solutions! *(To HELEN.)* DON'T STARE AT THIS PARTS, DESIRE IS SOAPED OUT OF EXISTENCE.

SAVAGE: Fifty…?

MACLUBY: Fifty, and the ground shifting, fifty and the air thick with falling categories! It snows old faiths, it snows old dogmas! Fragrant Troy forgives your misdemeanours, how clean are you?

SAVAGE: Not clean yet…evidently…

MACLUBY: But washed? *(He sniffs him.)* You have the odour of the will to compromise, which is acceptable… *(He goes out.)*

HELEN: I have this horror we will never fuck again… *(Pause. SAVAGE is staring.)*

HELEN: I said I have this horror we will –

SAVAGE: Heard…

HELEN: Not because it is forbidden but because –

SAVAGE: Fifty…!

HELEN: You have lost the will – are you listening?

SAVAGE: FIFTY AND NO KNOWLEDGE YET! *(Pause. HELEN stares appalled.)*

HELEN: No knowledge? Look at me. Sliced. Minimal. Reduced. Hacked. Slashed. Incapable. How dare you say no knowledge. I AM IT. *(Pause. He fixes her with a look.)* That isn't looking it's a fence.

SAVAGE: WHAT'S A LOOK, HELEN? *(Pause.)*

HELEN: What it is, I don't know. What it was, I will tell you. It was a thing as solid as a girder, down which streamed all the populations of our forbidden life… *(Pause. SAVAGE sobs.)*

CREUSA: *(Entering.)* I have to tell you this. I am to be your wife again. *(They stare at her.)* Do you think I wanted it? *(Pause.)* WELL, SPEAK, BECAUSE YOU KNOW IT'S POSSIBLE. Hatred could not prevent it. In that pit of contempt called bed we reached out sometimes like the drowning in the dark. EVEN COPULATION WE COULD DO.

HELEN: SHUT UP.

CREUSA: IT'S POSSIBLE AND IT HAPPENS IN EVERY PLACE. *(Pause.)* Clean Troy is to make divorce the only capital offence. And I, for all my maggot life am not ready to die just yet WE ARE TO BE A SHOW MARRIAGE. Life, yes, life in any mould, SPEAK THEN, you must admire me above all martyrs, I am a martyr to nothing but life itself, and in the end ONE MALE BIT IS MUCH LIKE ANY OTHER –

HELEN: I VOMIT YOUR –

CREUSA: You would, you are a monument to pain –

HELEN: VOMIT YOUR TOLERANCE. *(Pause.)*

CREUSA: The smell of Hyacinth…! In every bath and prison tub…Hyacinth, who could not make an entry while he lived, in table form swims through the lush of every woman's parts… *(To THE GAOLER.)* Let me out, please…! *(She goes. Pause.)*

HELEN: You did not deny. *(Pause.)* Did you? You did not deny? Or are my ears defunct in sympathy with other parts –

SAVAGE: I was so –

HELEN: Deny it then.

SAVAGE: Overthrown by –

HELEN: Indeed, but now –

SAVAGE: Disbelief –

HELEN: Now, though?

SAVAGE: Appalling and grotesque resuscitation of –

HELEN: So you won't –

SAVAGE: And yet it's possible. *(Pause. He looks at her.)* It's possible… *(He is aghast.)* Is it? *(Pause.)* HORROR! *(Pause.)*

HELEN: I am indifferent who – with which bitch you – devour time – all skirt's your garden, out and plunge there by the armful, and if I discover you fat and naked in the compost, red from exploration, good but NO RENUNCIATION, PLEASE. *(Pause.)*

SAVAGE: I am exhausted by –

HELEN: Yes –

SAVAGE: THE PLUNGING LIFT OF THIS INFATUATION.

HELEN: It's not infatuation –

SAVAGE: Floor after floor of –

HELEN: I HAVE NEITHER ARMS NOR LEGS, IT IS NOT INFATUATION. *(Pause.)*

SAVAGE: I think…let me speak…I think…you are a barrier to knowledge now, when once you were the absolute condition… *(Pause.)*

HELEN: All my life I was afraid I might recant, but never did. Always, it was the man who suffocated passion in the puddle. *(Pause.)* Don't be the grey-arsed priest, I beg of you, don't hide under the arch, squatting on your heels and with a withered finger trace the ancient hieroglyphs, all intellect and sterile. Let me be the board you chalk your meaning on, chalk screaming on the wet of my wounds… *(He doesn't respond.)* All right, renounce… *(Pause.)*

SAVAGE: Helen –

HELEN: No, shh, all words suddenly redundant –

SAVAGE: Helen –

HELEN: Can't hear you –

SAVAGE: I have to know what –

HELEN: Words, aren't they weapons? Aren't they wires? Keep your weapons off me! Look out, wires!

SAVAGE: RENUNCIATION ALSO MUST BE KNOWLEDGE. *(Pause.)*

HELEN: I don't persuade. I never have persuaded. They persuaded me. Helen never urged a man, he came, he drenched her in his fever, *(With a sudden wail.)* oh, undress me, no one's looking, I am maimed without you, and fuck all limbs, this is the torture…! *(He stares at her.)* What have you learned, then? That you hate Helen?

SAVAGE: Yes –

HELEN: Hate her, and could punch the sight out of her eyes –

SAVAGE: Yes –

HELEN: The feeling out of her lips –

SAVAGE: ALL RIGHT…!

GAOLER: *(Entering.)* Go home, now, citizens…

HELEN: OH, THE GROSS INTRUSION OF BANALITY…

GAOLER: Thank you, and take your bowls –

HELEN: Persist…

GAOLER: Towels to the laundry –

HELEN: Persist…! *(The infusion of the city.)*

SCENE TWO

A Public place. The cage is no longer visible. FLADDER enters holding a gong and sits.

GAY: *(Entering.)* The Concentrated Thoughts of a Great King Deposed Reviled, Neglected and Eventually Rehabilitated in the Interests of Universal Harmony! *(To FLADDER.)* Beat the gong if you deny my version. *(He gongs.)* Not yet, silly. *(Pause.)* My catastrophic marriage to a – *(He gongs.)* No, let me get started, gong at the end if you have to. *(She composes herself.)* My catastrophic marriage to a libidinous woman inexorably led to the death of thousands – *(He dongs.)* How can you gong that? Everybody knows that! It's a Historical Fact. If you are going to gong everything we will take the gong away from you. You abuse the privilege of age. *(She proceeds.)* When I was destitute I came to truth – *(He gongs.)* Give it to me! *(She snatches it and tosses it offstage.)* YOU ARE TRYING TO RIDICULE THE GOVERNMENT OF FRAGRANT TROY – *(He shakes his head.)* You are and we are not obliged to tolerate it! *(She rehearses.)* In poverty I discovered twenty truths –

One! In limitation lies the source of satisfaction.

Two! The question leads only to the next question.

Three! You have to die some time.

Four! The final end of equality is universal plastic surgery. *(FLADDER makes a noise in his throat.)* Shut up –

Five! To suffer is to be without soap! *(He gurgles.)* Shut up, I said –

Six! Dig your garden till the sun sets.

Seven! And when the soldiers have gone, plant it again.

Eight! *(To FLADDER.)* I SHALL NOT DESIST, NO MATTER HOW YOU GURGLE.

(Pause.)

Eight! If you must kiss do it with your eyes open.

Nine! The great joy is to concede.

Ten! Don't grieve after midnight.

Eleven! *(To FLADDER, who is frothing.)* THIS IS WHAT YOU DISCOVERED, ISN'T IT? KEEP

STILL, THEN. *(Pause.)* Eleven! Fornication is the aptitude of mongrels.

Twelve! Swans mate for life.

Thirteen! Violence is no solution.

Fourteen! Nor is justice.

Fifteen! Soap is experience. *(To FLADDER.)* YOU ARE DRIBBLING ON MY LEG.

Sixteen! *(Pause.)* Sixteen! *(To FLADDER.)* YOU SEE, I AM NOT SABOTAGED BY YOU! *(Pause.)* Sixteen! The majority are sometimes right.

Seventeen! It is perfectly natural to hate.

Eighteen! It is love that's artificial.

Nineteen! Marriage is the government. *(To FLADDER.)* NO, I WON'T STOP!

Twenty! *(Pause.)* Twenty! *(Pause.)* The Past never occurred! *(She pushes him off his knees.)* I did it! I did it, and I was not stopped by you! *(Pause. She looks at him.)* What does it matter if you thought those things or not? What does it matter? Clean Troy is not about truth. It's about me. Now, get off your knees and scarper. *(He climbs to his feet.)* Take your gong. *(He moves.)* Do you still love your mother? *(He stops.)* You do…You do love her…! *(Pause. She looks closely into him.)* Is there anything she could do – anything – would stop you loving her? *(Pause.)* Extraordinary. *(She walks a little, still looking at him.)* I once put corpses in her bed. Arms and things. By this I meant to say, this wrist, this bowel, you caused to howl, you caused to wither. But she was only irritated by the smell. Is that the reason for her power? *(HOMER enters, senile now, and with two sticks.)*

HOMER: Please, don't let them bath me again…

GAY: You must be bathed!

HOMER: Not so often, surely?

GAY: Yes, often and often! Do they scrub you?

HOMER: Yes!

GAY: That's good, I told them, scrub him in every crack and pore because that's where his misery collects, and his misery makes him sing those songs, oh, so miserable your songs are now, and anyone who hears you, they get miserable too! Why did Odysseus go back to Penelope? *(HOMER stares, bewildered.)* I asked you a question. I mean, hadn't he met this girl, this perfect girl? So why did he go back to Penelope? SHE MUST HAVE BEEN PROPER HAG BY THEN. *(Pause.)*

HOMER: No more soap!

GAY: Oh, take him away and wash him…

HOMER: No more soap!

GAY: *(Turning on him.)* I THINK YOU MUST DEFEND YOUR FICTIONS AND NOT TAKE THAT ARROGANT STANCE.

HOMER: *(As he is hurried out.)* Oh, God, not soap…!

GAY: *(To CREUSA, who enters with SAVAGE.)* I don't believe he has the slightest interest in art any more. He is interested in soap, and only soap. *(She smiles.)* Now, are you reconciled? You must consummate the marriage, and in public. And to think we once had public executions! No, this is progress –

CREUSA: I wonder if I can –

GAY: Please, don't throw up objections…! How girlish you are…!

CREUSA: Yes…

GAY: When you have been so – used – and flogged – and flung around like soldiers' baggage… *(She kisses CREUSA on the cheek.)* Your cheeks are maps of sordid life… *(CREUSA goes out. GAY watches her.)* The Troys are slipping away. So many errors…your sacrifice is a small thing compared to our survival.

SAVAGE: Sacrifice? I could not do it if it were a sacrifice.

GAY: What is it then?

SAVAGE: An education, obviously.

GAY: I might also be an education… *(Darkness falls on the stage.)*

SAVAGE: On Monday I washed the body of the old woman.

On Tuesday I cut the throat of a stranger.

On Wednesday I lifted potatoes from the allotment.

On Thursday I seduced the mother of my lover.

On Friday I was ashamed and unable to act.

On Saturday I read the works of great authors.

On Sunday I lay and wished I was a baby.

On Monday…

On Monday I washed the body of the old woman…

GAY: I'll take my clothes off, shall I?

SAVAGE: It's night…!

GAY: I will, if you will…

SAVAGE: The dictator stirs inside his bunker…

GAY: *(Removing her shoes.)* Shoes first…

SAVAGE: The executioners are checking their weapons…

GAY: Then socks…

SAVAGE: And intellectuals rip the membranes of humanity in their shuddering cots… ALL RIGHT, UNDRESS! *(Pause.)*

GAY: If I am naked and you are not, what then? *(SAVAGE shakes his head.)* One of us has the advantage, but who…?

SAVAGE: You ask questions like a man throws stones. You talk to fend off silence.

GAY: I have the advantage! *(She flings off her last garment. She stands naked. Pause.)* Stare at me, then. *(Pause.)* Stare. *(Pause.)* Consume me. *(Pause.)* Are you consuming me? *(Pause.)* You're not, are you? Or are you, I can't tell from – *(She sees FLADDER, sitting.)* Oh, God, there is a man still here! *(She covers herself with her hands.)*

SAVAGE: What's the matter? He can't speak.

GAY: He can see me – he – SEES ME.

SAVAGE: But what he sees he can't put into words. So what he sees he sees as the stars see. Or the stones. Do you hide yourself from stones? *(Pause.)*

GAY: If you do not respond to me, I shall be damaged. I shall be damaged and the onus will be on you! *(Pause. Suddenly she goes to grab her clothes but SAVAGE seizes them first.)*

SAVAGE: You look ridiculous. Beautiful and ridiculous. *(She goes to snatch them but he whips them away. She looks, uncomprehending. She attempts to smile.)*

GAY: What's this? Desire?

SAVAGE: DESIRE! Do you think beauty makes desire? Do you think you only need to STAND AND BE OBSERVED? *(She looks alarmed.)* It's night… *(She looks nervously to FLADDER.)* Don't look to him. He is a stone.

GAY: Are you going to – cut me into bits? *(Pause. He is bemused. He sinks to the ground. Extends a hand limply.)*

SAVAGE: Shh…

GAY: *(Horrified.)* ARE YOU?

SAVAGE: Shh… *(He shakes his head.)* Oh, pitiful…oh, unknowing… *(He beckons her with a gesture. Timidly she goes to him. He encloses her chastely in his arms. A figure enters from the darkness. It is GUMMERY, carrying SHADE in a small cage at his belt. He looks at GAY. He looks at SAVAGE.)*

GUMMERY: No anger but. *(Pause.)* I walk along the shore so full of kindness for the world. *(Pause.)* No anger but. *(Pause.)* We have our nightly stretch so kindness-sodden and we see his widow and our queen. No anger, obviously. Undressed. *(Pause.)* Much as old Helen might have been. *(Pause.)* Kindness is bruised and Hyacinth demeaned… *(He turns to go, stops.)* How hurt we are. No anger but. *(He starts to leave.)*

SAVAGE: How hideous you are. Without your anger. How crippled and deformed. So kind you make all kindness loathsome not that it seemed a very precious thing but now it stinks the corpse of undone actions all tumours in your lung you passive and colourless licker of fallacies I see when I look at you why heroes have to die, Homer was right in this at least he did not pursue the Greeks to their retirement, shuffle, stagger away you offend the landscape and my vocabulary withers in describing you, I, a doctor, too. Speechless, and in revulsion... *(GUMMERY is terribly still.)* Cart your shrunk mate off, you spoil a decent night. *(GUMMERY remains.)* And yet you stay. To test what, I wonder? *(GUMMERY is still. SAVAGE climbs to his feet.)*

GUMMERY: Once, I made my body iron. To hurt. And now it's iron to suffer... *(Pause.)*

SAVAGE: Suffer? For what? My student's gabble? There was panic in his trousers.

GUMMERY: TEST ME.

SAVAGE: And you were cruel...they told me... *(SAVAGE goes to GUMMERY, who is still motionless. He stands behind him.)*

GAY: *(Suddenly.)* CAN'T WATCH! *(She grabs her clothes, runs to FLADDER.)* CAN YOU? *(She rushes out.)* CAN'T WATCH! *(Wind. Darkness. The peculiar voice of SHADE, tunefully.)*

SHADE: Intellectuals also kill! Intellectuals kill! Intellectuals also kill! Intellectuals kill!

SCENE THREE

Bells. MACLUBY besuited. CREUSA gowned. They look over the city.

MACLUBY: Troy isn't what it was, when you last wed.

CREUSA: Nor Creusa, either.

MACLUBY: Troys have been, and Troys have gone...

CREUSA: And Creusas, they have been and gone, too...

MACLUBY: *(Smiling.)* This is the proper spirit for matrimony.

CREUSA: Yes.

MACLUBY: Accommodation.

CREUSA: Yes.

MACLUBY: No more climbing the greasy pole of personality, but –

CREUSA: Yes. Because I fell, and fell again… *(A blast of rattles and cheers as a massive bed descends. It is upholstered with twig or flint.)* WHAT'S THAT…!

MACLUBY: No one said it would be easy…

GAY: *(Entering.)* The territory of epic adventures! The poor man's empire! I am a romantic, at last I have kept that alive! *(To CREUSA.)* On the bed now, and good luck in the maze! I think it is a maze, with its dead ends and repetitions, but at the centre of which is – must be – for those who persevere – I don't know what! *(CREUSA is helped to the bed. Crowd applause.)* How Troy needed this! Listen! When all was disintegration and morals were exploding nebulae! The young particularly will appreciate this AFFIRMATION, hurry, make yourself comfortable, your husband is IMMINENT. *(CREUSA lies on the bed.)* This shows as nothing better can, the utter CIRCULARITY OF LIFE, the fact we teach in school that if you walk defiantly away from a fixed point, the earth's roundness ensures you will return to that same spot, no matter how terrible the journey! THE LOOP OF KNOWLEDGE. He's coming! *(Whistles.)* I could weep with that strange weeping women do at weddings! I could! *(SAVAGE enters, in a moth-eaten and devastated suit. Applause. He stares at the spectacle of the bed. Silence falls.)*

SAVAGE: It's twigs…

CREUSA: Not as bad as you might –

SAVAGE: It's twigs…

MACLUBY: Climb in, Dr Savage…

SAVAGE: *(A terrible connection.)* IT'S A PYRE!

MACLUBY: You are the one who wants the knowledge –

SAVAGE: A PYRE WHEN I'M NOT DEAD…!

CREUSA: All right, all right…

SAVAGE: NOT DEAD…

CREUSA: Shh…shh… *(He mounts the bed. He sits rigidly and apart from her. The occasional rattle from THE CROWD.)*

MACLUBY: And Odysseus went to Penelope, and slew her suitors, and having washed the blood from his hands, undressed her, and she undressed him, and as she did, his eyes travelled her worn and imperfect body, and her eyes saw his decay, and they wept, and pity was the source of his tumescence… what else could it have been?

CREUSA: Look at me with new eyes, or we shan't do it…

SAVAGE: I can't.

CREUSA: It can be done.

SAVAGE: Anything can be done, but not with new eyes…

CREUSA: Hold my hand, then –

SAVAGE: Trying –

CREUSA: Hold it – *(Se extends hers. THE CROWD whistles and claps.)* HOLD IT… *(With a spasm of pain, SAVAGE thrusts his hand into hers. More applause.)* It's all right…! It's all right…!

MACLUBY: The Political Fuck! Not for the first time, the Political Fuck! *(As THE CROWD chants its approval, HELEN appears pushed by HOMER.)*

HELEN: What can you see?

HOMER: You've got the eyes, not me –

HELEN: To the left!

HOMER: Some agony –

HELEN: The right then! *(THE CROWD obscures her view.)* Oh, shift you fragrant lawyers!

MACLUBY: *(Watching SAVAGE's agony.)* He squirms, he sweats, but that's the pain a rebirth brings, is birth was painless, would a child be loved?

HOMER: What do you see?

HELEN: *(Straining.)* A bed –

HOMER: A bed –

HELEN: A terrible bed...

MACLUBY: This is the union from which all stale and mothy marriages will suck their consolation!

GAY: *(Like a trainer.)* Kiss him, kiss him, do! MORE LAMPS, THEY ARE OBSCURE!

(Spotlight heat the bed.) The lips release the tongue, the tongue unlocks the fingers, the fingers free the fastenings, the fastenings ungate the flesh, oh, claim her, do...! *(With a desperate effort of will, SAVAGE flings himself on CREUSA. THE CROWD surges as the bed is drawn out of sight.)*

MACLUBY: *(Laughing.)* Knowledge...! Knowledge...!

HELEN: Oh, my own madman, does he grin or weep...?

SCENE FOUR

HELEN is alone, SHADE's cage at her feet. THE BOY enters, no longer a boy.

BOY: My father and my mother have been reconciled. And in spite of her advancing years, she has conceived. They are calling it a miracle.

HELEN: Miracles happen when desire's dead…

BOY: My father wanted me to be an intellectual, but I lean towards business. *(Pause.)*

HELEN: You are the soap maker.

BOY: I wash out minds as well… *(He peers into the cage.)* Is there meant to be a bird in here?

HELEN: Yes. He sings all day long.

BOY: Can't hear him.

HELEN: Really? I find him deafening. Why are you dressed like an undertaker?

BOY: An undertaker? No one has ever said that before. I think of myself as a bridegroom. May I tell you about soap? It is my obsession.

HELEN: How lucky you are to have an obsession. And you can't be more than thirty-two.

BOY: Oh, dear, I think you are going to interrupt me all the time.

HELEN: Isn't that allowed?

BOY: It breaks the flow.

HELEN: I don't like flows. The best things can be said staccato.

BOY: Nevertheless, I will persist.

HELEN: How can I avoid you? My nurse is old and falls asleep, and it's not as though an amputee has anything to block her ears with –

BOY: I came to soap thinking is a product –

HELEN: You would not believe the sheer variety of human innocence that foists itself on me! Poets, infertile women, men with agony inside their trousers, I have to tolerate the lot –

BOY: But it is not a product, it is a culture. For example –

HELEN: *(Conceding.)* ALL RIGHT, FLOW. *(Pause.)*

BOY: There has never yet been a society that could tolerate the smell of human flesh, can you explain that? The individuals who live with most intensity the odour of mankind have always been the outcast, the vagrant, the dispossessed. We are born with a profound revulsion for our own scent, an antipathy formed during some nightmare travel down the birth canal – I speculate – but certainly the odour of the mass can turn the stomach and I believe the essence of the human smell to be a lethal toxin. This soap's justification and the fulcrum of an honourable career. *(He smiles.)* But my concentration on the subject led me further, as indeed all concentration will, no matter how banal the subject. The great banker also knows the human heart. So soap revealed its laws to me. *(Pause.)* Your eyes are shut but you hear everything, I know –

HELEN: You have his voice, but without the edge of panic that clung to all his vowels…

BOY: My flow, please… *(Pause.)* Soap makes harmony, and made with proper inspiration, lets imagination compensate for impossibly demanding life. Which brings me to my point, that you might understand the need for what I hope to call Essential Helen, as Hogbin's body, all kindness and purity, pervades the Trojan spirit now. *(Pause.)* Respond, by all means. *(She is silent.)* Sometimes the horror of an idea is only the boom of its essential truth… *(Pause.)* And now you won't talk…! *(Pause.)* We see in your life spectacularly the price or Eros. I don't stoop to criticize, but simply draw to your attention the fifteen thousand orphans of the Peloponnese, the wail of widows and wounds of conscripts whose total ache would lift the mountains off their feet, I am not judging, you understand I am not ethical, the children of these wars eat murder with their breakfast. I don't judge.

HELEN: What you describe is consequence. I refuse the blame. Every conscript had his choice and every widow could have blocked her man. But if they died for Eros, where's the tragedy in that? In other wars they'll scream for flags, sometimes for banks, or even books, I've heard. No, cunt's a worthy cause as slaughters go.

BOY: You garb the argument! Beauty has this effect, it stirs the blood, and yes, it is a truth of sorts.

HELEN: Truth…? Oh, don't drag truth in, I'm over sixty –

BOY: Very well, but whether it's a truth or not, it cannot be a lie –

HELEN: Beauty is a lie! Of course it is a lie! *(He shrugs.)* It is simply the best available lie on the subject of truth… *(Pause. He smiles, shaking his head.)*

BOY: My flow…my flow… *(Pause.)* But I proceed. However great the pain your Eros brought, we cannot dispense with Eros. It lives in all of us. It cries, and breathes.

HELEN: In you? It cries, and breathes?

BOY: *(Charmingly.)* Now, that is sabotage –

HELEN: Preposterous claim –

BOY: All right, it cries in varying degrees, but because I don't stand out at passing skirt is no –

HELEN: He must defend his sprig!

BOY: Really, you will not disorganize me by –

HELEN: I won't disorganize him –

BOY: By some phallic contest which –

HELEN: He's not disorganized –

BOY: Is both grotesque, pernicious and –

HELEN: He's not, he's definitely not disorganized –

BOY: No –

HELEN: And I don't want to disorganize you, God knows the mayhem if you were, I shrink to think, the uncaging of, the swollen veins, no, no, you stay as you are! *(Pause.)*

BOY: *(Coolly.)* You are piqued.

HELEN: The flow, for pity's sake.

BOY: You are piqued and I know why.

HELEN: Me? Helen? Piqued?

BOY: Because I look at you with cool and level eyes. *(Pause.)*

HELEN: You do. I grant you that.

BOY: Which you are unaccustomed to.

HELEN: *(Pause. Then with inspiration.)* The story of the Actress in the Penal Colony! The star who had made a million men throb in the stalls found the interrogator unyielding and her breasts showing though the dirty quilted jacket moved his lust his pity his ambition NOT ONE BIT so solid and so thick the plating of his IDEOLOGY, and this made her weep. But when she had been returned to the cells he locked his door and stropped himself. AT

THAT MOMENT THE SOUL OF THE PARTY DIED. *(Pause.)* You are so oblique and so well-mannered, a proper skater, as black as a fly and impossible to swat. A man for the age. Why do you want my body?

BOY: To give all women, so all women may be, at moments of their choice, Hellenic… *(A terrible howl comes from HELEN.)* You howl – yes – you howl but –

HELEN: MY – OPIC PER – FUMIER!

BOY: The lending of transgression to the ashamed, the loan of passion to the guilty, the licensing of total love to the domestic –

HELEN: FASTIDIOUS SYCOPHANT!

BOY: YOU DON'T LIKE PEOPLE –

HELEN: No –

BOY: You scorn their simple pleasures, you mock the scale of their imagination –

HELEN: Yes, every day!

BOY: IT'S UNFORGIVABLE! *(Pause.)*

HELEN: Could I ever forgive myself if I were forgivable? *(Pause. He looks at her.)*

BOY: Your lonely and malevolent life… *(Pause.)* We terribly want to help you –

HELEN: Afraid –

BOY: Who –

HELEN: You. Afraid.

BOY: Afraid, of what?

HELEN: Afraid I'll cling in the imagination of a girl, or in a boy's head, make all his thoughts unscholarly… *(Pause.)*

BOY: Helen – if I may call you Helen –

HELEN: Well, don't call me anything else –

BOY: Helen –

HELEN: That's it, though you say it oddly –

BOY: You have not seen yourself for years.

HELEN: No. I have no mirror.

BOY: I think, if you were to – examine your appearance – you might understand that your capacity for mischief is now, sadly –

HELEN: You talk like a shrivelled priest, and the language shrivels when you talk it – do you mean I'm ugly? I was born ugly. You think that slipping and sliding word circumscribes my power? You're not – though a lipstick maker and a skin-cream bottler – so bereft of knowledge as all that surely? *(Pause.)* No, you cannot have my fat to let unsuffering women play at deepest life…better the crabs get dinner off me… *(He goes out. FLADDER comes in, carrying the gong.)* They want to smear themselves with essence, the new Trojans. Think with a soap called Helen they might temporarily contract desire. Sign nothing. And when I'm gone, in the sea with the remnants, they will boil me otherwise and use my fat to humiliate some unborn class… *(Pause.)* Tell me, is it possible for Helen to be old? *(He gongs. Pause. A CHILD enters, without arms.)* Oh, look, she has in her the same appalling gift…! *(HELEN grins.)* It's in her hip…the tilting of her head…OH, THE WRECK OF DOMESTICITY AND THE TEARING OF MEN FROM REGULAR EMPLOYMENT…!

CHARITY: What?

HELEN: Shh! Your mother!

CHARITY: Tear men from regular employment? How?

HELEN: I can't be told, it happens!

GAY: *(Entering.)* Listen! The Festival of Families! And we'll be late! *(THE CHILD runs off. GAY follows, then stops.)* May I kiss you?

HELEN: Kiss me…?

GAY: Yes. *(Pause, then GAY kisses her, goes out. Pause.)*

HELEN: *(Apprehensively.)* I think I am going to be killed. *(Pause.)* Beat the gong then… *(Pause.)* So they are killing me, WHO IS. *(Pause.)* You know and you're not telling me! *(Pause.)* WHO IS. *(Pause.)* You? *(Pause.)* Well why not you? Because it isn't in your character? WHAT IS YOUR CHARACTER? To think any one of us is knowable, when personality is only crystal grinding between stones, DON'T COME NEAR ME YET. *(He is still.)* I want to be killed. But in a gush of violence. I wanted to be beaten out of life by some mad male all red about the neck and veins outstanding like the protesting prostitute in the bite of the night, discovered all brain and sheet and stocking NOT THIS COLD POLITICAL THING, hacked to shreds among the bed things NOT THIS, the wonderful gore that trickled underneath the door, NOT THIS THOUGH! *(Pause. He is still.)* Who signed the warrant? *(She looks at him.)* THE ENTIRE POPULATION DID? Oh, come on, even the children? AND THE AS YET UNBORN? *(SAVAGE enters, stops. She glimpses him.)* Don't come near. I would rather be blind than see you again. Oh, suddenly the air is thick with stale longings, and sweats gone acid with betrayal, OLD HUSBAND AND OLD LOVER, I would prefer to be slashed by a passing killer than you two set about me kindly, considerate in strangling, considerate in suffocation, THE

CONSIDERATE LOVER WAS ALWAYS THE WORST – *(SAVAGE makes a move.)* DON'T COME INTO MY EYE LINE, I WOULD RAM MY SIGHT OUT RATHER ON A BRANCH! *(He freezes. She averts her face.)* Oh, this purgatory of flowerbeds, in Old Troy temper was the rule, I don't belong and – WHERE'S HOMER! *(Pause.)* Oh, my maker's gone… Someone has extinguished him… what for? A POET'S SOAP? *(She looks at SAVAGE.)* It must have been you…what was it? Did his weeping anger you? We do feel bitter, don't we, towards the genius whose final statements are so trite? But he was silent at the end…the spectacle of me…robbed him of speech… Whereas you…are shameless…which I loved… *(EPSOM enters, with a cloth. She sees him, from the corner of her eye.)* The knacker comes. *(She grins.)* One for the soap yard!

EPSOM: Got a job to do…

HELEN: A job, he calls it! Magnificent monster! And for a terrible hour I thought there was no one left who hadn't changed!

EPSOM: Change, for what?

HELEN: For what! Exactly! Look at him, as unredeemed as when a dirty boy he worked his snot between his tutor's teeth… *(Pause. EPSOM goes to HELEN.)*

EPSOM: *(Intimately.)* Be yer mate…

HELEN: *(Not grasping his meaning.)* Why not be my mate! What's a little strangulation between friends? I have seen torturers play chess with their victims, and the mothers of drowned infants fuck the perpetrators, no, it's all right, it is! *(He goes to cover her.)* SAV – AGE! *(Pause.)* Can you watch this? *(Pause.)* You can.

You can watch this… *(EPSOM silences her by dropping the cloth over her face. He puts his hands about her throat. He exerts. He stops. Pause.)* No, that's wrong, surely… *(He grimaces, as if at effort.)* The way you handle my neck, Les, I've been loved better –

EPSOM: DIE! *(He exerts.)*

HELEN: Yes, I long to, but –

EPSOM: DIE! *(A pause, her head drops forwards. An immediate cacophony of factory whistles.)*

FLADDER: The revolutionaries are flunkeys, too! The terrorists transport dominion in their handshakes!

WE KNOW BUT WE STILL ACT!

WE KNOW BUT WE STILL ACT! *(EPSOM drives away THE AUDIENCE which has gathered at the scene. FLADDER runs out.)*

EPSOM: Fuck off! Scarper! *(A WOMAN is going near THE BODY.)* Off yer vermin!

WOMAN: Cures tumours, whore's blood!

EPSOM: No, it's 'angman's spit yer thinkin' of! *(He gobs at her. She flees. He laughs. Others risk his blows to touch HELEN for luck, and run.)*

SAVAGE: I can watch. I can watch anything.

EPSOM: It's a gift, mate… *(THE PUBLIC are repulsed by EPSOM.)*

SAVAGE: I think to believe in every lie is better than to see through every truth…

EPSOM: *(Fetching a broom.)* Sweeping up…

SAVAGE: *(Draws near HELEN.)* In passion, the woman births the man. The convulsions of her flesh are births…

EPSOM: *(Sweeping.)* I wouldn't know…CLEAR OF THE BODY, PLEASE!

SAVAGE: Imagine, then.

EPSOM: Who, me?

SAVAGE: Why not you? *(EPSOM shrugs.)* I INSIST THAT YOU IMAGINE. *(EPSOM stops sweeping.)* To have had Helen, imagine it…

EPSOM: Trying…

SAVAGE: Yes, but to have had Helen, and to have no longer, IMAGINE THAT. *(EPSOM shrugs.)* The greater the love, the more terrible the knowledge of its absence. No sooner did she love me than I longed for her death, AND YOU CALL YOURSELF A MONSTER! *(Pause.)*

EPSOM: I think –

SAVAGE: YES!

EPSOM: I think –

SAVAGE: I AM WHAT YOU ARE ONLY IN YOUR DREAMS. *(He goes to HELEN, and takes her in his arms.)*

EPSOM: *(Horrified.)* CLEAR OF THE BODY!

SAVAGE: Down the tunnels of her ears, I whisper… *(He mutters.)* Down the chasm of her throat I murmur… *(He draws the cloth from her mouth and kisses her.)*

EPSOM: ALL RIGHT…! *(SAVAGE lets the cloth fall, goes out. Pause. Then EPSOM goes to HELEN and removes the cloth. Pause.)*

HELEN: Not dead…

Until he spoke…

Not dead….

WHY NOT, BASTARD…!

EPSOM: Search me –

HELEN: Any death I would have welcomed and you spare me to hear that!

EPSOM: I thought –

HELEN: What was it, pity?

EPSOM: I suppose –

HELEN: Pity…!

EPSOM: I take life and I'm criticized, I give life and I'm criticized, CAN'T I PITY SOMETIMES, TOO?

HELEN: Oh, utter decline… Helen pitied… And I thought…for a moment… I dared think you had spared me for lust… *(She laughs.)*

SCENE FIVE

CREUSA comes in, an old woman pregnant. SAVAGE is alone.

SAVAGE: It's time. *(Pause.)* It's time to write the book.

CREUSA: On what? Soap wrappers?

SAVAGE: Your interventions were always so mundane.

CREUSA: There is so little paper here and one time it was blowing down the gutters, wrapped around the lamp-posts, fine cartridge, too, but who remembers Paper Troy? Collect today for tomorrow may be barren! As for pencils…!

SAVAGE: Can't write the book, then…

CREUSA: And reading's out of date…

SAVAGE: *(Relieved.)* Can't write the book… *(She shrugs, sits on a stool.)* Inevitable. The greatest document fails to exist. *(CHARITY hurries in.)*

CHARITY: Skipped Hygiene! Skipped Good Citizens and Family Love! Don't tell! *(She is about to run out.)*

SAVAGE: Seen a bit of paper?

CHARITY: Paper? What's that?

CREUSA: You see…!

CHARITY: Oh, that stuff the soap comes in?

SAVAGE: *(Grinning.)* CAN'T WRITE THE BOOK!

CHARITY: Write a book? What for?

SAVAGE: To spread unhappiness, of course…

CHARITY: *(Inspiration.)* I'll be the book. They say that men in concentration camps learned poems of nine thousand lines. I can do that! *(She sits cross-legged.)* Ready! *(She gets comfortable.)* Now, you speak!

GAY: *(Entering with officers.)* You say you saw it happen –

FIRST OFFICER: Everybody did –

GAY: Where is she, then?

FIRST OFFICER: I REPEAT WE ALL SAW HELEN DIE.

GAY: All legless and armless women, fetch them in!

SECOND OFFICER: There's only one in all of Troy –

GAY: Bring her! *(THE OFFICER leaves.)* They say that Helen's dead –

SAVAGE: She is. I kissed her cooling mouth.

GAY: Then where's the body?

CHARITY: WE'RE TRYING TO WRITE A BOOK!

GAY: Be quiet you precocious little – and I can see your knickers, you are not to sit like that!

CREUSA: You were the same –

GAY: I was never –

CREUSA: You were just the –

GAY: IT IS NOT POSSIBLE I WAS LIKE THAT. *(CREUSA shrugs. THE OFFICER pushes in A POOR WOMAN on a trolley. She is armless and legless.)*

SECOND OFFICER: Do you mean this?

GAY: Yes. How did she lose her limbs?

SECOND OFFICER: She fell under a tram. To be precise, she fell under two.

GAY: When?

OFFICER: When –

GAY: Not you. *(To WOMAN.)* You.

OLD WOMAN: When there were trams, of course.

GAY: She's lying. When were there ever trams?

FIRST OFFICER: During Mechanical Troy.

GAY: Mechanical Troy… I'd forgotten Mechanical Troy.

FIRST OFFICER: It rusts in shady corners…

GAY: *(To THE WOMAN.)* Well, if you'd lived in Dancing Troy, you'd only have got bad feet.

OLD WOMAN: *(Creaking with laughter.)* Seen some of 'em! I prefer me truck.

GAY: This can't be Helen, she's far too sensible.

SECOND OFFICER: *(To THE WOMAN.)* Shove off! *(They start to leave.)*

GAY: Wait a minute! *(She stops.)* Which tram?

OLD WOMAN: The 3.

GAY: Which direction?

OLD WOMAN: Empty. To the Depot. *(Pause.)*

GAY: All right. *(THE WOMAN moves.)* Why do you live? *(Her trolley stops.)*

OLD WOMAN: Out of habit. Why do you?

GAY: You are impertinent for a thing on castors.

OLD WOMAN: Beg pardon –

GAY: What are you trying to make me do? Commit suicide?

OLD WOMAN: No, I just –

GAY: Isn't there enough suicide without you –

OLD WOMAN: All over the shop –

GAY: I could regard that question as an attempt on my life!

SECOND OFFICER: We'll bring charges –

GAY: No, get her out – *(SECOND OFFICER propels her.)* And see she's washed…! *(Pause.)*

SAVAGE: That was Helen…

GAY: Idiot.

SAVAGE: HELEN!

GAY: Do you think I don't know my own mother…?

CHARITY: I WISH YOU WOULDN'T INTERRUPT THE BOOK. *(GAY and THE OFFICERS go out. Pause.)* Chapter One! No! INTRODUCTION. *(She shuts her eyes.)* Ready. Expatiate!

CREUSA: *(Suddenly.)* It's coming –

CHARITY: Shh!

CREUSA: *(Stands.)* The child –

CHARITY: The book!

CREUSA: THE MIRACLE! SAVAGE! *(SAVAGE jumps up.)*

CHARITY: *(To SAVAGE.)* If you go, you will never write the book. *(He hesitates.)* You know that, don't you? You do know that?

CREUSA: THE CHILD, SAVAGE…! *(He stares, his mouth open.)*

CHARITY: 'This book was so nearly never written…'

MACLUBY: *(Entering.)* Examining your feelings, Dr Savage?

CHARITY: 'So nearly never written because I pretended feeling I did not posses…'

MACLUBY: She only wants her hand held…

CHARITY: Conscience delays all journeys, but especially journeys of the mind… *(She jumps up.)* That's it, first line! *(MACLUBY assists CREUSA away. SAVAGE watches.)* Refusal. That's the only way we learn. *(A high wind. SAVAGE turns impulsively on THE CHILD and starts to throttle her. By a twisting motion of her body, CHARITY escapes. SAVAGE reels. FLADDER enters, carrying a rule, a yard long. He places it against a wall and makes a chalk line. He turns, sees SAVAGE.)*

FLADDER: That low. *(Pause. SAVAGE reassembles himself.)*

SAVAGE: What…

FLADDER: That low. *(FLADDER goes off.)*

SCENE SIX

Under the city gate. THE OLD WOMAN, parked.

CREUSA: *(Entering with a mass of bundles.)* I did it.

OLD WOMAN: You did.

CREUSA: And it is whole.

OLD WOMAN: That's something all Troy knows.

CREUSA: Look, it feeds off me…its fingers reach for my flooding tit, which, as if to ridicule my age, is bursting. Sixty, and in surplus!

OLD WOMAN: Baldness and abundance. Arthritis and suck.

CREUSA: Don't wonder where these gifts come from…

OLD WOMAN: Enjoy your miracles and keep your mouth shut.

CREUSA: *(Hoisting her load.)* Off now.

OLD WOMAN: And by the same gate, Creusa…! Forty years since you last fled. *(Pause. CREUSA looks at her.)*

CREUSA: By the same gate, yes.

OLD WOMAN: Good luck!

CREUSA: Some dithering old peasant will lend me a corner of his sack, and if he don't speak Trojan, all the better, spare me his preamble, and swop dinner simply for the fuck.

OLD WOMAN: No note for the husband?

CREUSA: Once a quitter, always a quitter. Tell him that.

OLD WOMAN: Damn all reconciliations. It couldn't last. They say he had been Helen's man, so really it never had a chance.

CREUSA: It wasn't that.

OLD WOMAN: Once tasted, Helen spoiled a man for others –

CREUSA: IT WASN'T THAT. *(Pause.)* He had no hope. *(Pause.)*

OLD WOMAN: Hope? Can you eat that? *(CREUSA shrugs, sets off. FLADDER enters with his rule and chalk. He marks a wall, is about to go.)* First Troy was burnt by foreigners. But last Troy the people burn themselves.

FLADDER: That low! *(He departs.)*

OLD WOMAN: What…! *(THREE YOUTHS are hustled in. GAY enters.)*

FIRST OFFICER: Three more who say they have seen Helen and enjoyed her!

GAY: Where?

FIRST YOUTH: Down the docks.

SECOND OFFICER: When?

FIRST YOUTH: Between seven and eleven, I don't know exactly, time stood still –

GAY: What did she say?

FIRST YOUTH: Nothing.

GAY: Nothing? Neither mm or ahh?

FIRST YOUTH: She's dumb, ain't she? *(He looks to the others.)* Helen's dumb? *(THE OFFICER thrusts him away. He runs.)*

FIRST OFFICER: You!

SECOND YOUTH: I met her near the botanical gardens and she drew me in –

GAY: To what?

SECOND YOUTH: The lily house, we poured with sweat –

GAY: When?

SECOND YOUTH: Some time between – say, five and nine –

SECOND OFFICER: FIVE AND NINE?

SECOND YOUTH: I couldn't say exactly, time stood still –

FIRST OFFICER: *(Elbowing him away, addressing the next.)* Where?

THIRD YOUTH: On a bus –

SECOND OFFICER: Upstairs or down –

THIRD YOUTH: Upstairs, of course.

GAY: When?

THIRD YOUTH: Oh, anything between –

SECOND OFFICER: TIME STOOD STILL DID IT?

THIRD YOUTH: Yer know! He knows, so why –

FIRST OFFICER: And is she dark or fair?

SECOND/THIRD: 'er 'ead is shaved! *(They laugh and run.)*

GAY: Someone is chalking lines. All over Troy, a metre high. Both on the villas and the slums.

SECOND OFFICER: Not some one Mrs. Some many have been caught with chalk.

OLD WOMAN: Where is the harm in a line?

GAY: We don't know, but we think it has a message.

OFFICER: There's one! *(He goes to the wall and taking out a cloth, begins rubbing FLADDER's line.)*

GAY: And oddly, the suicides have ceased.

OLD WOMAN: That's good, if life is…

GAY: Not good! *(Pause. They look at her.)* No, not good, because the hate must go somewhere. The hatred must. If only we had Helen! She could be the object but now it's the state!

SECOND OFFICER: *(Seeing A YOUTH at a wall.)* Oi! *(He grapples THE YOUTH to the floor.)*

GAY: Oh, hold him! He stinks of cellars! And don't puncture him! Be careful of his blood!

SECOND OFFICER: *(Kneeling on THE YOUTH.)* What's this with chalk?

GAY: His spit! Be careful, all their fluids kill!

SECOND OFFICER: What!

FOURTH YOUTH: That low –

SECOND OFFICER: Come again, you –

FOURTH YOUTH: THAT – LOW – *(THE OFFICER looks at GAY.)*

GAY: Release him.

SECOND OFFICER: Release him?

GAY: Kill him, then, what difference does it make? *(Pause. THE OFFICER kills THE YOUTH. OTHER YOUTHS pass, running. SAVAGE enters.)*

SAVAGE: The Miracle has gone.

GAY: Into the park with its –

SAVAGE: Been in the park. Just dogs. Just starlings. And dirty youths marking the streets with rules.

GAY: And the mother? Where is she?

SAVAGE: Gone. Without a note.

GAY: Deserted you? But she's seventy! *(A sound of disintegration. FLADDER, with YOUTHS, hurtles in. They stop.)*

FLADDER: LAST TROY. *(Pause. She stares at hm.)*

GAY: I understood – you – had – no – tongue –

FLADDER: *(Opening a cavernous mouth.)* NO TONGUE. *(She stares.)* But I articulate the people. *(A fall of buildings. He thrusts out the ruler.)* THAT HIGH. The ruins. THAT LOW. The city. *(People pour out the city, with or without bundles. THE OLD WOMAN is buffeted. FLADDER departs in the surge of the crowd.)*

OLD WOMAN: Oi! Mind my trolley! *(She is knocked.)* That hurts, idiot! *(And trodden.)* Bite your arse! WHAT'S THE RUSH? It's no different over the hill, I know because I been there! *(She shouts.)* THEY BUILT ELEVEN TROYS AND EVERY ONE WAS FAULTY! I LOVED ELEVEN MEN AND EVERY ONE WAS FLAWED. BUT DO I SURRENDER?

EPSOM: *(Passing with a sack.)* Save breath, four wheels…

OLD WOMAN: Oh, my second father!

EPSOM: Ta ta, four stumps…

OLD WOMAN: Don't go, I still got lips –

EPSOM: Fuck it –

OLD WOMAN: Fuck it, yes, what's in the sack?

EPSOM: *(Departing.)* Daggers.

OLD WOMAN: YER CAN'T EAT DAGGERS. *(He goes.)* Teach a man a trade, and he'll find hirers…

SAVAGE: *(Seeing.)* Helen…

OLD WOMAN: Oi! My trolley! *(Some women start to tip her.)* Come off it, girls, steal from the wealthy if you must – rob yer enemies –*(They lift her off, dump her on the ground and place their bundles on the trolley.)* WELL, THAT'S NOTHING IF NOT PREDICTABLE! *(One slaps her.)* Sorry! Suffer in silence! Sorry!

SAVAGE: Helen…

OLD WOMAN: *(Now in the midst of the torrent.)* Sorry – can't move…beg pardon… *(A sack is dropped, abandoned. Tablets of soap spill out over the ground. THE OLD WOMAN cranes to smell them.)* Hyacinth! I smell you, Hyacinth!

SAVAGE: *(Beside her.)* It's you…

OLD WOMAN: No, it's not.

SAVAGE: It is…it's you…

OLD WOMAN: Not me. And never was. *(A shattering of masonry.)* No Helen but what other people made of her. I deny the body exists except within the compass of another's arms… *(A rush of fugitives. CHARITY glimpses SAVAGE.)*

CHARITY: Come on! We've not finished yet!

SAVAGE: No, nor started…

CHARITY: Chapter One! *(He stares at her.)* But I'm the book…! *(He doesn't move. THE CROWD moves on, CHARITY with them.)*

OLD WOMAN: Give us a lift, somebody! Give us a lift! *(She is spun round.)* I go in a pocket! I go in a bag! Oi! *(She is knocked onto her back, She lies, laughing. THE CROWD thins to individual scattering.)*

MACLUBY: *(Appearing with a sack into which he pops the soap tablets.)* All gone except the cripples…

OLD WOMAN: 'ho are you calling a cripple? *(He looks at her with supreme detachment.)* I suppose if birds shit in my mouth I might be fed… *(She opens her mouth. Pause.)* Come on, sparrow, I chucked pastry at you once… from honeyed beds…from honeyed balconies…my fingers crumbled over-abundant cake…SHORT MEMORY! *(SAVAGE looks at THE OLD WOMAN. He looks around him. Pause. MACLUBY tosses him a spade)*

OLD WOMAN: Terrible shortage of sparrows…come on, pigeons, divest! *(She opens her mouth wider still.)* Crows? *(SAVAGE goes to her. He flings on a shovel of earth.)* Anyone! *(He flings on another.)* Oi! *(And another.)* I GOT NO POWER, WHY MUST I BE DEAD? *(He smothers her with earth, breathless. She is silent. He walks back to GAY, flings the shovel at MACLUBY. GAY wraps SAVAGE in her arms. He is still.)*

SAVAGE: All that I know…and all you don't…

GAY: Shh…

SAVAGE: The long length of our quarrel yet to come…

GAY: Shh…

SAVAGE: Shallow reconciliations and lingering angers in the dark…

GAY: That's love, isn't it? *(He looks at her.)*

SAVAGE: Cut that short, then.

GAY: Love…hammered out thing…shapeless thing…

SAVAGE: Cut that short, then.

GAY: Bashed out like copper…warped like yew…

SAVAGE: CUT THAT SHORT, THEN. *(She kisses him, but silently. He throttles her, letting her body lie over him. Pause. The wind. THE BOY enters, with a stiff bag. He looks at his father.)*

BOY: Find what you wanted?

SAVAGE: Thank you, yes… *(THE BOY turns to go.)* Kiss me…? *(THE BOY looks at him, blankly.)* All right, give us the plate! *(THE BOY looks puzzled.)* Broken plate… *(SAVAGE indicates with a nod the shards of broken plates which lie among the litter. THE BOY picks up a piece, gives it to him, goes. SAVAGE attempts to slash his own throat.)* Can't… *(He braces himself, but fails.)* Can't! *(And again.)* HOW DID THE OLD MAN DO IT? CAN'T! *(He chucks down the shard.)*

MACLUBY: What do you think suicide is, a solitary act? It's peopled with absences.

SAVAGE: I have absences.

MACLUBY: You murdered everything, and long for nothing. Aren't you already dead? *(He picks up his bag and walks away.)*

SAVAGE: That's knowledge, then… *(Pause. Whistling offstage. ASAFIR enters, sees SAVAGE.)*

ASAFIR: Hey! We are having a picnic here.

SAVAGE: Don't mind me.

ASAFIR: *(Off.)* Hey! *(JOHN enters, bowed by hampers.)* This is the picnic place.

YORAKIM: *(Entering.)* Oh.

SAVAGE: Don't mind me.

ASAFIR: But this is a picnic place!

SCHLIEMANN: *(As guide.)* The University! What a terrible place this was! The little rooms suggestive of a gaol, the –

YORAKIM: Erm –

SCHLIEMANN: The corridors of inordinate length where tortured thinkers thrashed each other in pursuit of a deity they called Truth –

YORAKIM: Erm –

SCHLIEMANN: A deity without shape or form, of course, these were not primitives – *(He looks at SAVAGE.)* Are you on the tour? *(An inordinate pause. Black.)*

BRUTOPIA
SECRET LIFE IN OLD CHELSEA

Characters

SIR THOMAS MORE
An Intellectual

ALICE
His Wife

CECILIA
His Daughter

MEG
His Daughter

ROPER
His Biographer

THE SERVANT
Nurse to CECILIA

HENRY VIII
The Monarch

BERTRAND
A Suitor

BONCHOPE
A Heretic

THE COMMON MAN
An Occupant of the Garden

THE DOCTOR
An Inhabitant of Utopia

THE WORKMAN

DAKER
A Scholar

FACTOR
Lout to the King

LLOYD
Lout to the King

HOLBEIN
A Court Painter

BOLEYN
A Queen

SERVANTS

CARTERS

PRINTERS

MONKS

NUNS

THE SICKNESS

SCENE 1

The garden at Chelsea. The King of England standing in moonlight. About him, a body of men assemble a massive telescope and its cradle. Others sprawl on the ground.

THE CAPTION

Thomas More published *Utopia* in 1516. It describes the perfect society. His daughter Cecilia composed *Brutopia* in secret. Only now has the text been discovered.

A figure appears pulling on a coat. He kneels before the monarch.

CECILIA: *(Aside.)* My father did not love me. Therefore I chose to cease loving him. Once I accomplished this, so much confirmed me in the wisdom of my decision. And so it was in Brutopia, that all the reasons one might discover for affection were seen equally to be good reasons for contempt. In Brutopia love was impossible and anger took its place. This anger was in certain ways, indistinguishable from love.

KING HENRY: I'm here to look at the moon.

MORE: It's late.

KING HENRY: Of course it's late you academic bastard, when else can you look at the moon?

MORE: Forgive me, I'm more than half asleep.

KING HENRY: No, I saw your lamp on, you scholarly bastard, you were in your study.

MORE: Sleeping, yes.

KING HENRY: Sleeping in your study? You theological bastard I saw your shadow pass the light or

I should not have pestered you. Don't you want to entertain me?

MORE: Want, yes, but –

KING HENRY: That's as I thought, the genius longs to entertain me, so down to Chelsea for a discourse on the moon. Get up now and fix your eye to the lens, you see I come equipped, I come with all astronomy's impedimenta. Gawp.

(MORE is manoeuvred to the eye-piece. HENRY speaks quietly into his ear.)

Do you miss me?

CECILIA: *(Aside.)* In Brutopia there was neither lie nor truth. Everyone believed everything.

MORE: Profoundly.

KING HENRY: Profoundly. He misses me profoundly!

MORE: But scholarship abhors society and –

KING HENRY: *(Squeezing his shoulder.)* Look –

MORE: I am looking –

KING HENRY: The moon, the moon…!

MORE: Yes –

KING HENRY: Are you looking?

MORE: Yes, of course I'm looking –

Yes –

Yes –

Why do you like the moon so much?

KING HENRY: Don't know

(MORE leaves the eye-piece.)

Discourse, then.

MORE: I'm no astronomer.

KING HENRY: I have astronomers, I'm here for wit.

(Pause.)

MORE: *(Returning to the lens.)* The moon has long been honoured for its female character –

(A terrible cry is heard.)

A charismatic symbol which in pagan cultures represented –

KING HENRY: What's that?

MORE: What? Charismatic?

KING HENRY: No. The yell.

MORE: Yell…

KING HENRY: Yes, I heard one.

(Pause, MORE leaves the lens.)

MORE: You traipse all the way from Westminster in dead of night to –

KING HENRY: Somebody yelled.

(Pause.)

MORE: Bonchope. He preaches heresy.

KING HENRY: The moon has truly entered him.

MORE: I don't know why but regularly this sound issues from him, as if in contempt of speech, I'd say the devil was squatting in his gob but –

(The cry.)

there it goes again – I don't credit the devil – shall we proceed, I –

(He returns the eyepiece.)

KING HENRY: Where is he?

MORE: In the lock-up.

KING HENRY: Gag him.

MORE: *(Leaving the lens again.)* Gag him? Now?

KING HENRY: His clamour's messing up the moon.

MORE: Gag him?

KING HENRY: Yes, you know, a wad of cloth which inhibits speech –

MORE: I – I –

KING HENRY: *(Taking a cloth.)* I will. Where do you keep him?

MORE: On the bottom lawn.

(HENRY sets off. The sprawling men jump to their feet and follow.)

Should I – do you want me –

CECILIA: *(Aside.)* And the Brutopians, believing everything, sometimes laughed and sometimes wept at the same spectacle. They were luckily, bereft of tenderness. This made them perfect citizens. In Brutopia, you cannot be unkind. So much hypocrisy is spared by this!

(CECILIA's face is seen between the trellis, still, observing, like a mask. After the passage of the royal party, MORE limps by.)

SCENE 2

MORE's garden gaol. HENRY addresses its occupant.

KING HENRY: You explain to me the transmigration of souls and I will explain to you the paternity of Christ. You first, and remember I am a rampant theologian, one slip from orthodoxy and I hasten your ordeal, speak, I am all monarchic ears.

(BONCHOPE, gagged, is seen at the grille of a rustic prison. MORE watches.)

BONCHOPE: Mmm……mmmmm……mmmmm….

KING HENRY: *(Stroking his chin.)* Possibly….

BONCHOPE: Mmm….mmmmmmmm….!

KING HENRY: *(Walking up and down contemplatively.)*

Possibly………

(The followers, propped against trees, laugh.)

Yes……

BONCHOPE: Mmm! Mmm! Mmm!

KING HENRY: Steady! Controversial!

BONCHOPE: Mmm! Mmmmm!

KING HENRY: HERESY! HERESY! WE ESTABLISHED THAT AT TRENT YOU INVETERATE LIAR AND MANIPULATOR OF THE DOCTRINE!

(He goes to the grille.)

Look… there is a moon… Placed in its waters by the supreme being … do fix your dirty gaze on it, do …

(BONCHOPE's eyes rise to the moon.)

Is life not infinitely sweeter than a single thought? For all that got you here is no more than a thought, though you prefer to call it truth, another truth is on its way behind you, shouldering your truth into the truth pit, LOOK OUT MORE TRUTHS! I do assure you, nothing holds, and it hurts to burn, you've seen it…

(MORE, unable to contain himself, hurries up to the prison and stares at BONCHOPE.)

MORE: Oh God, how I do hate him.

KING HENRY: Yes.

MORE: I try to hate his sin, but also I hate him.

KING HENRY: Yes.

MORE: HATE!

(Pause, BONCHOPE's eyes are full of terror.)

KING HENRY: Worship the moon, now.

MORE: What?

KING HENRY: Up there.

MORE: You are in a jaunty mood tonight.

KING HENRY: No, no, do it.

MORE: You strain my faith, but I will compose a sonnet.

KING HENRY: Yes, in Latin.

MORE: *(After the slightest pause.)*
Ad lumen, mater et filia –
Lumina et regina stellorum –
Sub canopis aeterna noctum et stabile –

KING HENRY: *(Holding MORE close.)* You don't like girls, do you? *(Pause.)*

MORE: No. Not in the way you mean.

(Pause. HENRY goes to BONCHOPE.)

KING HENRY: *(Intimately.)* Sir Tom won't jig.

MORE: I think you –

KING HENRY: Your persecutor. Your spiritual whatnot. He won't jig.

(BONCHOPE's eyes move from HENRY to MORE, and back again.)

Sir Tom wants me to feel the monkey in his presence. He wishes me to feel the ape.

MORE: Not in the least –

KING HENRY: To experience the humiliation of the hungry in the presence of the never-hungry – HAIR SHIRT!

(He pulls open MORE's gown. He wears a hair shirt.)

Hair shirt! I knew it! He mortifies the dirty packet we call skin! He flagellates the sack of gristle we call body, WHO CAN COMPETE WITH SUCH AVERSION?

(Pause. He releases MORE's gown.)

No, it's magnificent. It's mastery. He could stare at woman's belly and think – rot waiting its hour. He could see her hips and think – death's hiding place. Etcetera. No, it's magnificent. Clearly, there is nothing which can stop the mind of More. He is himself a god.

(The moon comes from behind a cloud and floods his face. He turns to BONCHOPE.)

Good night, idiot. Do you know who I am?

(BONCHOPE nods.)

And admire me?

(He nods again. KING HENRY leads the way from the lawn.)

They blinded in Byzantium.

MORE: So I understand.

KING HENRY: Little execution. Much blinding.

(Pause.)

More, come to court more often, and show off.

MORE: Show off?

KING HENRY: Yes, you know, show off!

(MORE bows his head. HENRY embraces him, holding him tightly.)

Why do you pretend to be a bore?

MORE: *(As if puzzled.)* I – I –

KING HENRY: Do you want to disenchant me? Do you think a bore is never pestered? Awful error.

(HENRY releases him, strides away, followed by the rest. MORE watches them depart.)

CECILIA: *(Aside.)* In Brutopia, they know no pity.
So when hurt, they seek no comfort, but
find another to inflict their hurt upon. This
eradicates preposterous sympathy!

(MORE's wife appears.)

ALICE: Are you –

MORE: *(Turning on her.)* CAN'T I WALK IN MY OWN GARDEN! CAN'T I LURK A LITTLE IN MY PLOT!

(Pause.)

ALICE: How powerful the moonbeams are tonight, I –

MORE: CAN'T I STROLL AT ANY BARMY HOUR WITHOUT YOU IN FLAPPING SLIPPERS –

ALICE: Yes –

MORE: FLAPPING –

ALICE: Yes –

MORE: SPY AND SIMPERER!

ALICE: Yes –

MORE: *(Pointing.)* THERE IS YOUR GARDEN, THERE!

(Pause. He swiftly embraces her.)

ALICE: I understand… I do… I understand…

MORE: Yes…

ALICE: I only feared –

MORE: You feared. That is the function of all wives. To fear. Fear on and good night.

(He releases her. She turns to go.)

I am very grateful to you. Thank you. You are perfect and considerate. Thank you.

(She creates a smile. She starts to go.)

I am writing a description of the perfect world and consequently cannot sleep beside you. You understand that, obviously.

ALICE: I understand.

MORE: Good night now and kip well, dear one.

(Again she turns.)

HOLD HANDS!

(Pause. She returns, takes his hands. Pause. He closes his eyes.)

Perfect now. The equilibrium of marriage.

(Pause.)

ALICE: Your daughter never sleeps.

MORE: *(Opening his eyes.)* Meg never sleeps?

ALICE: Meg sleeps. I mean the other.

MORE: Other?

ALICE: They are your daughters, both of them.

MORE: Never.

(He laughs.)

How could she, she denies me.

ALICE: Not the paternity.

MORE: No, not that. But the rest. The imitation and the admiration. That she withholds.

(ALICE turns to leave.)

BUT I'M NOT CHAGRINED!

SCENE 3

Sun in an arbour. CECILIA sits with MEG. ROPER, a young man, shrugs and grins.

CECILIA: I dislike you. Shall I tell you why? Because you tell jokes all the time. I have no sense of humour, so why do you persist?

(He shakes his head, smiling.)

You want to control me. That is why you want me to laugh. One day I can see whole populations laughing, their heads will go back as if on a single hinge. Laughter! And they will be incapable. They will be enslaved. Do stop nodding, you are so –

(He smiles.)

All right, you have seen my naked arse, do you think that gives you an authority?

(He shakes his head.)

STOP SMILING YOU CAREERIST.

(Pause.)

I wish someone would talk to me who was extraordinarily intelligent. Whose eyes. Whose mouth. Radiated like a sun boiling. But washed. But clean. You seem to think neglecting yourself is some evidence of moral strength, to me it is rather –

(ROPER gets up, walks slowly away, CECILIA turns to her sister.)

How can you love that man, he is a –

(MEG smiles.)

Shh! His master walks! Shh! His mentor exercizes!

(She peers through the foliage. MORE is discovered.)

MORE: *(Through the trellis.)* Do you find nothing funny in the whole wide world? Cecilia?

CECILIA: Nothing.

MORE: Not the absurdity of the posturing prince? Or the monkey's habits?

CECILIA: Neither.

MORE: How hard you are to love.

CECILIA: Impossible, I hope.

MORE: It is a pity we can't talk. It is an indictment of us both, for I can talk to anyone.

CECILIA: I've seen you.

MORE: I have brought workmen crashing off their ladders with an apt remark.

CECILIA: It is an odd talent.

MORE: And left the coarsest labourer choking on my wit.

CECILIA: An extraordinary talent.

MORE: AND YOU DON'T GIGGLE.

(Pause.)

My own dear one. My own implacable and adamantine one. My loved one, my obdurate. Have you seen spit on a flint? So it is with you. GIRLHOOD! Where is it? GIRLHOOD! I saw it! There!

(He laughs, turns to go away.)

CECILIA: Who is in the lock up?

MORE: Nothing

CECILIA: Nothing? I said who, and you say –

MORE: Nothing. *(He smiles, goes out.)*

SCENE 4

A Maze. It is raining. CECILIA enters.

CECILIA: *(Calls.)* Are you here?

(She goes into the maze, stops.)

You are! I know you are!

(She marches on, to the centre. A woman is seated on a bench. She is drenched, but still.)

Mud. Much mud in Brutopia.

(Pause. She sits beside her, embraces her swiftly.)

How cruel are you today?

(Pause.)

Oh, bitterly, I can tell.

(She stares at her.)

Warped by resentment, stained by malice, she crouches on her grudges like a hen on eggs…!

(Pause.)

Is there war in Brutopia?

THE SERVANT: All the time.

CECILIA: Continuous? The thrashing of the populace in endless struggle! What sort of war?

THE SERVANT: Civil.

CECILILA: Civil war! Yes!

THE SERVANT: The rich against the poor, and the poor are guilty.

CECILIA: *(Inspired.)* The poor are guilty! Yes! Of what, though?

THE SERVANT: Poverty.

CECILIA: Poverty, of course! Their poverty is ugly, and the ugliness of their poverty arouses the indignation of the rich! Yes! The poor rich! The angry rich! So the rich lash the poor, and then?

(Pause.)

What?

(Pause.)

THE SERVANT: You don't understand, do you?

CECILIA: I'm trying to.

THE SERVANT: The poor are guilty.

CECILIA: Yes. I said yes.

THE SERVANT: How can you understand Brutopia if you are witty?

CECILIA: I'm sorry.

THE SERVANT: Wit has nothing to do with Brutopia.

CECILIA: No.

THE SERVANT: No wit in Brutopia.

CECILIA: None at all. Forgive me. Anything else?

(Pause.)

THE SERVANT: The poor erupt. They kill the rich. But not only the rich. They kill each other.

CECILIA: Horribly.

THE SERVANT: Horribly. It is their only pleasure.

CECILIA: Yes.

THE SERVANT: This the rich both fear and yet encourage.

CECILIA: They encourage it, why?

THE SERVANT: BECAUSE THEY NEED IT, OBVIOUSLY!

(Pause.)

CECILIA: They need it, yes.

(Pause.)

Forgive me, why do they?

(Pause.)

THE SERVANT: I can't tell you everything.

CECILIA: No, but –

THE SERVANT: It assures them they are correct. Because in Brutopia nothing is seen to be good unless it is opposed.

CECILIA: Anger is the proof of its correctness! Yes! I'll write this down!

(She goes to move.)

This mud! Everywhere, mud!

(She looks at THE SERVANT, who does not move. She stands on the bench, looking over the hedge of the maze. The heads of the Brutopians are seen, plastered by rain, in all the alleys.)

They're not happy. They are sullen. So sullen…!

SCENE 5

A sunny place. MEG is reading. Her father appears behind her. He leans on her chair.

MORE: How does my daughter love her husband?

MEG: So admiring is my husband of my father, I might almost say it is my father I have married. Your words ring out in the strangest places, your phrases trickle on our pillow. Peculiar.

(She grabs his hand.)

Promise not to die.

MORE: Never.

MEG: I think to wake and know you cannot be discovered somewhere, in the kitchen or the library, would wreck my –

MORE: *(Demonstratively.)* Thomas More! His tomb!

(Pause. He pretends to contemplate.)

A thing deceptively simple. Severe. A table without embellishment. MORE. His title, in stark and livid letters. MORE. Who dreamed the greatest dream, who overcame the monk, the monarch and the scholar. He dwarfed his peers, and in a cheap time stood a rock of – you finish it –

MEG: I refuse to flatter you, it –

MORE: Indelible and incorruptible –

MEG: No – I said –

(MEG takes his hand playfully. He bites her hand.)

Ow! Ow!

(He laughs.)

Oh, God, you've – ow, you've bitten me! You bite, why do you bite? Look, blood! Why do you bite?

(He laughs.)

MORE: More's a wolf!

(Pause. He stops laughing.)

I can't apologize.

MEG: *(Wrapping her hand.)* It hurts, it really –

MORE: Yes, but I can't apologize. Don't ask me to apologize…

(He walks away, leaving her seated. A wind tugs at the foliage. He walks through covered ways. He stops, seeing a group of figures. He looks at them.)

SCENE SIX

A cloaked and hatted FIGURE is sitting on a low stool staring into a bowl, wide but shallow. Sitting behind him THE SERVANT. A third figure, THE COMMON MAN, is squatting behind them, MORE approaches them, looks into the bowl.

MORE: What's that?

THE DOCTOR: The solution.

MORE: To what? *(Pause. THE DOCTOR does not reply.)* I like the way you keep your hat on it lends you an authority you might otherwise lack, and never meeting my eyes is calculated also, don't forget you are dealing with a genius, where are you from, Spain?

THE SERVANT: I got him in.

MORE: You got him in but where from? He pretends to be a doctor, but suppose he is a murderer?

DOCTOR: You have a fever.

MORE: I have a fever, do I? Who told you?

THE SERVANT: I did.

MORE: I am sometimes feverish but that stuff is green. In any case I've never taken medicine. Why doesn't he speak, is he Spanish?

THE DOCTOR: I'm from Utopia.

MORE: *(With a laugh.)* There are no doctors in Utopia!

THE DOCTOR: Why, is there no sickness?

MORE: How could there be, there is no disharmony.

THE DOCTOR: I promise you, my hands are full.

MORE: With what? Childbirth? And please look in my eyes it is discourteous to stare at the ground, clear evidence to me you never set foot there, it is a society of honest men, without rank, shame or hierarchy. If you think I'm drinking that you are mistaken.

THE DOCTOR: Study the solution.

MORE: Study it? How? What is there to study? *(He kneels.)* All right, I study it. It's opaque. It's odourless. Its colour I have already established.

THE DOCTOR: Nothing else?

MORE: There is a life sized reflection of Sir Thomas More in – *(Pause.)* Oh, Jesus, I have put on years...

SCENE 7

The rustic prison. BONCHOPE at the grille. CECILIA is looking at him.

CECILIA: Are you the devil?

(Pause.)

Are you, though? Have you got a LONG TONGUE?

(He extends it.)

Not long, is it?

(Pause.)

I hear you read the Bible in English, why?

(Pause. He retracts his tongue.)

BONCHOPE: It is God's will His words should –

CECILIA: Do you know God? How do you know His will?

BONCHOPE: It is self-evident God would want His flock to understand –

CECILIA: Nothing is self-evident.

BONCHOPE: You interrupt me when I –

CECILIA: I have to interrupt! I hear such fallacies what can I do but interrupt?

(Pause.)

BONCHOPE: Why don't you cut out my tongue?

CECILIA: Well, of course, that is what they will do, but I am satisfied with interrupting you.

(Pause.)

I love the Latin bible. Latin is music. I don't understand a word of it.

BONCHOPE: Then you are kept from God –

CECILIA: No, I'm nearer –

BONCHOPE: How can you be nearer when you cannot understand the words that –

CECILIA: That's it!

BONCHOPE: When the words are –

CECILIA: That's it! Not understanding. That is it.

(She extends her tongue.)

BONCHOPE: MADNESS!

(He turns away from the grille. CECILIA goes nearer.)

CECILIA: I think there will come a day you can't hear Latin anywhere. And you will burn the Latin. Because you also are a burner.

(Pause.)

Listen! Oh, do come out! Listen! My father sailed to Amsterdam. He went to all the shops and bought up all the Bibles. Your Bibles. The English ones. Hundreds of Bibles! And he went into a field and burned them. Stoke, prod, like the bonfires in the Autumn. But hardly was his back turned and – yes! He didn't understand this thing called printing. Printing really wrecks all discipline! Do you know printing?

BONCHOPE: Yes. It's done with metal.

CECILIA: Metal, is it? Scarcely was he on the boat and they ran off another hundred!

(Pause. She grins.)

So I think it's time to ban paper.

(Pause.)

You don't talk more than you have to.

BONCHOPE: I'm horrified.

CECILIA: Horrified?

(A terrible cry comes from the prison.)

Recant, then! Just recant!

(Pause.)

Do come up again…

(Pause. She looks through the grilles. She turns away.)

It's vile in there…!

IT'S NOT A DOVECOTE, IT'S NOT A DOVECOTE!

(She hurries away.)

SCENE 8

MORE is staring into the solution.

MORE: There is no Utopia. I invented it.

THE DOCTOR: It exists.

MORE: Where, then! Where?

THE DOCTOR: You think you can imagine, and there be no consequences? If a thing is imagined, it is born! I alone escaped Utopia. The place exists.

MORE: You are a Spanish liar and this liquid is trick, I'm not as old as this!

THE SERVANT: I discovered him outside the gate.

MORE: Yes, well, I'm famous, aren't I? Quacks will queue for me.

THE DOCTOR: I landed at Deptford.

MORE: Deptford, did you? Off what boat?

THE DOCTOR: 'The Angel of Deliverance'.

MORE: I'll check that! I have friends in all the harbours! 'Angel of Deliverance'! Write that down! And then what? Walked?

THE DOCTOR: Exactly.

MORE: Long walk. Deptford to Chelsea. Awful walk. Show me your shoes!

(He peers over the bowl.)

MORE: No shoes…!

THE DOCTOR: No footwear in Utopia.

MORE: No footwear, why? I never specified the abolition of the cobblers!

THE DOCTOR: No, but it occurred.

MORE: How?

THE DOCTOR: It was a consequence.

MORE: Of what?

THE DOCTOR: Utopia is all consequences.

MORE: You are a Spanish liar! Give its latitudes!

THE DOCTOR: How practical you are, in some respects…

(CECILIA appears, breathless.)

CECILIA: He's standing in shit!

(Pause. She looks at THE DOCTOR, then back to MORE.)

MORE: *(Standing, brushing his knees.)* Well?

CECILIA: That's all right, is it?

MORE: Not only all right, but a good thing. Shit comes from his mouth.

CECILIA: His mouth?

MORE: Therefore he stands in it.

CECILIA: Ah…

(Pause.)

Thank you…

MORE: *(To THE DOCTOR.)* I shall study the bills of lading, Spanish doctor, and God help you…

(He walks with his arm round CECILIA, leaving THE DOCTOR seated.)

We must hate evil, we must not extend to evil any tolerance or pity which would stimulate its growth, or even enter into conversation with it, for then it dares assume equality with good, and posturing its legitimacy, corrupts the weaker minds, for some minds are weaker just as some bodies are, it is God's will and we can't dispute it, but to those of us with swift intelligence is lent a natural authority to sort the ideas into heaps, the good and bad heaps, and let the bad heap burn –

(He stops.)

Cecilia, if you withhold your admiration from me is it any wonder I am unkind? Is it? I can embroider what you find hard to speak, but offer up some, do you see, I am being realistic, I am being terribly frank, say you understand me.

(Pause.)

CECILIA: You want – you have to be –

MORE: The focus of your adoration, yes.
SIMPLE ENOUGH!

(Pause.)

CECILIA: Yes.

(Pause.)

If only I could be – impulsive.

MORE: Yes. Impulsive, yes. That's what you need. Make Meg your model!

(He smiles at her, squeezes her cheek, goes off. She sees ROPER hurrying towards her.)

ROPER: Sir Tom!

(CECILIA intercepts him.)

CECILIA: Give us some paper.

ROPER: *(Who is holding an armful of documents.)* Paper, why?

CECILIA: Old stuff. Junk will do.

ROPER: We must account for paper.

CECILIA: Account for it by all means.

ROPER: Four sheets.

(He draws the sheets from his sheaf.)

CECILIA: Four sheets! You reckless and dissolute man! No, even four's too much, your instinct was correct, I will write it on a SINGLE SHEET.

ROPER: What?

CECILIA: The Fyrste and Most Remarkable Account of the Geography and Society of the Unknowne and Terrible Kyngedom of – Brutopia! Because what is love but emulation? That's love, surely?

ROPER: You should marry.

CECILIA: *(Sarcastically.)* I should have, but you opted for my sister. You married her and not me because she more closely represents my father, isn't that so? He led you to our bedroom and pulled off our covers, and there we were, all arse and breast exposed, and quite honestly, there is not a deal of difference, is there? So it must be –

ROPER: The personality of Meg has always –

CECILIA: No, that's codswallop, you thought she was more completely Thomas More.

(Pause.)

With necessary adjuncts. Reproductive parts and all female etceteras but him, in essence, whereas I –

ROPER: I think you know so little about love.

(Pause.)

CECILIA: Little? I know nothing.

ROPER: *(Wryly.)* A man will come and steal you. Without your noticing. Steal your whole world. And you will see nothing but him on every page or window.

(Pause.)

Hell it will be, I think.

CECILIA: Obviously love's hell, why else would you want it?

ROPER: *(Slipping away.)* Shh! I think he's coming! *(She grins. He disappears. CECILIA turns, and finds a man close and staring at her.)*

CECILIA: Who are you?

THE COMMON MAN: The Common Man.

CECILIA: Then go a common place. This is a private garden.

THE COMMON MAN: Nothing's private any more.

CECILIA: That must depend how many dogs you've got.

THE COMMON MAN: I tame dogs.

CECILIA: How, by suffocating them? You stink and I hate the way you look at me. BOB!

(Pause.)

THE COMMON MAN: Bob's my mate.

(Pause. She looks at him a long time. A wind whistles through the garden. Suddenly CECILIA slaps his face violently, time and time again. He

staggers backwards, disappears. CECILIA holds her hands in the air.)

CECILIA: Soap!

Somebody!

SOAP!

(THE SERVANT appears with a bowl and towel. CECILIA plunges her hands in, washes them, dries them, gives back the towel. She turns, and through the trellis, catches sight of MORE sitting at a table with THE COMMON MAN, talking avidly and laughing. She stares.)

THE SERVANT: Your dad. He loves my class.

CECILIA: Why?

THE SERVANT: My thieves. My criminals.

CECILIA: Why?

(Pause. CECILIA embraces THE SERVANT.)

You are my love.

(THE SERVANT strokes her head.)

Do you hear me? I have no other.

(She frees herself.)

THE SERVANT: I bathed and dressed you once.

CECILIA: Yes.

THE SERVANT: And slapped and powered you. And while you slept, skirts up for somebody!

(CECILIA smiles.)

CECILIA: Good. I trust no one but the two-faced and corruptible. Now say you detested me, even as you spooned my infant mouth.

THE SERVANT: I was near to infanticide.

CECILIA: Oh, nurse, you bitch!

THE SERVANT: Spitefully made pinpricks in you, and hid sharp things underneath your mattress!

CECILIA: *(Wide-eyed.)* You –

THE SERVANT: Sprinkled you with ice-cold water –

CECILIA: Oh, immaculate –

THE SERVANT: Burst paper bags behind your ear –

CECILIA: And no one knew! No one spotted!

(Pause. THE SERVANT smiles.)

The world's foul, obviously…

(The cry of BONCHOPE is heard over the gardens.)

First premise of Brutopia…

(She suddenly slaps THE SERVANT over the cheek.)

That's for all that, then. Quits.

(She turns away, smartly.)

SCENE 9

CECILIA walks through the overhung garden.

CECILIA: *(Aside.)* Brutopia is a republic, but with a monarch. The population is literate, but there are no books.

(She stops.)

No.

(She continues.)

There are books, but these are written in Brutopic. The rules governing this language are extremely complex!

(Inspired.) Yes! Utterly complex and obscure, and there are no dictionaries!

(She comes up to the gate of the maze. The heads of the BRUTOPIANS appear among the hedges, complaining.)

No dictionaries, and no grammars, either!

(She goes into the maze.)

Complain away, complaint is the music of Brutopia!

(They mob her. She rebukes them.)

Do you want everybody getting knowledge? What would you do with it? UPSET BRUTOPIA! Oh, yes, you would, I know you would, it would UNSETTLE you.

(She moves on, stops.)

Books can be discovered, yes, they can, but it entails appalling effort. Terrible effort, yes. So those who want must suffer. Knowledge is acquired through pain.

(They groan.)

That's perfectly correct! That's wholly proper!

ALICE: *(Offstage.)* Cec-ilia!

(Pause. All is still.)

Cec-ilia!

(Pause. A FIGURE climbs a ladder, stares at her over the hedges.)

BERTRAND: Is she small?

(Pause.)

Is she pallid?

(Pause. She stares back at him.)

I am in the Russia trade.

(Pause. ALICE joins CECILIA.)

ALICE: *(Sotto voce.)* This is a man with a future and good legs.

BERTRAND: *(Deliberately.)* Whalebone. Timber. Fur.

ALICE: *(Sotto voce.)* Twirl a bit.

CECILIA: You twirl.

ALICE: Flick something.

BERTRAND: Leather. Grease. Elkhorn.

ALICE: He has a seat in Parliament. Ask him.

BERTRAND: Resin. Hide. Esparto grass.

ALICE: *(Nudging CECILIA.)* Say something! Don't you want a husband?

CECILIA: Welcome to Brutopia.

BERTRAND: Where's that?

CECILIA: Here, of course.

BERTRAND: What happens in it?

CECILIA: Everything.

BERTRAND: And who is the monarch?

CECILIA: The worst swine.

ALICE: His parliamentary seat, ask him.

BERTRAND: And do the people suffer?

CECILIA: Appallingly.

ALICE: *(Nudging her.)* What constituency, say.

BERTRAND: Is there beauty in Brutopia?

ALICE: Oh, yes. It is an instrument of torture.

BERTRAND: I understand this country. I will be its first explorer. I will draw its maps.

(Pause. He climbs off the ladder, disappears from sight.)

ALICE: He's coming!

CECILIA: Yes.

ALICE: He likes you.

CECILIA: Yes.

ALICE: *(Holding her.)* Marriage is a desert. But some find oases.

CECILIA: Yes.

ALICE: And he has wonderful legs!

(She hurries away. BERTRAND appears. Pause. A thin wind rattles the foliage.)

CECILIA: *(Looking coolly at him.)* Brutopia is imperfect, and where perfection appears, it is eradicated.

(He looks at her.)

How, did you say?

(Pause.)

By a committee of eradicators, of course!

(Pause. She takes him by the arm and leads him down a walk.)

Well, they call it a committee, but only one member has a vote. And only one can speak. The same one. The others must applaud, and the first one to stop applauding –

DEATH!

(She fixes her mouth to his, passionately kissing him. She stops, swallows.)

As for death....

(He looks at her. Pause.)

The horror of it is exaggerated here.

(Pause.)

Do you like women?

BERTRAND: Women? How you generalize!

CECILIA: We do in Brutopia. It's the law.

BERTRAND: I delight in female company.

CECILIA: Do you? Why?

BERTRAND: The female mind is a subtle, sensitive, instinctive and –

CECILIA: No, I mean do you like us? Never mind the inventory of the virtues of the gender, do you like women undressed?

(Pause. He looks deeply into her.)

I long to marry you, obviously, but are you coarse enough?

BERTRAND: I try.

CECILIA: You try! Can you try to be coarse? It's a gift, surely?

(Pause. She looks at him.)

I think you are full of kindness.

(Pause.)

What's called kindness.

(Pause.)

Aren't you?

ALICE: *(Sweeping in.)* That's it, then! This way, and mind the thorns!

(BETRAND is led away by ALICE.)

BERTRAND: I love her.

ALICE: Excellent!

(She draws back a bramble.)

Mind your eyes!

BERTRAND: She's ugly. Terribly ugly.

ALICE: Do you think so? I always have, and yet –

BERTRAND: I love her.

ALICE: This all needs trimming back –

BERTRAND: Love her.

ALICE: I heard you –

BERTRAND: *(Stopping.)* UGLY AND I LOVE HER.

(Pause.)

ALICE: Speak to her father, then.

BERTRAND: But what's Brutopia?

ALICE: I wouldn't know.

BERTRAND: She's touched, surely? Be honest, is she touched?

ALICE: *(Coldly.)* Marry and risk it.

(She smiles.)

SCENE 10

MORE enters the fountain garden at night. He holds up his palm to falling snow.

MORE: Are you still here?

(A shadow moves over the snow.)

Listen, you are a liar and now I can't sleep.

(He discovers THE DOCTOR sitting under a wall.)

Look!

(He points.)

Bare feet!

(He smiles.)

More the sufferer!

(He stops smiling.)

There is no boat called 'The Angel of Deliverance', I checked it with my many friends and the boat's a fiction, there!

(Pause.)

A fiction!

(Pause. Sound of drunken hooliganism in the distance. A broken bottle. MORE stares at THE DOCTOR.)

What's gone wrong in Utopia?

THE DOCTOR: The flesh.

MORE: Whose?

THE DOCTOR: The body.

MORE: Whose?

(A burst of LOUTS.)

THE DOCTOR: Erupted.

MORE: Erupted…?

THE DOCTOR: Bodies overflowed the gaols.

MORE: What gaols?

THE DOCTOR: You don't know about the gaols?

MORE: There are no gaols!

(He flings himself down beside THE DOCTOR.)

You see, you have not been there! Read the book! NO GAOLS!

(He thrusts a copy of Utopia *at THE DOCTOR.)*

THE DOCTOR: *(Coolly.)* That is an early edition…

MORE: Just off the presses!

THE DOCTOR: No, we have a different binding.

MORE: Oh?

THE DOCTOR: With your profile on the cover.

MORE: Oh?

THE DOCTOR: Every Utopian has one.

MORE: Really? Expensive!

THE DOCTOR: No, cheap and uniform. And inside, a picture of you seated.

MORE: Really?

THE DOCTOR: Your body in repose stares wisely at the reader. Your body, for some reason. The only body in Utopia. Officially.

MORE: Only body? What are you –

(A window is broken. Jeers and laughter. MORE bounds to his feet and tears over the snow. As he hurtles by, CECILIA, dark, freezes against a trellis. She opens her eyes. Sounds of protest nearby.)

THE COMMON MAN: *(Off.)* Oi!

MORE: Oh, yes!

THE COMMON MAN: *(Off.)* Oi!

(MORE appears again dragging THE COMMON MAN with him, fixed in a headlock.)

MORE: Oh, yes, my eloquent and articulate –

THE COMMON MAN: Oi!

MORE: My monosyllabic deity for whom all alleys are his just imperium –

THE COMMON MAN: Oi!

(They pass CECILIA, who follows with her eyes.)

MORE: To stagger and vomit freely in as the whim inspires!

THE COMMON MAN: Oi!

MORE: Yes, yes, my subtle bruiser, my darling criminal spewed from the gob of squalor, luscious delinquent –

THE COMMON MAN: And arch-enemy of silence – there!

(He forces THE COMMON MAN to the ground in front of THE DOCTOR, retaining his hold.)

You were describing the Utopian. You argued that he had both a body and no body. Do elaborate. Shh!

(He tightens the stifling grip on THE COMMON MAN.)

THE DOCTOR: In Utopia half are gaoled and half are gaolers.

MORE: How? There are no criminals in Utopia because there is no property.

THE DOCTOR: Is the body not a property?

MORE: They steal bodies? Why?

THE DOCTOR: Is it not the site of all our hopes?

MORE: No, it is the pit of all our instincts! In Utopia all instinct is contained by thought, thought is the civilizer.

THE DOCTOR: And bad thought?

MORE: Bad thought has no place in Utopia!

(A LOUT's cry nearby. Breaking glass. MORE stops. Bitterly, he thrusts THE COMMON MAN into the snow and climbs to his feet.)

SCENE 11

A part of the garden. A window is broken. THREE FIGURES lurch in the darkness. Two are bawling hooligan songs. CECILIA, concealed, watches MORE hurtle by.

MORE: I claim my peace you –

FACTOR: Oi!

(MORE seizes FACTOR by the throat.)

MORE: Muck-mouth and arse-faced breaker of all contemplation –

FACTOR: Oi!

MORE: Up my garden, will you, gobflash, I –

(He sees the third hooligan is HENRY, who stares at him. MORE, holding FACTOR in a headlock, freezes. Slowly, he releases him, and slowly sinks into a posture of obeisance. FACTOR sniffs. Pause.)

KING HENRY: I am no respecter of property.

(Pause.)

MORE: Who is?

KING HENRY: Or chastity.

(Pause.)

MORE: Who is?

KING HENRY: Which also is a property.

(Pause. He looks at MORE. FACTOR blows his nose. A fine wind scatters snow.)

MORE: No moon tonight, I was not expecting –

KING HENRY: I love night, when the enemy is drowsing. Down I come THE MONARCHY! They shiver in their gowns. Beautiful disorder and women trembling. THE MONARCHY! Women in their hanging hair and tumbling servants. THE MONARCHY!

(He nods in the direction of the others.)

This is Factor. This is Lloyd.

(They bow.)

I cannot move without my murderers, but Tom, I must get a mob behind me. How can I do this?

MORE: Moral example.

KING HENRY: Tosh, I have to hand out land.

(Pause.)

MORE: What land?

(Pause.)

KING HENRY: I read you my new poem.

MORE: Poem? At two in the night?

KING HENRY: WHY NOT POEMS AT TWO IN THE NIGHT?

(Pause.)

I feel in the night. So I write in the night.

MORE: Yes.

KING HENRY: Come, walk.

MORE: Walk?

KING HENRY: Yes, up, while I recite, a poem in three stanzas put to music by me obviously, a love whine, a love whimper, a love howl –

(MORE climbs to his feet. LLYOD tunes his lute.)

Dedicated to I SHAN'T SAY WHICH BITCH –

(The LOUTS laugh.)

but I paw her glass like a dog in a lather.

(They follow HENRY into the dark.)

Oh, English weather I adore you, damp and clammy mask of murderers, for without it there could be no woman skin such as we long to lap with out insatiable gobs –

(He stops.)

That's not the poem –

(The hooligans laugh.)

Play, Lloyd – listen, this is my tune –

(The tune begins in earnest. The cry of BONCHOPE echoes across the garden. It is ignored. After an introduction, HENRY sings, walking.)

So shall I dream of her pale breast
Half exposed to the eye of swine
And her thin mouth so closed and stitched

Which grumbles yes to the infant's cry

(He explains.)

She has a child you see, which she never wanted –

(He sings.)

Oh, distressed mater – nity,
Oh, encumbrance of my life,
Oh, maternity in which I walk
Like the caged wolf howling.

(LLOYD beats a new intensity. HENRY stops walking and turns to MORE, delivering the last stanza with a cruel and relentless violence.)

Oh, fang my back and tear my flesh
You hungry and unnourished she,
Your thin wrists will struggle with me
In the dead light of the mor-ning!

(The music stops. Pause.)

The clean version.

(Pause.)

You don't understand, do you, Tom?

(MORE shakes his head.)

It is the single flaw in your genius.

MORE: May I sleep now?

KING HENRY: That you do without disturbance, do you?

MORE: So I predict.

(MORE bows, turns and walks.)

KING HENRY: Obviously, after her, there'll be another!

(MORE stops.)

Which proves nothing.

MORE: The shallowness of your affections, arguably…

KING HENRY: No.

MORE: Gratification as a single end is near to comedy, I daresay –

KING HENRY: No. It is the wordless presence of a god.

(Pause. MORE smiles patiently.)

MORE: What is?

(Snow falls lightly. HENRY comes to him.)

KING HENRY: The clash of unknown parties in desire…

(Pause.)

MORE: I don't know…

(He looks frantically at HENRY.)

I don't know…

(He walks away.)

KING HENRY: Go to bed, then…

(Pause. The cry of BONCOPE.)

LLOYD: Sir Tom has never suffered love.

FACTOR: He loves God.

KING HENRY: No man loves God who has not suffered women.

(FACTOR laughs.)

I say so! The best priests make a wreck of all their vows. And the best atheists.

LLOYD: Home, James?

(HENRY doesn't move.)

KING HENRY: More's death is on him like a growth…

FACTOR: And ours…

KING HENRY: And everyone's, ole! And everyone's, you embroidered disembowellers, and everyone's!

(He walks swiftly, followed by the hooligans, past the hidden faces of CECILIA and THE SERVANT, who follow with their eyes.)

CECILIA: He grows coarser…

THE SERVANT: Yes.

CECILIA: Is that because –

THE SERVANT: Nothing is denied him.

CECILIA: I too shall be coarse. Young and coarse.

Brilliant and coarse. Help me.

(She looks at her, kisses her quickly.)

Shall I marry the parliamentary member? He pesters me with notes.

THE SERVANT: Shh!

(THE DOCTOR walks silently through the garden.)

CECILIA: *(Aside.)* In Brutopia, nothing is what it seems to be. This is universal and a source of comfort. Where nothing is expected, disappointment is unknown, and hope entirely redundant.

(The cry of BONCHOPE pierces the night. THE DOCTOR stops, listening.)

CECILIA: Who is he?

THE SERVANT: He is from Utopia.

CECILIA: I long to meet him!

THE SERVANT: Shh!

(THE DOCTOR kneels in the snow, and sobs, noisily. CECILIA watches, transfixed. He ceases, gets up, walks on into the dark.)

His children are dead. His wife is dead. His brother is in prison.

(The sound of mass laughter. THE SERVANT disappears in the dark. CECILIA looks over her

shoulder. The BRUTOPIANS are massed in a sunken garden, gazing up at her.)

CECILIA: Laugh by all means.

(They do.)

The most comic thing in all Brutopia is – yes – the person who believes –

(They laugh.)

The very word – yes –

(They laugh.)

Ridicule – derision – yes –

(They stop.)

In Brutopia all pain is an act. The legless beggar acts discomfort. The orphan performs despair. HOW ELSE CAN YOU GET ATTENTION?

(They begin protesting their individual cases. A cacophony ensues. CECILIA watched with bemused satisfaction.)

SCENE 12

The silence of a thaw. The single sound of a workman tapping at a broken window to remove the glass. MORE and MEG in the sun.

MORE: *(Promenading.)* What is the relation between justice and the court?

MEG: None.

MORE: None, for the court merely dispenses punishment. What is the relationship between punishment and crime?

MEG: None.

MORE: None, for crime is an effect of property. Without property, crime has no function.

MEG: Does crime need a function? Can't crime exist for itself?

(He looks at her. They are beneath the ladder.)

MORE: *(Calling up.)* It can't be, can it?

WORKMAN: Wha'?

MORE: Can't, can it?

WORKMAN: Sir?

MORE: Property and crime? Insidiously linked?

WORKMAN: Wha'?

MORE: NO STUFF NO NICKING. Come on, don't ape ignorance, I put a proposition to you, weigh it, test it, the glazier is not without opinion, surely?

(Pause.)

WORKMAN: Sir, I –

MORE: WHAT SIR WHAT SIR WHAT SIR WHAT?

(Pause. Then with infinite patience.)

If I have, and you don't have, must you have what I have?

(Pause.)

WORKMAN: Erm…

MORE: Now, don't give me the answer you think I want, give me the answer that accords with your opinion.

(Pause.)

WORKMAN: No, sir.

MORE: No, he says, why not?

WORKMAN: No, or I would crack your head now, surely?

MORE: And what prevents you?

(Pause.)

WORKMAN: Erm…

MORE: *(Sprinting up the ladder he presents his head.)*

Skull!

(He takes the man's tool.)

Hammer!

(He poses, sacrificially.)

Tension.

(Pause.)

Still alive…

WORKMAN: I do not sufficiently dislike you.

MORE: Liking? Liking's inapplicable, it's fear of punishment!

(Pause.)

WORKMAN: Could be, I suppose –

MORE: You fear capture –

WORKMAN: *(Thinking.)* Could be –

MORE: THE SANCTION STAYS YOUR HAND.

(He gives him back the tool.)

Thank you. Glaze on.

(He rejoins MEG at the bottom.)

The sole protection of all property is fear of violence –

WORKMAN: No, not fear of punishment. Sorry, no.

(MORE and MEG stop. A faint irritation spreads over MORE's features.)

MORE: What, then? Obviously, you want what I have, not having it yourself.

WORKMAN: No.

MORE: Yes. You would rob me of my brain were it not most securely in a box.

WORKMAN: No –

MORE: No? No? It's the best brain in Europe, why don't you want it? It would be certain proof of your imbecility if, seeing the special nature of my brain and the – I mean this in all kindness – relatively mundane nature of your own, you did not covet it –

WORKMAN: I don't covet it –

MORE: You do –

WORKMAN: Don't covet it, I promise –

MORE: Envy, envy it!

(Pause.)

WORKMAN: Forgive me, but I don't want your brain, nor any other of your property.

MORE: *(Coolly.)* Then you are glazier through and through.

(He bursts out laughing.)

Through and through!

(He nudges MEG)

Through and through!

SCENE 13

CECILIA's breast, the object of BERTRAND's fixed stare. A groan comes from his depths. Swiftly, she lets her garment fall over it.

CECILIA: Enough, and what did you do today?

BERTRAND: *(Moved to an ecstasy of frustration.)* Oh… Cecilia…

CECILIA: In the House of Parliament?

BERTRAND: Oh…

CECILIA: *(Perplexed.)* You lie. You exaggerate. It is only –

(He hides his face in his hands. She watches him. Pause.)

Or does it make you really ill?

(Pause.)

Does it?

(She goes to him.)

Are you ill with me?

BERTRAND: Mad women always did excite men, though they took them in secret, whereas I –

CECILIA: I AM NOT MAD! I AM THOMAS MORE'S DAUGHTER. *(The voice of MORE laughing with his peculiar tone drifts nearer. The moment he appears, BERTRAND releases her hand.)*

CECILIA: The House of Parliament, you said –

BERTRAND: *(Recovering.)* We passed a resolution on the subject of the limitations of continental cloths, silver thread from Nimes and coarse wool from Ravenna, both stuck at seven thousand ells, and went on to discuss apprenticeships, reducing wages and whipping for football, it was a hard debate, some said footballers had their uses, they made good infantry, but I was eloquent, I said in my experience footballers fled at the first sight of a horse…

(MORE and MEG enter.)

MORE: *(Grinning fatuously.)* My loves, my loves, my love, my loves, my loves, my loves, my loves, my loves,

(He turns in a convoluted dance, slowly sinking to the ground, singing to the tune of 'Greensleeves'.)

My loves, my loves, my loves, my loves, my loves, my loves, my lo-oves …!

(He lies on the floor, watched by BERTRAND, MEG, CECILIA. Pause. He is rigid.)

And in Utopia, the act of reproduction was perceived as half-distasteful, half-absurd, the necessary but eminently fatuous prelude to the better business of rearing future citizens…

BERTRAND: *(Boldly to CECILIA.)* When I meet you again you must submit, and I will submit to you, God help the consequences…

(He bows, hurries away.)

MORE: It's Spring, my season! Spring, I swear!

(A figure is seen advancing waving a sheaf of paper.)

Daker!

DAKER: The preface!

MORE: *(Still turning on the ground from one posture to another.)* The preface to Utopia! Oh, Daker, I do hope it's kind and complimentary!

DAKER: It is!

MORE: I hope it honours me immensely!

DAKER: As far as I could honour you without it seeming –

MORE: What?

DAKER: Obsequious and reverential –

MORE: What's wrong with seeming so? Don't you revere me? Are you not obsequious?

DAKER: Well, that may be, but –

MORE: Stuff but, if I am worthy, praise me!

(He holds it out.)

DAKER: Read it and see.

(Pause. His hand remains outstretched.)

Do read and judge for yourself. If I offend you, it's only that I –

(MORE takes it, and tears it across. CECILIA laughs. Pause.)

MORE: Are you my ally, and my friend, dear Daker? And have I not educated you?

DAKER: You know it.

MORE: Away, then, to your stool and inscribe this preface without consideration to humility. Only the fullest praise, only the highest compliment, for *Utopia*'s a book commanding reverence and obsequy. Admit its greatness and stop shuddering for fear someone will call you creep, be honourable and praise it to the skies, how else can great work make its mark but by the unreserved devotion of its addicts?

DAKER: Yes.

(MORE smiles, hops up and clasps him round the shoulder.)

MORE: Meg! Feed Daker! Meg!

(CECILIA watches the three of them, arm in arm, prance down the arcade.)

CECILIA: *(Aside.)* The word most common in Brutopia is WE. I is forbidden. I is severely punished. But WE is everywhere! WE MUST. WE SHALL. This produces such a climate of mutual celebration! Endless mutual celebration until your ears are singing!

SCENE 14

A leafy place, intimate. BONCHOPE is standing before a laden table. ALICE is seated. She looks up.

ALICE: Mr. Bonchope!

(She hops up.)

Do have a seat! Or do you find you sit too much? Stand if that suits you better. This is chive, and this is cucumber, they are fresh from the garden, that's shrimp, and that's a little dip I make myself from medlar, do you know medlar? I don't expect someone like you goes in much for medlars! It should be clearer, more a jelly, but in some ways it's better when it's thicker, is it terribly uncomfortable in there?

(He is filthy.)

I haven't seen it but they say it's tiny.

BONCHOPE: Tiny, yes.

ALICE: Oh, dear, and that thing there is fish in a glaze, I didn't make it so I'm not responsible – do have a glass, would you like a stem, or do you like the straight ones? People are funny about glasses.

BONCHOPE: A straight one.

ALICE: And do you get plenty of food?

BONCHOPE: Very little food.

ALICE: Oh, goodness, well, tuck in, napkins over there and knives. I never feel hungry myself at lunch times, no matter what I have prepared, I only pick, why do you squawk, by the way?

(Pause.)

If it is a squawk?

(Pause.)

Perhaps I shouldn't call it a squawk? Is it a signal?

(He sits, stiffly.)

I tell you why I ask, because when you're just getting into bed it can be terribly disconcerting, as I suppose you –

BONCHOPE: I can't help myself.

ALICE: You can't –

BONCHOPE: Can't help myself, no.

(Pause. MORE appears, picks up a plate and helps himself to food.)

ALICE: *(To MORE.)* That's hot, that's spicy, that one –

(To BONCHOPE.) Let me fill a plate for you, let me pile it up, you must be so –

(She fills a plate.)

You really must –

(MORE is seated and eating.)

How's that?

(She puts a plate in front of him. He looks at the food.)

This is pleasant isn't it?

This is.

We haven't dared to eat outdoors, this is the first –

(Pause. She closes her eyes.)

Obviously I am your persecutor, too.

Obviously you are shit mouth in my estimation.

I think the heretic must die. I think the wrong must suffer.

(A long pause. MORE dabs his mouth.)

MORE: Did you enjoy *Utopia*?

BONCHOPE: It brought Heaven nearer to my mouth.

MORE: How's that?

BONCHOPE: By showing tolerance to be supremely beautiful. Though I stood in my own dung by failing light, it brought tears to my eyes.

(MORE studies him. Pause.)

MORE: Is that pickle sweet?

ALICE: Which one?

MORE: The yellow one.

ALICE: Yes, the yellow one is sweet.

MORE: She calls it sweet, wherein the sweetness, love?

ALICE: *(Tasting it.)* Well, I – yes, that's surely –

MORE: *(To BONCHOPE.)* Tolerance appeals to you, then, does it?

BONCHOPE: I think it is the mark of civil society and the glory of all culture.

MORE: You sing its praises, then…

BONCHOPE: It is the pinnacle of political society and the highest moment of –

MORE: He hymns! He hymns!

(To ALICE.)

Then what is that one there?

ALICE: That's hot.

MORE: Give me that.

ALICE: It's hot –

MORE: Tolerably, though? Tolerably hot?

ALICE: Well, how do I know what –

MORE: *(Tasting it.)* It's tolerable, certainly. My tongue is quite content… but what if it were… suppose my tongue were burned? Would that be tolerable, Mr. Bonchope?

(Pause.)

BONCHOPE: If your tongue burns, drink some water.

MORE: I am the wit, Mr. Bonchope. What are you?

BONCHOPE: A simple preacher.

MORE: No, chuck false modesty, what's your intention?

BONCHOPE: Intention? Must one have intention?

MORE: One must if one goes preaching illegality! One might fake innocence but one has intention!

BONCHOPE: Yes.

Yes.

(Pause.)

To make God's word ring clear in every –

(MORE scatters some crockery with his elbow. The noise shocks and shatters. A tin plate rolls over the paving, and stops. Pause.)

MORE: You only love tolerance because it lets your filth flow.

(Pause. BONCHOPE stares at him.)

Tolerate me, says the miscreant, that I may come nearer to your throat. You would have me and my family in the gutter, dirt and ash.

ALICE: *(To THE SERVANT who has appeared.)* We've had an accident, would you just –

(THE SERVANT kneels and collects.)

BONCHOPE: It's not Utopia, this, then?

MORE: Not Utopia, no…

(He turns in his chair. Across the lawn he sees THE DOCTOR, a distant figure, strolling.)

ALICE: *(To THE SERVANT.)* It's too early for a picnic but I thought, risk it, put a shawl on…

BONCHOPE: It's death, then, if I –

MORE: Yes.

ALICE: *(As THE SERVANT sweeps up a broken plate.)* Oh, what a pity, I so liked the pattern on that rim!

BONCHOPE: I recant.

MORE: *(Rising.)* That's sensible.

(BONCHOPE rises also.)

ALICE: *(To BONCHOPE.)* Take a napkin with you, fill it up, here –

(She stuffs items of food into a napkin.)

Mr. Bonchope is going back to his little den –

MORE: Scripture is a ground, Mr. Bonchope, that's all. A ground of struggle. Later, there will be other grounds, and other books from which the likes of you might wring wrong meaning. What these grounds will be I cannot – even I – imagine.

BONCHOPE: Utopias?

(MORE leaves, watched by BONCHOPE. THE SERVANT is clearing the table. Suddenly BONCHOPE seizes on the food, stuffing it into his mouth. He catches sight of ALICE, looking at him. He stops, smiles, then proceeds with his feasting.)

SCENE 15

MORE is walking through the trellis ways. He is pestered at the heels.

THE COMMON MAN: A joke, Sir Tom!

MORE: *(Walking.)* Not every day can jokes be manufactured. Not every day is funny.

THE COMMON MAN: Must laugh, Sir Tom!

MORE: I see you are determined to reflect the cosmic mockery rained down on us by our intellectual pretensions –

(THE COMMON MAN bursts out laughing.)

No, that's not a joke!

(He cackles.)

That is merely a reflection on the futile nature of –

(And cackles.)

Not a joke, I say!

(He leaves THE COMMON MAN behind. As he swiftly walks, he hears a voice.)

KING HENRY: More.

(He stops. He turns. HENRY is seated in a secluded rustic niche.)

MORE: You?

But it's daytime!

(He smiles, bows. HENRY looks at him.)

Much luck with the poem?

(Pause. HENRY merely observes him. MORE is uncomfortable.)

It is a sad fact that the loved object is more often than not more susceptible to force than poetry.

(He grins, weakly. Long pause.)

Sometimes, when you look at me, I know why I so loved being a priest …

KING HENRY: NO SAFETY IN THE CLOISTERS!

MORE: No?

KING HENRY: I look at the cloisters. And I think, what a lot of bricks…!

(MORE looks puzzled.)

MORE: Yes, a lot of bricks, but…

KING HENRY: I think, there's an asset…

(Pause.)

MORE: An asset? The bricks? Surely, it's the thought that is the asset, not the bricks…?

(Pause.)

The accumulation of philosophy…

(Pause. HENRY looks at him.)

The aggregation of analysis and sensibility…

(Pause.)

KING HENRY: No, the bricks.

(HENRY drops a copy of Utopia *onto the pavement with a definitive slap. Pause.)*

MORE: Ah. Not your –

KING HENRY: Pox.

(Pause.)

MORE: You are frank today. Fortunately I am not without endorsement. Today I had a letter from Erasmus of Rotterdam fulsomely applauding its ambition and congratulating me on the maturity of my Latin style. He welcomes me into the –

KING HENRY: Shh –

MORE: Hallowed circle of the discoursers on faith and government, I–

KING HENRY: Shh!

(MORE contains himself. Pause.)

Where's the politics?

MORE: I replaced it with goodwill.

(HENRY looks at him.)

KING HENRY: Where's the parties?

MORE: Parties?

(He is patient.)

There are no parties because there are no contradictions. And no contradictions because there are no separate interests –

KING HENRY: Pox.

(Pause.)

I want to get divorced and you must fix it.

(Pause.)

MORE: I did, I think, fix –

KING HENRY: Yes, you did, and thank you, but now I want to get divorced again.

MORE: Again?

(Pause.)

I am sure you know what you are doing, but –

KING HENRY: I do, and everybody must agree.

MORE: Everybody?

KING HENRY: The peasant, the factory hand, the shepherd and the sailor.

MORE: Yes, but –

KING HENRY: The roofer and the gutternsnipe, the butcher, and –

MORE: Yes, but –

KING HENRY: AND ALL THE GENIUSES OF THE CLOISTER!

(Pause.)

MORE: You are very modern.

KING HENRY: Modern, yes, to the buckle on my boot.

(Pause.)

MORE: You see how I prefer to prune and prattle here among the climbing and the twining –

KING HENRY: Everybody inside. Nobody outside.

MORE: What?

KING HENRY: Solidarity.

(Pause.)

MORE: Solid – arity?

KING HENRY: Good word. I found it in the dictionary. It means you must.

(Pause.)

MORE: Forgive me, but I much prefer the –

KING HENRY: YOU ALWAYS HAVE TO BE STANDING ON THE EDGES. *(Pause.)* SNOB. *(Pause.)* AND NOW THERE ARE NO EDGES. *(Pause.)* SNOB. *(Pause.)* Down now, in the puddle with the rest of us. *(Pause.)* I'm insecure. My dad got power with an axe... *(Pause.)* How black you are, which is the colour of self-confidence. And me, all colours, all flash. I stick my emblem in every gap, HENRY, HIS ROSE! HENRY, HIS MONOGRAM! Vulgar, like a yobbo bawling in the night, as if by scrawling on the fence I might keep history off... *(Pause.)*

MORE: History? Don't you mean time?

KING HENRY: I mean whichever bastard's waiting in the alley. *(Pause. He reaches into a pocket.)* I want your signature on this. *(He draws out a paper.)* Sign and you can plant begonias until your eyes are fields of cataract... *(Pause. He holds it out to MORE.)*

MORE: I don't like naked documents.

KING HENRY: No envelopes.

MORE: I don't like letters pointing at my heart.

KING HENRY: My arm is suffering.

MORE: I don't like –

KING HENRY: *(Withdrawing it petulantly.)* Too late! You had your chance but you preferred to stutter! Too late! *(He stares at him.)* No immunity for genius! *(And MORE stares.)* Genius wants to pontificate from floral havens, but reputation carries risks. You are a great-headed flower, and when the wind blows down must come the stalk. The bigger the head, the poorer the stalk, I am the wind and you damned well asked for it, you snob! *(Pause.)*

CECILIA: *(Aside.)* Brutopia, among its highest achievements, abolished the surprise. In Brutopia, nothing was surprising. To even appear surprised was certain evidence of immaturity or weak-mindedness. *(Pause.)*

MORE: If you killed me they'd name you barbarian from Greenland to China.

KING HENRY: If I killed you, the intellectuals would shudder from Greenland to China too. OH, THE WIND BLOWS ON US ALSO. Many monarchs would delight. Many of the second-rate would dash for empty chairs. *(Pause, then he rises to his feet, looks around him.)* The genius must share the garden with the yob. No world yobfree. No world geniusfree.

(He goes away, down the path. Instantaneously it rains.)

MORE: *(In despair.)* MEG! OH, MEG! *(CECILIA enters. She watches him.)* OH MEG! *(He is weeping. CECILIA's face is taut with pain and confusion. She hurries to him. He clasps her in his arms.)* Oh, Meg!

CECILIA: I'm not Meg –

MORE: GOING TO DIE, MEG!

CECILIA: Die…?

MORE: DIE, DIE!

CECILIA: Why die?

MORE: Because I'm honest! *(He buries his head in her hair. The rain runs down.)*

CECILIA: Be dishonest, then… *(Pause. His face emerges from her hair.)*

MORE: You're not Meg…

CECILIA: No, I'm Cecilia… *(He searches her face.)* FORGIVE ME, I'M CECILIA. *(She stares at him. His hands grip her by the shoulders. A long pause. She trembles.)*

MORE: Oh, wonderful…her womanly nature yields to see my ashen mask for the last time… indelibly stamped on memory the visage of her doomed father, Thomas More…

(She frowns.)

CECILIA: Who is Thomas More…?

(He does not relax his grip.)

What are you –

(He stares.)

You are –

(Pause. It dawns on her.)

Are you – instructing me – in – sham life?

(He merely stares.)

Are you – for love – teaching me to lie – and lie – even to myself?

(Pause.)

You are…

(Pause.)

You are trying to save me from the world…

MORE: *(Booming.)* MEG!

(CECILIA frees herself from her father as MEG appears, running.)

MEG: Father!

MORE: DEAD!

MEG: What –

MORE: *(Grasping her in his arms.)* DEAD, MEG!

MEG: Oh, God –

MORE: Ripped from your adoration by manic power!

(As he recites, his eyes meet CECILIA's, who is slowly drifting away from them.)

MEG: Oh, great soul, what –

MORE: DEAD!

DEAD!

The Recovery.

SCENE 1

The garden.

MORE: *(Offstage.)* DEAD! DEAD!

(CECILIA walks backwards from the spectacle. She is unaware of BETRAND, and collides with him. He seizes her wrists.)

BERTRAND: Shh.

CECILIA: Not now.

BERTRAND: Shh.

CECILIA: No, not now, I –

(He draws her back into a niche in the wall.)

No –

CECILIA: *(Aside.)* The Brutopians suffered more than any other race from love, which was not called love, but anger. 'I am angry with you' was an expression of deepest desire. But when this anger was relieved by carnal acts, the Brutopians experienced despair. Thus men and women seemed either furious or sunk in grief, according to how far their passion had progressed.

(CECILIA emerges, adjusting her skirts. BERTRAND leans against the wall, staring out over a lawn on which distantly, THE DOCTOR is discovered staring down at a single point on the turf. CECILIA leans beside BERTRAND. Pause.)

CECIILIA: You speak.

You speak now.

BERTRAND: What?

CECILIA: Anything. Timber if you wish.

(Pause.)

Or skins.

(Pause.)

BERTRAND: I –

CECILIA: Tallow. Fur.

BERTRAND: I –

CECILIA: Your voice, for God's sake.

(Pause. She puts her hand on him.)

BERTRAND: I apologize for any –

CECILIA: *(In despair.)* No, not that. Anything but that.

(She walks away from him, along a path. She encounters ALICE, distraught, but does not stop.)

ALICE: Have you heard!

CECILIA: *(Striding.)* Yes –

ALICE: And he says death, death all the time, what can we –

CECILIA: I heard –

ALICE: Meg is powerless!

SCENE 2

The maze. A cacophony of BRUTOPIANS. CECILIA stares, goes through the gate. They press on her. She forces her way to the centre, where THE SERVANT is sitting. Perfect silence prevails at the centre. THE SERVANT looks up.

CECILIA: I'm pregnant

(Pause.)

Pregnant by a lout.

THE SERVANT: I'll cure it.

CECILIA: No. This is Brutopia, where nothing comes except by error, and the wanted is simply what occurs.

THE SERVANT: I'll attend you when it comes.

CECILIA: *(Amused.)* That's to risk its life I solemnly predict!

SCENE 3

MORE is walking towards the rustic prison, with ALICE and MEG at his heels.

ALICE: You will die of pneumonia –

MEG: You must prepare an argument on the basis of Nihil Autoritatem, the Juridicium of Aquinas –

ALICE: You have been coughing all the winter, your lungs are tissue paper as it is –

MEG: The absolution of the clergy under the Edicts of Diocletian –

ALICE: What are you going to do in there? Die? Do you want to die?

MEG: Or Maximum Imperium! Yes! We invoke the clauses of the limitations!

ALICE: IT ISN'T FAIR ON ME!

MEG: Be quiet! How can anybody think!

SCENE 4

The centre of the maze. The BRUTOPIANS are kneeling as a congregation. CECILIA passes among them with a gracious smile.

CECILIA: *(Aside.)* The Brutopians were never silent except when sentimental. And how sentimental they could be! They held childbearing in such high esteem, whilst frequently killing children! And funerals they loved, whilst indulging murder!

SCENE 5

MORE is in the rustic prison. He hangs his arms through the grille, staring at the ground. ALICE is weeping.

ALICE: Please sleep in your bed. I will keep to my own side. Please sleep in your bed. I will not disturb you by tossing.

MORE: Your napkin of a mind…

ALICE: Yes, but do as I ask, I'll lie silent as a graven image…

MORE: Your table cloth of a mind…

ALICE: It is, but –

MORE: Your ironing board and breadknife of a mind –

ALICE: ALL RIGHT, BUT I HAVE SOME RIGHTS AS WELL AS YOU.

(Pause.)

MORE: Gaol is what I always wanted. Even lying beside you in a mattress plump with affection, it was gaol I ached for.

ALICE: You will have all the gaol you want, why anticipate it?

MORE: I have always been one step ahead in the imagination, and now go in, your head is wet.

ALICE: The last occupant of this place apologised, why don't you? The last occupant is smothering his children with a slobbering love, why don't you? The last occupant walks the streets intoxicated with freedom, WHY DON'T YOU?

MORE: He will be back.

ALICE: No. He is swallowing life by the lungful.

MORE: I SAID HE WILL BE BACK.

(He looks into her face.)

Fireside, piss on it. NO SWEET LIKE THIS.

(He slaps a fistful of mud over his cheek. She winces. Pause. She withdraws.)

ALICE: *(Suddenly.)* I love you.

(She stops. Pause. She looks back. His eyes are tight shut, his face filthy.)

MORE: In what way?

(He gives nothing. She goes. MORE hangs in this posture.)

CECILIA: In Brutopia everyone is sentenced to death. Without exception. The death sentence is handed out at birth and hangs above their beds, framed as a certificate. This dispenses with all the paraphernalia of courts and trials! At various times, as the need arises, these sentences are enforced.

(CECILIA approaches the rustic prison. MORE remains with his arms propped and his eyes closed. She examines him.)

CECILIA: I have a child.

(His eyes open. Pause.)

MORE: It's easily done.

CECILIA: Yes! Very! So easily I scarcely –

(She stops, looks at him. Pause. Suddenly she takes his face in her hands, thrusting her arms through the bars.)

MUST YOU DIE WITH ME HATING YOU?
MUST YOU TAKE MY CONTEMPT –

MORE: Ow –

CECILIA: I AM SO COLD AND –

MORE: Ow –

CECILIA: DEAD IN FEELING TO YOU –

MORE: Ow –

CECILIA: DEAD AND –

MORE: Ow –

CECILIA: INDIFFERENT.

(Pause. She releases him. ROPER is behind her, with an artist, HOLBEIN, who holds a sketchbook.)

ROPER: Mr Holbein will begin his preparatory drawings now.

(Pause. CECILIA withdraws from the grille. She looks at HOLBEIN.)

CECILIA: You drew me when I was a child.

(HOLBEIN inclines his head.)

Why not draw me now?

ROPER: Mr Holbein is very busy –

CECILIA: I know he is! BUT WHAT ABOUT MY GRIEF?

That needs catching, surely?

(Pause. HOLBEIN nods.)

Thank you. You see, a great artist does not miss an opportunity. What shall I wear?

ROPER: I don't think –

CECILIA: Black, presumably?

(HOLBEIN nods. She goes.)

MORE: She envies me my death. She knows how well I shall die, and envies me. Are you drawing yet?

(He leans against the grille.)

Last time…

(The chalk works on the paper.)

How different it was last time…!

(He laughs.)

HOLBEIN: Not so very.

MORE: Then I was mighty. Then I was a power. How different it was last time!

HOLBEIN: Not so very.

MORE: Why do you say that? I have fallen, I am dragged to the floor. Why do you say that?

HOLBEIN: Because last time you were swollen with power. And now you are swollen with the absence of power. But swollen, still swollen.

MORE: As you draw me I draw you, not with pencil, but I criticize, I am your critic and my eye is fierce as a gull's scanning your features as it will be on the axeman's too, he also will experience a shame for fear he is not so good an axeman as I am a poet...

(Pause. HOLBEIN draws.)

ROPER: *(Gaily.)* I have taken down all that. I have a record of all that –

(He turns a page.)

Isn't it a fact that in extremity a man will say things possibly better composed, possibly better conceived, than he could have in the comfort of his study?

MORE: COMFORT OF HIS STUDY?

ROPER: Yes –

MORE: COMFORT? IT WAS A CHAMBER OF PAIN!

ROPER: Yes.

(Pause. MORE smiles.)

MORE: Have you got that?

ROPER: *(Writing.)* Yes...

MORE: It isn't true. My study was heaven, and the best things I wrote were written in heaven...

(Pause. ROPER stops writing.)

SCENE 6

A niche in the wall. THE SERVANT is dressing CECILIA in funeral garments.

THE SERVANT: I think in my unsatisfactory life my finest pleasures come from executions.

CECILIA: What does the head do on its separation from the body?

THE SERVANT: I saw a bishop's, and that was excellent, because it murmured.

CECILIA: What? What did it murmur?

THE SERVANT: Stand me up. It saw the World from upside-down, and was obviously uncomfortable.

CECILIA: *(Piqued.)* Are you trying to –

THE SERVANT: It did not say the least thing philosophical.

(Pause.)

But your father may be different. He may mouth some wit or wisdom. Or a stream of filthy epithets. There! You are wonderful in black.

(She goes to leave.)

CECILIA: Don't leave our employment…!

THE SERVANT: Leave Brutopia?

CECILIA: If you give notice, I shall follow you and beg a slave's job in your slum.

THE SERVANT: Yes, and I'll beat you, even for perfect labour.

(THE DOCTOR stands before them. She looks at him.)

He won't plead guilty to Utopia. Not now. He's arranging his funeral.

(THE SERVANT goes. THE DOCTOR looks at CECILIA. Pause.)

CECILIA: Were you in Utopia?

(He looks, silently.)

You can't have been, there is none!

(Pause.)

I see you wandering the estate, limping and intellectual, a pose I have to admire, I admit, since I adore good poses, and crippled brilliance surely is the best, but tell me, what's your trick?

(Pause.)

THE DOCTOR: You are not as shallow as you seem.

CECILIA: I am. More shallow.

(Pause.)

As for your spectacles, they're false.

(She tears them off his nose, and wears them.)

Yes! Plain glass!

(She clasps his hand.)

I do admire you!

THE DOCTOR: All doctors must wear spectacles, whether their eyes are weak or not.

CECILIA: That isn't in his book!

THE DOCTOR: Not written, no. But in the book. The seeds of all our comic pains are in the book.

(She suddenly holds him in her arms.)

CECILIA: Yes! Yes, it's true! I know it is. You're ill, and maybe dying… it's death, isn't it? That's smeared on you…?

(HOLBEIN appears.)

Draw me like this. With this man's head here, in my lap.

(She draws THE DOCTOR's head into her lap.)

And a little fruit…festooning him…

(She draws down a trailing bramble. HOLBEIN sits on a folding stool, and begins. Silence as he works.)

HOLBEIN: *(At last.)* I was talking to Meg…

CECILIA: Meg? Oh, Meg…

HOLBEIN: Who plans an exhaustive translation –

CECILIA: Remarkable Meg –

HOLBEIN: Of your father's correspondence with Erasmus.

CECILIA: Never throw away a letter! It will make a scholar's lunch!

(He brushes the paper with his hand.)

HOLBEIN: This is, I think, the first time I have seen you as a woman in repose…

CECILIA: I am not in repose…

HOLBEIN: It will be about ten guineas, who shall I bill?

CECILIA: *(Gazing down at him.)* Look, how his eyelids dip, like overladen coasters, get that, can you?

HOLBEIN: I assume Sir Tom's debts will be honoured –

(He blows chalk dust away. CECILIA has observed a book protruding from THE DOCTOR's pocket and is fixed by it.)

You –

Your head has shifted –

(Pause. She stares.)

Miss –

CECILIA: Yes –

(She draws the book from his pocket.)

What is this?

(She extends it to HOLBEIN.)

HOLBEIN: *(Wiping his hands on a rag, takes it.)* It appears to be –

CECILIA: Yes –

HOLBEIN: A book.

(Pause.)

CECILIA: What book?

HOLBEIN: Handwritten. It's –

CECILIA: What?

(HOLBEIN examines the cover.)

HOLBEIN: My English is –

CECILIA: Just read it, would you?

HOLBEIN: 'A Proposal…for the…Governance… of… Just Society…' By… Emmanuel Salgado… MD…Utopia…

(Pause.)

CECILIA: His body is a rack of pain… thin and hammered like old tin... and yet no sooner does he get his paws around a pencil but he begins – he can't resist – to inscribe laws of new societies! I believe in every prison the victims of one system scratch plans for the next – on walls, in blood!

SCENE 7

BERTRAND, restless in an orangery. ALICE, observing.

BERTRAND: I am so sorry but – you have your problems, obviously – but she – Cecilia – is quite intolerable and I –

ALICE: Yes –

BERTRAND: Her moods and tempers I must confess I do not find at all endearing –

ALICE: No –

BERTRAND: On the contrary, she offends me and provokes me and I am obliged to ask myself the simple question IS THIS LOVE and I –

ALICE: Yes –

BERTRAND: Admit I am inclined to say – forgive me, you are in such turmoil but –

ALICE: No, no, you bubble –

BERTRAND: Inclined to say not love but something else and – oh, do forgive me, I am so self-regarding when you are –

ALICE: No, no, you froth –

BERTRAND: I find her quite unstable which is in its own way captivating but I have my own concerns to balance, what I require is partnership not struggle and –

(ALICE is staring over the garden at the figure of THE COMMON MAN, who is moving about in a massive overcoat.)

ALICE: You! *(He stops.)* You! Yes! *(He thinks, falters, turns to run.)* Here, I said! *(He stops, and surlily approaches her, his eyes on the ground.)* That is my husband's gown you're wearing. *(He shrugs.)* No, do not shrug like that. It is his otter. AND DON'T SHRUG LIKE THAT. *(BETRAND watches from the wall.)* Get if off this minute. *(He raises his eyes, cruelly. She meets them.)* You only stare like that because you have no power. How it hurts. You put your anger in your stare. But I stare also. Get it off. *(Pause. He does nothing. BERTRAND leans off the wall to threaten THE COMMON MAN.)*

THE COMMON MAN: He gave it me! *(Pause.)*

ALICE: He couldn't have...

THE COMMON MAN: TRUE. *(Pause.)*

ALICE: *(Thinly.)* He couldn't have because I bought it for him as a wedding gift. I wrapped it in fine tissue and I laid it on our bed. He walked into the room and sunlight flashed over its collar. It is a Pope of coats, he said. It is a Tsar of garments, GET IF OFF.

THE COMMON MAN: Who cares, it's mine now –

BERTRAND: GET OUT THE SHAFTING OTTER COAT. *(THE COMMON MAN smiles, cruelly. He undoes the tapes. It falls to the ground. He is naked. ALICE turns her head very slightly.)*

ALICE: He has nothing underneath.

THE COMMON MAN: *(Triumphantly.)* The Common Man.

ALICE: Yes, I know you are.

THE COMMON MAN: Steals where he can. But this wasn't stolen.

ALICE: I have my needs also. Cover yourself with your hands go quietly.

THE COMMON MAN: ISN'T A COAT FOR WEARING? *(Pause.)*

ALICE: No. *(He goes, naked, over the garden. They watch him.)*

BERTRAND: You are inspiring. In your ordeal. Inspiring. *(Her eyes remain on the diminishing figure.)*

ALICE: Of course he gave it to him. It's obvious he did. *(Pause. She looks at BERTRAND.)* He gave him my love gift. *(She shrugs.)* So what? *(Pause.)*

BERTRAND: You grow. You flourish, as if pain brought out some hidden self. May I say this? As if Sir Thomas, in his waning, brought out your subtler light.

ALICE: Oh?

BERTRAND: May I say this? May I? May I say that widowhood might be your chance? May I?

ALICE: Say anything. Say what you like.

BERTRAND: I hesitate, but –

ALICE: Don't hesitate –

BERTRAND: Tremble, even –

ALICE: Tremble, yes, but speak –

BERTRAND: Weren't you a widow always? *(Pause.)*

ALICE: What are you saying?

BERTRAND: I don't know.

ALICE: You do. *(Pause.)* You do know. Hold my hand if that will help. *(She stretches out a hand to him.)*

BERTRAND: I can't. *(The hand remains.)* IT IS IMPOSSIBLE, I CAN'T! *(He seizes it.)*

SCENE 8

HOLBEIN has completed the drawing. He holds it out, its back to CECILIA.

CECILIA: I rarely look in mirrors. But this is not a mirror, is it? This is a picture of the soul? *(He goes to turn it to her.)* Don't show me yet! *(He stops.)* Have you made me terrible? *(He offers it to her, and she receives it without taking her eyes from his. Pause.)* I think, if I like it, the reasons for doing so will be false. I think I shall like only what I believe myself to be, which is not what I am, of course.

(Pause. Then she coolly tears the drawing across, first one way, then the other, her eyes remaining on his all the time. Then she swiftly departs. Pause.)

HOLBEIN: I have never known such terrible self-consciousness. Such an agony of sensibility… *(The eyes of THE DOCTOR open.)*

THE DOCTOR: She is unloved. Do you think she could bear to see she is unloved?

SCENE 9

A part of the garden. CECILIA is hurrying with a package. She encounters HENRY. She stares. She curtsies.

KING HENRY: Cecilia More. Uncommonly sore. Bore to a bore. And cold to the core. *(Pause.)* I quote the common opinion. *(On an inspiration, she holds out the package.)*

CECILIA: License my book!

KING HENRY: Refer it to the censor.

CECILIA: But you're the monarch.

KING HENRY: I don't appoint officials so I may do their work for them.

CECILIA: *(Smiling.)* No, stuff all that, just –

KING HENRY: Authority is a pyramid, whose apex rests on functions no matter how obscure –

CECILIA: `You just put H there, on the cover. *(He declines to take it.)*

KING HENRY: You are weak on constitutional affairs but what a mouth you have. It burns. It quarrels with the air. What book is it? I love brilliant women.

CECILIA: Mine.

KING HENRY: Speak some. I love learning from a woman's mouth. Men detest intelligence in skirt but I swell on it. *(Pause. With calculation.)*

CECILIA: Sum – in – caelo – magister – *(Pause.)*

KING HENRY: In Heaven, are you? Why?

CECILIA: Because you're God. Why else? *(She stares at him.)* How fast I'm breathing, I – *(She closes her eyes.)*

KING HENRY: Don't come near me...

CECILIA: No.

KING HENRY: Because I'm savage.

CECILIA: Yes.

KING HENRY: So savage.

CECILIA: I know, yes. *(Pause.)* How could I anyway, when you are murdering my father?

KING HENRY: TRYING TO SAVE HIM BY FLIRTATION!

CECILIA: No –

KING HENRY: HENRY LIKES SKIRT SO YOU HAVE HEARD –

CECILIA: No –

KING HENRY: I HATE TO BE USED, I SQUIRM TO BE USED.

CECILIA: No, I promise –

KING HENRY: I WON'T HAVE MY SEX WRUNG FOR NOTHING, DEATH THAT WAY, SEE! NEVER! *(She trembles, her eyes still closed. HENRY rests, also trembling, against a bench. Pause.)* They use me, but I can chop skirt also... *(Pause.)*

CECILIA: I want him dead. *(He looks at her.)* I never said those words before. Or thought them, either. But I want it. Do it, or I think I will become so shrunk and mad. If I'm not so already... *(He looks at her a long time, then turns and retires the way he came, watched by her.)*

SCENE 10

The rustic prison, where MORE lies on a canvas bed, THE SERVANT beside him.

MORE: I tell you terrible things. These things I could not tell my wife.

THE SERVANT: The servant has her uses.

MORE: Promise you're illiterate!

THE SERVANT: I swear! The whole house knows it.
(He looks at her.)

MORE: I want to die. I passionately want it.

THE SERVANT: That's good, because –

MORE: I have created myself, and I am sick with my creation.

THE SERVANT: Create another. *(He looks at her.)*

MORE: How?

THE SERVANT: Pack a sandwich. Walk out the gate. Walk till you find a hag in a turf house. Live with her. Spit in the fire and kick the mangey mongrel. *(Pause.)*

MORE: You see, even you, a criminal's discard, thinks life's a brimming basket! Dip! Dip! If you do not like your life, pluck out another! THERE IS NO OTHER. *(Pause.)* I thought I was a hermit, and I thought I was a courtier, and ached to know which was my proper self. BOTH, came the answer. I thought I was a misanthrope. I thought I was a humanist, and ached to know which one was false. NEITHER, came the answer. *(She stares at him.)* Do you understand me? You look with unfathoming eyes, I could as well address the blanket. Don't you see? I have yanked the tongues from hypocrites while writing poems on the brotherhood of man. BOTH!

NEITHER! *(Pause.)* Which road, anyway? Which hag?

(He laughs long, absurdly. The door of the prison opens and CECILIA enters. His eyes find her.)

CECILIA: *(Extending a hand.)* Come and practise death with me. *(He stares.)* Come. Practise death with me...

SCENE 11

A wide sunken lawn in winter, snow covered. CECILIA and MORE at the edge. Their breath is visible in the cold air. MORE seizes CECILIA's hands, and she leads him, staggering, over the snow.

CECILIA: *(Aside.)* And it was Death that governed Brutopia, His imminence was everywhere proclaimed, so the old men, by their proximity to Him, had most respect, and the young were pitied and their shallowness bewailed...

MORE and CECILIA, unbalanced, revolve in a wide, comic and pathetic promenade, MORE's eyes fixed on the sky, silently. From a concealed place on the perimeter, BERTRAND sees. CECILIA leads MORE to the edge, and relinquishes him. She goes. He looks about him.

MORE: Meg! *(He staggers to his feet.)* Alice! *(MEG comes behind ALICE, who is watching from a different part, also concealed.)*

MEG: He's calling you.

ALICE: Yes. *(She doesn't move. MORE proclaims.)*

MORE: It's perfectly true the life of the genius is beset with pains, it is true betrayal is his destiny, and what is destined must be loved, and is not bitter, no, not bitter, but DID ANYBODY WANT ME, oh, admire me, yes, lap my brains, but WANT ME, copy, yes, and quote, but WANT IN NAKEDNESS? IN DIRTY SKIN AND BONE? *(He tears his shirt off, dragging it over his head.)*

ALICE: Oh, God...

MORE: Who did? Or called me beautiful? NOT MY THOUGHTS NO, NOT MY HARMONIES, BUT THIS! *(Pause. His eyes search.)* ANYONE!

BERTRAND: *(Catching ALICE's eye.)* Get him in, shall I?

ALICE: I will. *(She appears on the perimeter.)* Oh, there you are!

MORE: SHUDDUP.

ALICE: We were thinking cocoa would be –

MORE: SHUDDUP. *(Long pause.)*

ALICE: How long do you intend to –

MORE: *(Fixed in a position.)* Hours. *(She goes to cross to him.)* Don't wade into my sea. *(She stops. MEG appears, BERTRAND, SERVANTS, like bathers on the edge of a pool.)* Oh, I soil your memory, oh, I soil your pity, I soil it with my dead man's mischief, NO APOLOGY! *(Pause.)*

ALICE: Oh, how you wreck the greatness of your character.

MORE: My greatness... how essential mankind should own the mould of More to jam its clumsy limbs into... BE MORE LIKE MORE. He was so. He met his fate like. What a supreme example of. Oh, flawless, oh immaculate – *(He detects BERTRAND, moving.)* DON'T ENTER MY WATER! *(He stops.)* I do this for you, so that you may be ashamed... and see terrible aches in perfect men... *(As if by mute agreement, they surge over the snow and enclose him.)*

SCENE 12

Part of the garden. BERTRAND intercepts CECILIA.

BERTRAND: *(Dropping to her feet and embracing her pregnant belly.)* The genius dies... new genius! *(He covers her belly with kisses.)* Birth on his death day! Can you manage it? As the axe comes, so you burst! Their souls brush wings in passing!
(He stumbles away.)

SCENE 13

The maze, Brutopia. Snow, and a thin, cruel wind. CECILIA enters. In the centre, HENRY, cloaked and hooded like a monk. His LOUTS play draughts. She comes to where he is seated. He looks at her.

CECILIA: How beautiful you are.

KING HENRY: I've been called it often, but it was never meant.

CECILIA: Beautiful because you live the thought...

KING HENRY: And the thought, what is that now?

CECILIA: The thought is you would see me naked. That is the thought now. And later, the thought might be, she should be dead. *(Pause.)* Shall I undress myself, or will you?

KING HENRY: My fingers are too cold for buttons, I – *(She goes to unbutton herself.)* Wait!

CECILIA: I can't wait –

KING HENRY: No pleasure in too hasty –

CECILIA: Oh, quick, the thought's the action, quick! *(He seizes her hand, holds her firmly, a long time.)*

KING HENRY: There is some – unity among men – which – some fellowship which – and your father is not dead –

CECILIA: Fellowship?

KING HENRY: Not dead and I –

CECILIA: What fellowship? *(He falters.)* Oh, God... you... even you...are goodness-stricken... WHAT UNITY AMONG MEN, WHAT! *(HENRY jumps to his feet and calls to the draughts players.)*

KING HENRY: Beat her!

CECILIA: Beat me –

KING HENRY: Beat, I said! *(The LOUTS, abandoning their game, pull CECILIA away. The sound of struggle from the maze. HENRY sits at the draught board. The LOUTS return without CECILIA.)* I could talk to More of many things. How I shall miss More! But not all things. *(They wait.)* Tell her husband, or her nurse. Yobs beats her, say. Say Yobs climbed in. *(They go off. THE COMMON MAN appears.)*

THE COMMON MAN: Sir Tom loves me. *(HENRY looks up, judging him at a glance.)*

KING HENRY: Why?

THE COMMON MAN: I laugh at all he says.

KING HENRY: Not all he says is funny. *(THE COMMON MAN smiles. HENRY moves a piece. He does not look up.)* Listen, I hate the poor...

THE COMMON MAN: We can't be trusted, certainly...

KING HENRY: No, worse than that. Someone said God loves you, and it's made you vain. *(He moves a piece.)* Behind your abject eye lies some vanity you will inherit the earth. DON'T PUT YOUR HAND ON MY BOARD. *(THE COMMON MAN's hand hovers.)* Only the rich have humility, for they know they are condemned... *(His eyes rise to meet THE COMMON MAN's.)*

SCENE 14

The assembled FAMILY and SERVANTS of THOMAS MORE, arranged on the terrace according to rank. A wind tugs their garments. At last MORE appears, grey. They look to him, expectantly. He addresses them.

MORE: I was happy here. But that was a prison. I was loved here. But that was a cell. Your kindness was a barred window, and your respect a manacle. *(He smiles, He goes down, addressing the SERVANTS individually, warmly shaking their hands.)* Thank you. There is five pounds in the kitchen. Thank you. There is something for you in the kitchen. Thank you. Thank you. Look in the kitchen. Thank you. The kitchen for you, too. Thank you. I shall miss your sponges. Thank you. *(He stops at the end of the row of SERVANTS. He is level with ALICE.)* Oh, God... *(He looks into her face.)* Oh God, what am I to say to you? All I rehearsed is rubbish... *(She looks at him.)*

ALICE: Look in the kitchen...? *(Pause. He seizes her to himself with a terrible fastness.)* What...? What...? Give me a word...give me a word... *(He shakes his head. He moves on. He embraces his son. He moves on, to MEG.)*

MORE: How you will be maimed. How you will find a whole half of your being gone, like some rough butcher cleaved you down as well as me... *(She looks into him. He frees himself from her hand, and speaks to ROPER, who is next.)* Give her your little comfort... plug her wounds with little waddings of old husband love... *(He looks for CECILIA, who is absent. BERTRAND, next, speaks for her.)*

BERTRAND: She –

MORE: *(Silencing him with a finger.)* She.

BERTRAND: She –

MORE: She. *(He smiles. He places himself at an angle to the entire company, and with supreme calculation, bows. As he does so, a familiar cry is heard.)*

BONCHOPE: Hey...! *(MORE pulls his cloak around him, and walks smartly away towards the river, over the lawn. A FIGURE is seen hurtling towards him.)* I preach heresy! I preach! I preach the proper word of God and death so what I preach! *(BONCHOPE catches up with MORE and dogs his heels.)* I deny denial! I recant the recantation! God's honest arguments and death so what! *(MORE strides on.)* I speak Him, Lord, I am thy gob and death so what! I wag the Christ tongue in my mouth, His message lives so long as I, and death so what! *(He falls behind, onto his knees. The FAMILY are a small group in the distance. MORE stops. Pause. He goes back to BONCHOPE.)*

MORE: You could not resist, then? It pulled you, did it, from nest and loving marriage? DEATH'S TIT? *(BONCHOPE stares into MORE.)* We are so... We are so... Kiss me, enemy... *(BONCHOPE stares.)* My boat's waiting. Quick! *(BONCHOPE climbs to his feet, goes to MORE. They embrace. They go off.)*

ALICE: *(To THE SERVANT.)* You don't sob...

THE SERVANT: I shall if you require it. To keep my post I'll sob buckets...

ALICE: No, sob for proper or forget it. *(She turns to go to the house.)*

THE SERVANT: Nor you neither, I observe... *(ALICE stops. She looks over the garden.)*

ALICE: This will be a dead house, now.

THE SERVANT: Or mad, maybe...

ALICE: Grief-stricken and all gloom...

THE SERVANT: Or giggle, maybe...

ALICE: The garden slips... and old walls heave... moss in the unused bedrooms... LIFE WITHOUT THE MASTER. *(She looks at THE SERVANT.)* Preserve his things as if he were about to come back any minute. A clean shirt daily by his bed. And change his books around, the order of them. His inkwell, do not let it dry, and ask the postman in, whether or not he has letters. Give him brandy, as my husband did. LIFE WITHOUT THE MASTER. *(She holds the eye of THE SERVANT, then hurries away.)*

SCENE 15

A quiet place in the garden. BERTRAND sedulously attends to CECILIA's bruises with a bowl of balsam and a lint.

BERTRAND: I like this... *(He dabs.)* I do like this...!

CECILIA: Why do you?

BERTRAND: Because you are in need of me. Because you're still. And for one shred of a moment – weak! *(He dabs.)* They found the louts, and they were thrashed.

CECILIA: What louts? I identified no one.

BERTRAND: No need. They confessed.

CECILIA: To what?

BERTRAND: Beating. Trespass. I forget. Is that enough?

CECILIA: *(Smiling at him.)* Yes.

BERTRAND: *(Putting down the bowl.)* I am so full of delight! I am childish with the thought of the child! *(He looks at her, moved.)* Hold my head. Do place an affectionate paw on my head. Though we conceived it crudely I aspire to your kindness.

CECILIA: Yes. I can do that. *(She puts a hand on his head.)* I can because I think so slightly of you. I can massage you like a dog... *(ALICE appears, smiling at them.)*

ALICE: He missed you, did Bertrand say? Or not missed. It is so hard to tell the actual feeling of a genius. Perhaps he merely registered your absence. May I sit? *(She sits on the wall.)* And it's ours. *(She swings her ankle to and fro.)* The whole damned thing. *(She laughs lightly, bites her lip.)* I have this absurd feeling! Of course, I shall be ill, of course at some stage I shall utterly disintegrate, but at this moment I feel... A RUSH OF INFANTILE DELIRIUM. *(She laughs. Pause. She swings her foot.)* I can tell you. I can tell you because you aren't at all censorious. I could not tell Meg. Who could tell Meg anything? She is so censorious. I shudder at the march of Meg! Shall I go? *(She hops up.)* I am forever interrupting, which is the function of the widow, I suspect? I'll go. *(She does not move. CECILIA rises, holds her close.)* How wonderful to have a baby. How I hate and envy you... *(She smiles, and goes. CECILIA watches her departure.)*

CECILIA: She loves you. You have done something with her.

BERTRAND: Me? What?

CECILIA: No, you have.

BERTRAND: Me?

CECILIA: Words, or something. You have set her on.

BERTRAND: I –

CECILIA: *(Briskly.)* It must be time you visited the Commons, the committees will be frothing, and you have horribly neglected the Russia trade.

BERTRAND: It proceeds without...

CECILIA: It proceeds without? Then what are you for? No, you must get on, and I will harvest the baby when its hour comes, all this rurality ruins you. YOU ARE NOTHING LIKE THE BASTARD YOU WERE ONCE.
(She smiles, the smile fades.) I am certain there is goodness in me. But this goodness cannot emerge in the company of the good, who sicken me. *(Pause. He walks, stops, turns.)*

BERTRAND: MY CHILD ALSO.

CECILIA: I know that. *(He walks, stops again.)*

BERTRAND: MY TINY PROPERTY.

CECILIA: Yes. *(He goes.)*

THE CAPTION

Sir Thomas More was executed on 6 July 1535. His final joke was made with his executioner.

SCENE 16

The garden in a neglected state. CECILIA is standing with HENRY, whose arms are wrapped about her.

CECILIA: These rare visits. These expeditions in dark clothes. And great anger in your act. I don't criticize. *(He kisses her passionately.)* These nocturnal raids. These depradations in me. I don't criticize. But the book's not printed.

KING HENRY: A king might lavish so much on a woman...!

CECILIA: No castles, thanks...

KING HENRY: Might deck her out in such – *(He nuzzles her.)*

CECILIA: The book, though...

KING HENRY: Shh...down now... *(He explores her.)* I suffer you... I squirm in aches which arch over the skies...

CECILIA: Me, too...but where's the book, I –

KING HENRY: *(Freezing.)* NO BOOK. *(She stares at him.)*

CECILIA: No book?

KING HENRY: It's too much gloom.

CECILIA: Gloom?

KING HENRY: Yes. Mankind is fouled in it. *(She smiles, disbelieving him. She reaches out an exploratory, seductive finger. He slaps it away.)*

NO.

YOU.

GRIM.

HAG.

(She is horrified. He runs his hand through his hair, anxiously.)

Can't print it though you can cut me off from cunt for ever more. Can't license it though you shut me out of all your little doors. It can't be done.

CECILIA: You licensed More. *Utopia* swamps all the bookstalls, and in new editions since you murdered him. Why him, and why not me? *(He looks at her with cross irritation.)* They are sweating at the printers, fanning themselves with inky paws, everywhere *Utopia*, where is mine? *(Pause.)*

KING HENRY: Literature must make us love ourselves. That is its function. And yours don't. *(She stares, bitterly.)*

CECILIA: No, that's false. *(She shuts her eyes, desperately.)* I wish I could – scoop up the arguments, but – it's false...!

KING HENRY: Sir Tom praised Man. Oh, good Sir Tom...! *(She is speechless for some seconds, aghast.)*

CECILIA: No, listen – listen, THAT'S PREPOSTEROUS, YOU HAD HIM –

KING HENRY: His democracy is luminous before our weary eyes –

CECILIA: LISTEN!

KING HENRY: Is not Utopia wonderful, for us base killers to see hovering like a mirage on the stinking draught? *(As if disintegrating, CECILIA sinks to the ground.)* No, don't splay like that, it's not womanly. *(She is like a fallen doll.)* Up, I said, you look like a scrubber. *(She does not move.)* It's possible to cease requiring you, it must be said, I – *(He turns to go.)*

CECILIA: Don't go! *(She struggles to recover, brushing her skirt. He waits, his back to her.)* How could you want me so, how could you show such greatness in wanting...and yet... hold such mundane and shallow beliefs...?

KING HENRY: *(Turning on her.)* WON'T PERMIT THE BOOK! *(He stamps and shouts.)* YOU USE ME! WON'T LICENSE THE BOOK! *(The sound of an alarmed hunting dog.)*

CECILIA: Now you've done it. *(It barks, it approaches. An expression of unease crosses HENRY's features.)* Perhaps dogs lick your palms. I would. *(It comes nearer.)* Let me be your bitch, all teeth in abeyance, fawning up your hip... *(The bark comes nearer. THE COMMON MAN appears from cover.)*

KING HENRY: Call off that thing.

THE COMMON MAN: I've no authority.

KING HENRY: Then find some, quick.

THE COMMON MAN: I stoop. I wheedle, only.

KING HENRY: Then get on dog level and plead. *(The barking becomes a low running growl. THE COMMON MAN and HENRY regard each other tensely.)* Christ help you if it marks me, you're for the block... *(A moment of recognition. THE COMMON MAN plunges to all fours.)*

THE COMMON MAN: Dog! Dog! Gnaw me! Hound, rip! *(The animal trots into sight, is placated by the spectacle of THE COMMON MAN on all fours, and licks him.)*

CECILIA: So I'll be with you, when I am wild... *(HENRY goes to leave.)*

THE COMMON MAN: Drink, sir! Tom did! Sandwich, sir! Tom did! *(HENRY leans intimately to him.)*

KING HENRY: If you knew me, forget me, lout. *(THE COMMON MAN makes a button of his lips. HENRY goes. CECILIA turns to go to the house.)*

THE COMMON MAN: Room for another? *(She stops.)* Room for another?

SCENE 17

The maze in a high wind. CECILIA enters in a shift, as if prepared for birth. A cacophony of street carnival and laughter.

CECILIA: *(Aside.)* The sound of Brutopia was roaring. Day and night it roared, and things were falling, things were breaking constantly, which was a sort of anthem in the unkind air...

(She looks for THE SERVANT through a mob.) JANET!

THE SERVANT: *(Appearing beside her.)* Childbirth here's a spectacle, and hundreds have to witness it, not only husbands but whole factories, whole regiments and schools!

CECILIA: *(Grasping her.)* Support me, I'm the queen –

THE SERVANT: *(Leading her.)* You see, what everybody hates is privacy, all acts must be seen! *(She assists her to a bench. Whistles and raucous applause.)*

CECILIA: Protect me, I'm the queen! *(An immediate silence. The CROWD disappears. CECILIA sees a WOMAN coming towards her. They are alone. The WOMAN stops, smiles.)*

BOLEYN: Everybody nowadays has a maze. I knew this one would be different, since a genius designed it. But genius abhors the arbitrary, so I found in a short time, it had its rules. It's a right turn after every three. Why three? His daughters? Or the Trinity? *(Long pause. She smiles, her eyes fixed on CECILIA, not unkindly.)* It is not simple for me, this. Whilst I am forever doing it, each time it burns. *(Pause.)* Do you know me? I am Ann Boleyn. I made the last queen's bed, and then I simply entered it. So might you, with mine, and I am here to threaten you, is that his baby you have there? I am the final queen I state categorically. Speak if you want to. *(Long pause.)* I don't accuse, I merely threaten, whilst perfectly aware endangered love affairs are the most clinging, I found it so myself we also were a risk and probably you aren't the only one, whose is this child? Do speak. *(Pause.)*

CECILIA: Not his.

BOLEYN: Whose, then? You are not married I know, I investigate before these missions, and so would you. It helps to face the enemy to know their night time tricks.

CECILIA: Bert Caldwell.

BOLEYN: Him!

CECILIA: Him, yes!

BOLEYN: It is a small world!

CECILIA: Small? It's microscopic, listen, obviously you frighten me –

BOLEYN: That's my intent –

CECILIA: I promise you I've no designs upon your place –

BOLEYN: They all say that –

CECILIA: No, but proof, I'm queen already, thanks –

BOLEYN: Of what, his heart?

CECILIA: Brutopia. *(Pause.)*

BOLEYN: Where's that? *(Pause. CECILIA smiles.)* You're not sane.

CECILIA: I'm certain that is my whole attraction. *(Pause.)*

BOLEYN: Try to be sensible, your father was. I immensely liked him, and though he was a snob he never leered.

CECILIA: He did leer. It was himself he leered at.

BOLEYN: He paid me many compliments, and sweetly put –

CECILIA: He did so many things with a straight face – *(BOLEYN lashes a slap. CECILIA reels. Pause.)*

BOLEYN: The times I've done this and always said on setting out, Ann Boleyn, no violence! And yet no sooner do I set foot on the property

I see red swimming in the bottom of my eyes! Do let's be sensible I hate to strike the pregnant.

CECILIA: Oh, don't be kind for – *(BOLEYN lashes her again. CECILIA holds her face. Pause.)* Don't hit me again, I will give up your husband. *(Pause.)*

BOLEYN: Poor love, that repudiates for two little slaps... and he is mad for you... *(She gets up.)* That's simple, then. Write him a letter.

CECILIA: Dictate, and I'll put my signature.

BOLEYN: No. You are the scholar. I'm from the scullery. You do it.

CECILIA: Me? A scholar?

BOLEYN: Yes, you're Meg, aren't you? Who has your parent's cranium? *(CECILIA laughs with resignation, disbelief, shame and bitterness.)* You are not Meg... You are another of...

CECILIA: I'm another, yes...

BOLEYN: Of his...

CECILIA: Another of his, yes... *(Her eyes meet BOLEYN's. Her nose is bleeding. BOLEYN turns to go.)* Wait... *(She stops.)* You have the body of the King and may it give you pleasure, but give me something for my sacrifice.

BOLEYN: I'm not buying my own husband, dear.

CECILIA: No, but I think it will be hard to keep him off me, and for all the slaps I'm still susceptible, so bribe me, will you? Help me desist?

BOLEYN: How?

CECILIA: By balancing a greater thing against desire?

BOLEYN: And what is greater?

CECILIA: A book.

BOLEYN: Book? But you're not Meg –

CECILIA: I'M NOT MEG BUT STILL I'M LITERATE.

I'M NOT MEG BUT STILL I'M PERFECT.

CERTAINLY I AM NOT MEG. *(Pause. She grins.)*

I have this work, you see, which your husband calls inhuman. Get it licensed. You know the bishops. Get them to pass it for the printer. Do it for me.

BOLEYN: *(Measuring her.)* I could not do what you have done. When I loved I'd tear my gums against flint walls to reach my wanted one. *(Pause.)*

CECILIA: Yes... I am not passionate.... *(BOLEYN inclines her head, formally and departs. THE SERVANT appears beside CECILIA.)* A queen's been here... smell the air... a queen...

THE SERVANT: To plead?

CECILIA: To prostrate herself. To bow before the powers of my belly where her unruly husband knocks like tree trunks in high seas butt the harbour wall... *(She laughs.)* I AM A TERRIBLE LIAR AND I MEAN TO HAVE BOTH. *(She turns desperately to THE SERVANT.)* MAN AND BOOK! BODY AND BOOK! *(She stops, alarmed.)* Is this a birth pain? *(She feels herself.)* I think the effort's brought me on. What's a birth pain? Call Meg! I awfully wish Meg to do my drudgery – *(THE SERVANT turns.)* Oh, listen – *(She stops.)* Was that – what I just did – was that politics?

SCENE 18

A child crying. THE SERVANT walks up and down with the swaddled infant. CECILIA is draped in a wooden lounge chair, convalescent. She wears spectacles, and attempts to read.

CECILIA: Oh, do stop bouncing it..! Did you bounce me like that? No wonder I'm so. No wonder. *(She opens her arms for the baby. THE SERVANT gives it to her. She looks at it.)* I shan't name the child, because I am not keeping her. *(THE SERVANT stares in disbelief.)*

THE SERVANT: Not keeping her...?

CECILIA: That's what I said. *(She looks at THE SERVANT.)* Oh, my tutor in malevolence, you are outbid. And your expression tells me all your wickedness is shallow. You are appalled. You are no further use to me. *(She smiles.)* Which is correct! The student must surpass the teacher, or what's the use of knowledge?

THE SERVANT: I'll bring her up.

CECILIA: Silly.

THE SERVANT: No, let me bring her up, I'll –

CECILIA: You! *(She stares.)* With your Utopian ideas? Do you think I'd give my loved one into you? You would load her back with such – CONVICTIONS! No, I have a better parent. *(She lifts the child, now silent, in the air, and smiles.)*

THE SERVANT: She needs you...

CECILIA: No, she exaggerates, we all do...

THE SERVANT: *(Unable to contain herself.)* I think you are a wicked and ill woman and I should have strangled you at birth!

SCENE 19

THE COMMON MAN, waiting in a place. CECILIA approaches with the child. He waits. She gives it him.

CECILIA: Make her imperfect. Make her ache for the impossible. Teach her to detect the liar but never contradict him. Forbid her wisdom. Teach her to draw her consolation from the stars. And say her mother talked too much to make a decent whore. *(THE COMMON MAN takes the child, wraps it like an item of shopping, and bounds off. HENRY appears, interrupting her thoughtfulness. He removes her spectacles.)*

KING HENRY: I hate the spectacles. They shout SCRUTINY at me. I am not to be looked into. The long look's critical. *(She looks down.)* The child thrives, then?

CECILIA: It lives, and yet I've lost it.

KING HENRY: Lost it? To whom?

CECILIA: Nature. *(He looks at her, puzzled.)* You see how spoiled I am, how arid in the very heart of feeling. You drink her nourishment. *(She unbuttons her dress.)*

KING HENRY: *(Putting his hand on her wrist.)* What have you done?

CECILIA: Drink me murderer... *(He is uncomfortable.)*

KING HENRY: Cecilia, you will be arrested...

CECILIA: In my arms, she lay, thinking, THIS IS THE LIFE! She chuckled with a sickening complacency. But I saved her. *(Pause. She pulls his mouth to her breast.)* Rob! Plunder, then! *(They engage, passionately. Then they are still. A voice, over the gardens.)*

THE PRINTER: Miss More! *(She opens her eyes. A FIGURE in an apron is seen coming towards them.)*

KING HENRY: Hide me!

THE PRINTER: Miss More! *(CECILIA bundles HENRY beneath her skirts.)*

KING HENRY: Hide me!

CECILIA: *(To THE PRINTER, who is waving a bill.)* You must want Meg. She gets all the letters.

THE PRINTER: No, it says Cecilia.

CECILIA: There are Cecilias all over Chelsea.

THE PRINTER: Yes, but here?

CECILIA: Not if here means here, but there is Cecilia who makes the pastry in –

THE PRINTER: No, it's you, Miss –

CECILIA: Or the hag who lives in the beer barrel –

THE PRINTER: Look – *(He holds out a calf-bound book, slipping off its wrapping. She sees the legend* 'Brutopia' *on the spine. HENRY, concealed by her skirt, remains in a posture which excludes him from the conversation. A pause of depth and confusion. CECILIA makes a move of her head to indicate THE PRINTER should go. He fails to perceive its meaning.)* I have a cart outside with seven hundred –

CECILIA: Loaves! I don't want seven hundred loaves – *(She jerks her head again.)* You see, you must mean –

THE PRINTER: *(Confused.)* I –

CECILIA: Cecily! Not Cecilia! You see, there's your error! Cecily, the baker, she has a place beside the gate and you've misjudged the turning – *(She thrusts the book back at him.)* She is the loaf enthusiast – this is not the first time she's – so off you go – *(She waves him away.)* Turn right, and right again – TAKE YOUR LOAVES AWAY! *(He withdraws, faltering. She looks keenly into his eyes. He recedes. HENRY lifts his head, sits contemplatively.)*

KING HENRY: When More lived this place was all seclusion...

CECILIA: The walls are falling down and dogs jump in...as well as monarchs... *(She is in a state of passionate excitement at the appearance of the book. She kisses HENRY spontaneously.)* I'm so – look at me – I am delighted! *(She kisses him again.)*

KING HENRY: You are. With what, though?

CECILIA: With you!

KING HENRY: Me? Solely?

CECILIA: Solely? Now, that's ambitious! No, the sun shines and the blossom blows and I – *(Pause.)*

KING HENRY: I only love you because I do not know you, Cecilia.

CECILIA: Yes.

KING HENRY: And when I know you –

CECILIA: Then we're done. And that's good. That's proper. *(Pause. Then HENRY gets up.)*

KING HENRY: Down the river, now, to Hampton. Diplomacy and tennis. And as I bash, it's you. And as I smash, it's you.

CECILIA: Call my name, but half-obscured, like a curse.

KING HENRY: Bash. Smash. I carve your body on the yew hedge. Henry. His thing. *(He smiles, kisses her tenderly, withdraws through the garden.)*

SCENE 20

TWO PRINTERS gazing at CECILIA. Seven hundred copies of the book BRUTOPIA stacked in a neglected greenhouse. CECILIA, the object of their amazement and contempt, runs her hands over the bindings. She takes a copy. She inhales it. She is without shame. She nurses and fondles the book. She meets their eyes over the cover's rim.

CECILIA: Scotch leather. *(She inhales the pages.)* And the paper?

FIRST PRINTER: Dutch.

CECILIA: Dutch?

SECOND PRINTER: All we could get, we –

CECILIA: No, I love the Dutch... *(With immaculate care she opens the book on a bench, runs her finger tips over the page.)* And what of the ink.

FIRST PRINTER: Clerkenwell. We make the ink. *(Pause. She turns the leaves.)*

CECILIA: How much you print, and how little you read...

SECOND PRINTER: We don't do books. We are handbill printers.

FIRST PRINTER: The pages came. The licence came. And then the money. Anonymous, the lot.

SECOND PRINTER: Off we went.

CECILIA: How satisfied you must be. I am so happy for you. How gratified.

SECOND PRINTER: It was good money –

CECILIA: No, no, I mean – to have at long last found an object worthy of your skills. *(She looks at them for the first time. They shift uneasily.)* This is no poster for a sordid dance, is it? Or handbill for a quack? All your apprenticeship, and years of craft, at last discover a fit task. *(They look blank.)* Midwives! Allies in great birth! *(She seizes them in her arms. She hugs them, releases them.)* Come now, you must have read some of it as you laid the type, what did you think?

SECOND PRINTER: No, it's – you rarely read when setting the –

CECILIA: Of course not, no, but when you – read the proofs, the galleys, what are they? You – surely then you – *(Pause.)*

SECOND PRINTER: We thought the margins were a bit broad, didn't we, John? *(Pause. They turn to go.)*

CECILIA: What is the use of craft if it – of industry, if it – invention, if it – you are the printers! *(She follows them to the door.)* The page is also you! *(They step into the garden. She follows them. They retreat.)*

CECILIA: Your craft is not immune! *(They ignore her.)* THE PRINTERS WILL BE KILLED AND RIGHTLY, TOO! *(They disappear through the hedges. ALICE appears beside CECILIA.)*

ALICE: Sir Tom would give them liquor.

CECILIA: Yes.

ALICE: He knew the fence that runs between labour and imagination. He knew better than you.

CECILIA: Yes.

ALICE: May I read the book?

CECILIA: *(Turning to her.)* I don't know. There are so few.

ALICE : And you are saving them?

CECILIA: Yes.

ALICE: For better readers?

CECILIA: *(Holding ALICE tenderly by the arm.)* Obviously it must be read by those already predisposed to understand it. Otherwise it might as well be thrown up in the air, to drift down in obscure places where – *(She stops.)* Yes, I think that is perhaps what I should do! I should not sell them, since then the rich will know everything as well as owning everything. It would not be good for them. *(She smiles, thinks.)* On the other hand, to give them to the poor would be to have them wrongly employed, as jambs for windows, draught excluders, and the like, no, that would demean my labour, obviously the books should reach their readers arbitrarily, rather. Only then can I be assured one copy, and only one perhaps, might reach its loved one and enrich his life. I will fling them over the wall.

ALICE: Over the wall?

CECILIA: Yes. Bookshops are prisons, after all. The books are gaoled. And there's a highway over there, beyond the gate.

ALICE: Yes...

CECILIA: So many people pass, of all descriptions, to and from the city. Of these, the vast majority are shallow and incapable of dream, but one! One might, a single soldier in a platoon, a merchant bored with wealth, who knows, but one! *(She smiles.)* I am an optimist, you see... *(ALICE looks at her.)*

ALICE: Cecilia, you are not well, the birth –

CECILIA: The birth? I had forgotten the birth! *(She looks distantly for a moment.)* Why do you call me ill when what I say is true? Why do you? Surely the ill are the liars? Hold my arm... *(ALICE takes her arm. They walk in silence.)*

ALICE: I have so much to tell you... so much to talk about... *(They walk.)* It's strange how, because you are so single-minded, I feel – I – who am not single-minded – feel I have to – odd, isn't it – confess to you... *(They walk. Silence, they walk.)* I want you to know things and yet I am certain in my heart these things you know already! *(She stops suddenly.)* I want to confess. *(Pause.)* And yet I know, when I do confess, you will say – oh, so typically of you – you will say, oh, that! I knew that! I already knew that! *(She laughs. Pause.)* So –

BERTRAND'S VOICE: *(Enraged over the lawns.)* WHERE – IS – SHE!

ALICE: Oh, God –

BERTRAND'S VOICE: I SAID WHERE –

ALICE: Oh, hell – *(BERTRAND enters furiously.)*

BERTRAND: I GO TO THE COT AND –

ALICE: Shh, you –

BERTRAND: I GO TO THE COT – I RUN TO THE COT OF MY – AND SHE'S – THE SHEETS COLD – WHERE –

ALICE: You have chosen the worst possible –

BERTRAND: I ASK THE NURSE AND SHE SAYS –

ALICE: I also am enquiring and you –

BERTRAND: MY BASTARD DAUGHTER WHERE IS SHE THE LITTLE LOVE! *(He stares at CECILIA.)*

ALICE: Enquiring, but more subtly...

BERTRAND: *(Not looking at her.)* Shut up.

ALICE: You are so horse-like, but that's to malign the horse.

BERTRAND: Shut up.

ALICE: You are so bull-like, but that's to malign the bull.

BERTRAND: *(Not removing his eyes from CECILIA.)* Shut up, I said...! *(Pause. There is a moment of recognition in CECILIA's eyes. She smiles.)*

CECILIA: You two are lovers! It's obvious! *(She laughs. He slaps her violently.)*

ALICE: DON'T DO THAT.

CECILIA: *(Recovering.)* How wonderful... your fingers touch on landings... oh, the ecstasy of the lingering, illicit touch... *(He stares.)* Marry my step-mother. Marry her and grow together like hard woods, gnarl like yews. She is a brilliant woman whom my father crushed... *(He stares.)*

BERTRAND: I want the child...

CECILIA: *Utopia* was false, and yet its falseness did not impede its progress. And your feelings for our bastard, perhaps they're false, too... *(She walks away from them. BERTRAND looks at her. Pause.)*

BERTRAND: Shall you send for the constable, or shall I? *(ALICE does not reply. Night falls.)*

SCENE 21

A pile of books. CECILIA seated by them, under a wall. It is night. MEG comes, joins her, pulling a gown closer for the cold.

CECILIA: *(In a whisper.)* I toss them over the wall. Like this. *(She chucks one, blindly.)* At intervals. Irregular, or some dealer will stand there with a net and so prevent the LEGITIMATE READER gaining access to the text. *(She smiles.)* Who this reader is, God knows. But that must be the point of printing, surely? The anonymity? *(Pause. Without taking her*

eyes off MEG, she spontaneously chucks another.) Three hundred and sixty-six to go. *(Pause.)* I know what kindness is. It is something done to the self. But when this self is made, give it to others. *(She chucks again.)* Shh! *(She cranes her head to the wall.)* Footsteps! Someone collects! Some scampers off, amazed... *(ALICE comes through the darkness, and sits with them. Pause.*
A distant sound.)

MEG: Look, a comet! *(They all look. CECILIA suddenly throws a book. The sound is repeated.)*

ALICE: The last wolf in England....shh.. *(They listen. The sound of oars in water. ALICE puts a hand on CECILIA's knee.)*

CECILIA: Oars.

Oars in the water.

I think the boat's for me. *(She stands up.)*

The agents of Utopia... have come for me...

SCENE 22

CECILIA waits in the moonlight on the sunken lawn. Some figures appear on the perimeter. They are NUNS. One approaches her, kindly.

CECILIA: Be careful, I am the king's mistress. *(The NUN nods, slowly.)* So one false move and – *(She nods patiently.)* Lay a finger on me and – *(CECILIA draws a finger gruesomely across her neck. The NUN nods again. CECILIA whispers.)* Got *Brutopia*? *(The NUN looks uncertain.)* Not got one yet? It's passed around, you see, in brown paper covers, hand to hand, in alleys or upstairs in pubs...

NUN: *(Smiling.)* We have such a nice room for you...

CECILIA: They said that to my dad! *(She grins.)*

NUN: Oh?

CECILIA: Same words exactly, and listen, do stop smiling, I can't be good in the company of the good and that smile is only violence, I'll get you a copy – *(She turns to go.)*

NUN: Not now.

CECILIA: Not now? Why not now?

NUN: It's late.

CECILIA: It's late, but you came late, so don't complain about the lateness!

NUN: You are full of wit, I do like you.

CECILIA: Good. So does everyone. For different reasons, obviously. Only my father failed to like me, and I arranged his death, which was what he wanted. I say I arranged it, no, I exaggerate, I blocked his pardon. *(The NUN takes a step.)* Be careful, the King does tend to – *(She makes the gruesome gesture again.)*

NUN: Shall we go? *(Pause, then suddenly CECILIA slaps her across the face. The NUN reels. From the perimeter, other NUNS hurry to her aid. The NUN gestures for them to stay back.)*

CECILIA: I'm sorry, I really cannot stand that smile. *(Pause.)* Go where?

NUN: This room.

CECILIA: I have a room.

NUN: We want to care for you.

CECILIA: You mean, I am to be loved whether I want it or not?

NUN: We will love you, yes.

CECILIA: When it's soldiers, isn't that called rape? *(Pause.)*

NUN: I think you are much too clever for your own good.

CECILIA: YES! MUCH TOO CLEVER! YES! And everything I know, I thought. From the bottom to the top. From the cellar to the attic. I did not borrow. I did not quote.

NUN: How lonely, how lonely you – *(CECILIA's eyes fill with tears. The NUN makes a subtle signal. The other NUNS hurry forward and pinion CECILIA with ropes, spinning her round to bewilder her. CECILIA is gagged, and held still. The moon shines down. CECILIA's eyes turn from side to side. A FIGURE comes into her eyeline.)*

KING HENRY: Yer boat's stuck in my mooring. *(The NUNS look alarmed as HENRY walks onto the lawn. FACTOR and LLOYD hang back. HENRY looks at CECILIA.)* And you've trussed my tart.

NUN: We are the Collectors of the Convent of –

KING HENRY: Yes, well, I am running out of patience with the convents, aren't we all? *(The NUNS bow to him. He sings.)*

Oh, she who walks upon the night

Shall see such things as stop the heart – *(He ceases abruptly.)*

You are not to handle lunatics in future. I am putting lunacy out to tender. Good night. *(The NUNS turn to go. One stays to unloosen CECILIA.)* No, leave her trussed. *(They depart. He sings.)*

We'll slice the moon into two parts

And lick the blood from the wet grass, *(They look back.)*

My love and I we will be wild

Unshamed and undefiled, *(FACTOR and LLOYD clap the rhythm.)*

I CAN KEEP GOING!

Off the grey corpse of charity

We'll take our dinner and our tea –

Not good –

Who dares impede our wet embrace

Let him go wary of his face,

Into her skirts my hand will be

The silent pilgrim of the faith...

I came to kill you. Or to fuck you. I did not know which. And I find others. Killing or fucking you. I did not know which. *(Pause.)* How beautiful to find you silent. *(The sound of oars in the water.)* Boleyn's been here I know, and done a deal with you. I know everything. I have to. *(Pause.)* How wonderful you cannot speak. Already you are diminishing, you are evaporating in the heat of my indifference, like a puddle in the sun. How small you are! How mild you are! How did I ever? Nothing so absurd as spent passion... *(He goes close to her.)* Speak, then. I saved you from the madhouse. *(LLOYD and FACTOR laugh loudly.)* Oh! They laugh the contrary! They say I am the madhouse! *(He looks into her eyes.)* Speak...

CECILIA's eyes look into his, and as if she had spoken, he nods, kindly, and turns away. The moon goes behind a cloud.

THE FORTY

(Few Words)

I do these things
Oh how I persist I am at least persistent

And I ask
Does anybody want them?

The answer comes back
Nobody at all

So I go on

1

A WOMAN folds a sheet. A MAN enters.

MAN: I do not wish to be hurt again

(She proceeds, as if unaware of him.)

I do not wish to be hurt again

(She completes the task, folding the sheet over her arm. She is still.)

I do not wish to be hurt again

(The woman allows her head to fall. She gazes at the floor. The man observes her. At last she lifts her head and goes to walk from the room. The walk becomes a run. Almost at once she runs back in. She is still, her gaze on the floor. Suddenly the man tips forward, convulsed in tears. The woman watches him. The man recovers, finds a handkerchief, and cleans his face. The woman walks smartly past him. He seizes her by her free wrist and stops her abruptly. She declines to look at him.)

WOMAN: You do not wish to be hurt again

(He says nothing, but neither does he release her.)

You do not wish to be hurt again

(Now he releases her. She walks out smartly. Again she returns. She rises to her full height, the sheet clasped to her chest, her back presented to him.)

MAN: I do not wish

WOMAN: *(Speaking over him.)* You do not wish to be hurt again

(She turns swiftly to face him. They exchange a long stare, concluded when the man thrusts two fingers into his mouth and whistles raucously. He stops.

Now he violently disorders his hair, scratching like an animal, and stops. She is apprehensive.)

You do not wish to be hurt again

(They watch. Now he circles her. She clings to the folded sheet. The strain tells.)

You do not wish

MAN: *(Speaking over her.)* I do not wish to be hurt again

(He stops. He extends a hand, palm uppermost. She is slow to respond. The hand falls. His head inclines. They remain still.)

*

2

A MOTHER holds an envelope, opened. A SON enters. He reads her expression. He recognizes the envelope as a letter of conscription.

SON: If I go I shan't come back

(She bites her lip. He frowns…)

I know

I know if I go I shan't come back

I know

I know

(His eyes assure her of his assertion. He looks away. He walks violently around the room and stops.)

If I go

If I go

(And resumes the walk, stopping at last. His eyes seek hers.)

If

If

(She avoids his eyes. Her husband enters. The woman extends the letter. He recognizes the envelope. His shoulders lift and fall. The woman's arm droops. They are all still, the old couple stare at the floor, the son looks at them, one after the other…)

If I go

(The father looks up.)

If I go I know I shan't come back

(The father frowns… the son persists.)

If

If

(The father looks away. His eyes travel to the eyes of his wife. He leaves the room. The son is still. He stares at the floor. After a long time he goes to the mother, and taking her by the shoulders, draws her close to him. With his right hand he draws her head into his shoulder. He strokes her hair like a lover.)

I shan't come back

(Her sigh is vast and fills her.)

I know

I know

*

3

Three men enter bearing a fourth, bound and blindfolded. They put down their burden, and stand around him, heads tilted to the ground like pall-bearers at a grave. The bound man arches his back, squirms, struggles in his bonds, but finding them too strong, ceases his futile efforts and is still…

BOUND MAN: So sorry

So sorry

So sorry

(The silence bewilders him. He rises into a sitting position, his head turning, acutely listening, sensing he might be alone but not certain…)

So sorry

So sorry

So sorry

(He is about to resume his struggle when he hears a woman enter. He is still. The three men go to the woman, and queuing, kiss her formally. They return to their places. She walks down to the bound man. She looks down at him and weeps. The bound man turns his head to understand. The woman pulls out a handkerchief to absorb her tears. The bound man knows her by her crying. He lies prone, and puts his mouth to her shoe…)

So sorry

So sorry

So sorry

(His apology draws more tears from the woman. In their discomfort the three men turn away their heads. Silence returns. She walks away, as she had entered. The three men close on the bound man and destroy his life, without anger. They step

back. They leave, arm in arm as mourners at a funeral…)

*

4

A beggar stands at the side of a road, one hand extended. An elegant couple pass. After a few paces, the man falters and stops. He reaches into his pockets, returns to the beggar and gives him a small coin. The woman, contemptuous, stands with one hand on her hip. The man returns to her, suffused in his own generosity. She declines to move on. Instead she returns to the beggar, who lifts his eyes with a certain apprehension. The woman looks cruelly at him, then with a supreme gesture, draws up her skirt, showing herself, a provocative pose which she maintains for some seconds, then, letting fall her dress, returns to the man, who seethes. Now it is him who declines to move on. He goes back to the beggar and slaps him once over each cheek. The beggar reels but does not fall. The man returns to the woman. They stare at one another, a hatred passes between them… the woman allows her eyes to fall… the man takes her arm and they leave…

*

5

A hospital bed. An elegant woman sits beside a mortally ill man. The woman nervously fingers a costume bag.

WOMAN: Nothing more to say

All said

All said and nothing more to say

(She writhes on the chair. She retrieves her composure. A nurse enters and performs a perfunctory routine at the bedside.)

All said and nothing more to say

(The nurse looks at the woman. The woman laughs in her anxiety, a short, disturbed laugh. The nurse withdraws. The woman stands as if to move swiftly but sits again, and is immobile, the bag clutched on her knees. Suddenly she lets out a short cry and suffocates it. The taut stillness returns. Now she stands desperately and topples the chair. She clutches the bag in front of her. The left hand of the patient rises slowly in the air and falls, unseen but sensed… the woman draws herself to her height. With the bag in one hand, she draws up her skirt with the other, presenting her arse to the patient. Her magnificence inspires the patient to utter a long, slow cry of love. The nurse appears. The woman does not move. The nurse lifts a hand as if to signal disapproval but the fingers curl in sympathy, and are restless…

*

6

Three women laughing uncontrollably. They perambulate, or stop, tossing back their heads, their hands on their hips or pressed to their cheeks. A fourth woman enters whose arms are folded tightly on her chest. She walks slowly, stops, and gazes at the floor. The women drift around her, erupting as soon as they meet one another's eyes, weeping, issuing strange cries, breathless, stamping their feet, until at last they come to a standstill and a relative silence descends, punctuated only by a sniff or a clearing of the throat. A substantial pause elapses…

WIDOW: I miss my husband

(At once the three women collapse in laughter, shaking, bent in two, streaming with tears… again they slowly recover. The widow affects a modest smile…)

I miss him

(This time the reaction is less severe… the women succeed in repressing much of their laughter by not meeting one another's eyes and covering their mouths, so that they cannot infect one another… then from the silence, one laughs loud and long and the others collapse in sympathy. The widow walks to the first and smiling observes her as she struggles with her seizure, now a cause of embarrassment to her. At last she subdues herself, looking at the floor. She lifts her eyes to the widow. At once the laugher explodes again, and she turns her back to avoid the sight that caused it… the widow is uncomfortable but not ashamed, the innocent smile still hangs on her lips as she walks to a second woman, who, even as she approaches her, begins to shake her head, lifting a hand and shaking it in a futile gesture of reluctance, but then emits an uncontrollable cry of mirth and surrenders to the torrent that follows it… the widow's smile fades at last, she lets her hands hang at her sides, her head tilts forward as the laughter, either low or bold, rolls on…)

*

7

A young woman in few clothes. She stands in a posture of modesty. A man enters. He is at ease, also patient. He folds his hands in front of him. The young woman lifts her gaze to his. A substantial pause…

WOMAN: Apparently I'm ill

(Her look is seductive. Suddenly she giggles, and stops.)

Apparently

(She tilts away from him, gazing…)

Apparently

(Her breath is long and studied… the man looks at the floor, unable to sustain their gaze. He runs a hand through his hair. He alters the position of his legs…)

Ill

Ill

Ill apparently

(The man breaks his pose, launching himself towards her as if over a gulf. As he seems about to embrace her he swerves. She giggles, her hand to her mouth. The man observes her over his shoulder, taking her in from a fresh angle. She remains motionless. Again she breathes long and deeply…)

MAN: Ill

(The barely perceptible tilting of her body first in one direction, then another…)

Ill

(He lifts one hand, the fingers active in his contemplation. He drops this hand and lifts the other, massaging his cheek. The woman tilts increasingly, as if she might topple but stays on her feet. The man's movements repeat themselves and quicken. Now he marches defiantly away from her, stops and regards

her from a distance, his fists closed. The woman is quite silent, observing him, and her movements cease as a second man enters, and stopping, looks from the woman to the man…)

Ill

(The second man looks back at the woman…)

Ill apparently

(Both men stroke their faces. The woman giggles, staring at the floor, and stops. An older woman enters, severe in expression but not unkind. She extends a hand to the young woman, who goes to her unresistingly. They walk out. The two men seethe. One takes out dice. They crouch. They shake the dice with a desperation…)

*

8

A woman enters reading a book. It is extended in front of her but she frequently peers over the top of the book, turning on her heel so she takes in all her surroundings. When she turns a page it is done with pointed deliberation. Her movements cease. She appears to concentrate. A youth passes, barely noticing her. Suddenly the woman throws down the book, so it slides to his feet. He looks down. He looks at her. The woman postures with her hands on her hips, expecting the book to be returned to her. The youth seems reluctant, as if his own pride were at stake. The tension is broken at last by her speaking…

WOMAN: Do you know Barescu the great Roumanian?

(The youth is suspicious… his gaze drops from her to the book… since he still declines to pick it up she swaggers a little, turning on her heel at the end of each pass. Suddenly she stamps her foot.)

Bar – escu

Bar – escu

(She sings… low and then falsetto.)

Bar – escu Bar – escu Bar – escu

Bar – escu Bar – escu Bar – escu

(The youth smiles, folding his arms and shrugging with a surprised pleasure. By contrast, she regards him severely. With deliberation she removes one of her leather gloves. When it is free, she tosses it at his feet…)

Do you know Barescu the great Roumanian?

(The youth is made uneasy. His eyes move restlessly from the woman to the glove. She is about to peel off the second glove when he smothers his head in his hands, writhing as if in a fit. Her hands remain extended in mid-action, as he staggers about the stage, stroking his head in a continuous movement,

uncoordinated and always in danger of falling… again she sings…)

Bar – escu Bar – escu Bar – escu

(The youth lurches away offstage… the woman takes out a compact. She pulls her hair in the mirror as if frustrated by a curl…)

*

9

A man seated on a chair. He has one leg crossed over the other. His hands lie comfortably in his lap. A second man enters and stands before him. Their eyes engage.

SECOND MAN: Oh, you were very different once

(A pause. The first man stands with a swift action and putting his hands in his pockets, walks, his eyes still on the second man. He retraces his steps and stops. He leans on the back of the chair, tucking one ankle behind the other. He stares the second man into submission. The second man drops his gaze, at the same time making a gesture of emptiness and futility with his hands. A pause, then the first man sends the chair flying over with one movement. The second man looks up, shocked by the violence of the act. The first man repeats his walk, and the second man, cowed, stares at the floor. At the end of the walk the first man bellows with laughter, a laughter which continues and is evidently false. The first man seeks to draw the attention of the second man, turning his head to one side or the other, whereas the second man defies him, staring fixedly at the floor. In the following silence the first man makes pigeon steps round the room, staring all the time at his antagonist, who will not favour him with a look. Suddenly he stops, bends forward and bares his arse. He remains in this position for so long he comes to possess the quality of statuary. Neither man moves, but the tension affects the second man. He emits a low moan, and shakes his head slowly and perpetually, his hands hanging at his sides. When the scene has accumulated its whole quota of despair, a third man enters and in a routine way flings a hood over the second man, who is unresisting. A fourth man enters and with a practised move, covers the first man with a cloth of the

same material… they depart… the moan continues under the hood…)

*

10

A man apprehensive but from a conviction he knows can only be unwelcome.

MAN: I realized something has changed

(His head droops…)

I realized something has changed

(He lifts his head defiantly. He looks from one person to another as if expecting an endorsement. His mouth tightens, he senses his solitude. Suddenly he grabs his head in his hands and walks violently in tight circles, stops, his head still clasped. Very slowly his body softens, the tension falls away, his hands fall. He turns to look half over his shoulder. He no longer fears his knowledge…)

I realized…

(He does not feel the need to communicate. A private smile passes over his face. He strokes his face in an affectionate manner. He walks out slowly, one hand stroking the wrist of the other.)

*

11

Bad light. An embracing couple, whose passion isolates them from the world. Their moves are slow, not snatched or urgent. A man passes, looking but ashamed to look. He disappears and immediately returns, pauses, confirms a sense of dread, and without direction, retraces his steps, not looking, filled with the effort of not-looking. Nothing disturbs the lovers. After some time the man returns, as if idly. He stations himself, his back to the couple, and folding his arms, leans his chin in a hand, an affectation of patience. Nothing disturbs the lovers. Now the man with a swift, arbitrary move, sits on the floor, his knees drawn up and begins to laugh, smothering his laughter with his hands. The lovers are unaware of him, and he, since his back is turned to them, can only imagine their actions. His mischief again comes to the relief of his pain. He lies back full length, his arms at his sides. He remains thus for some time, until an uncontrollable sob of laughter causes him to lurch onto his side. The woman is immediately alerted, turns her head only, observes her husband, and strictly and smoothly, pushes her lover away. She keeps her hands in the air, her palms to the lover, who bows and withdraws, stops, bows again and leaves… at last she speaks, her body still averted…

WIFE: It's nothing or nothing much

(The husband is still, and on his side. The woman, unabashed, walks a pace or two, but arrives at the side of the man from which she cannot be seen.)

Not nothing

Not nothing

(She tilts up her chin, folding her hands behind her, girlish, abolishing criticism.)

Nothing much

(Because the husband is silent, she walks around him, to be seen. His face is hard against the floor, but his eyes rise. Her mouth opens. She swallows. Not meeting his eyes, she lifts her skirt a few inches. A single breath of hers, audible. He is agonized, then turns over, ridding himself of her sight. A pause, then

she sobs, letting go her skirt, her hands hanging at her sides. The husband allows her sobbing to continue, then slowly lifts one arm, the hand outstretched. Her tears cease. She looks at the uplifted arm, its pitiful appeal for reconciliation… something in her resents its innocence… she sits, swiftly, drawing up her knees, and nursing herself, strokes her upper arms, downward and downward again. The arm of the husband does not move or drift…)

*

12

A man goes to perform an act of homage. He walks discreetly, his hands before him, loose and very slightly turning one in the other. His gaze is on the floor. He stops. He removes his hat in a conventional way and holds it against his chest with one hand. After some seconds in this posture of fidelity his head looks surreptitiously from one side to the other. He ascertains he is not observed, and lifting his head addresses the object of his homage.

MAN: I'm insincere

(His tongue moistens his lips. Again he ascertains he is alone.)

I'm insincere

(His head drops. He is still, then with a decisive movement, he thrusts his hat on his head and turns to go. As he sets off a woman enters swiftly, and collapses at his feet. He stops. He looks at her inert form. He walks round her, dubious, apprehensive. Her continuing immobility suggests she is either dead or ill. Again the man looks swiftly about him. He ascertains he is alone. He kneels. He grabs the hat off his head. He kisses her, lifting her head between both hands, passionate as if they were profoundly known to one another. Then he lays her head softly on the ground. He runs out and runs back, retrieving his hat. He runs out again, without a second glance…)

*

13

A man at the end of his tether. As he walks his arms extend slightly behind him. His fingers reach and close. He stops.

MAN: I will say it and go

(His hands reach and close…)

Say it and go

(His hands open, stretch and go rigid. He remains fixed in this position, tilted slightly forward. His body sways. A woman enters, wiping her hands incessantly on her skirt, in long, open-handed moves as if shaping her own body. In contradiction to this her moves are light and swift. She repeats a long walk, turning as if gaily at each end. She stops suddenly in mid-movement. She glares at the man.)

WOMAN: Say it

(He turns to look at her. His hands are loose. He takes her whole life in his glance. The woman begins wiping her hands again, suffering the pain of his scrutiny, but not removing her eyes from his, a pride and a pain. Her stiffness grows as his subsides.)

Say it

(Because he does not say it, her anxious moves slowly decrease until her hands hang loosely at the end of her arms, and her gaze falls. They are both suffused with calm, reassured by the not-saying. They come together, putting one arm round the shoulder of the other, like lovers. They walk slowly out, but his one free hand is stiff, and her one free hand wipes her skirt…)

*

14

A gallery. Some pictures at which three figures look with varying degrees of interest. One, a man, observes another, a woman, with a sidelong glance. The figures change positions, reversing their order. The third, with idle moves, departs. The man and the woman study, apparently absorbed. Now it is the woman whose glance includes the man. They move again, to study other pictures.

MAN: I am here today but only today

(The woman does not remove her eyes from the picture. It is as if the man had not spoken. She goes as if to leave but only to stop at a further picture. The man now looks directly at her, ignoring the pictures.)

Today but only today

(The woman looks at him. Her look causes him to slowly turn away and examine the picture adjacent to him. She looks again at her picture. They are perfectly still in their imitation of study. Simultaneously they turn to one another. A third party enters, but seems uninterested in either them or the pictures, and leaves again. The couple have not moved or let their eyes wander from the contemplation of each other. At last she looks sideways to see if they are observed, and ascertaining she is safe, draws up her skirt, widening her stance. The man goes to her unhurriedly to take her from the rear, his hand loosening his clothing. He is about to act when the third party returns, with the same anxious movements. He appears not to have discerned their imminent intimacy and leaves. The man goes to act again, his hand to his clothing. Now a further individual enters the scene, with slow, scholarly moves, and engages with the first picture. The woman stamps once on the floor in her frustration, a sign not noticed by him. The man, seething, lets his head sink and lifting his hands, nurses his temples, slowly as if to relax his

taut nerves. He removes himself a little from the woman and pretends to observe the picture closest to them. The woman disdains to let fall her skirt but maintains a defiant immobility. The scholar's intense concentration prevents the slightest activity on his part. Time hurts the unfulfilled lovers. The man looks at the scholar with the most intense hatred, as if to wither his existence. The woman, staring at the floor, becomes yet more determined to maintain her pose, a contest with the world which takes on a terrible tenacity. The man, observing her, is troubled by the extent of her determination. He looks around him, his courage falters, his hands twitch, he suffers the cruel and deflating sense the woman is mad. With glances in several directions he departs. After some time, the scholar moves to the next picture…)

WOMAN: I am here today but only today

(The scholar seems not to have heard. The woman with infinite sadness lets fall her skirt. She puts her fingertips together. She lowers her face to them. She resumes her relations with reality…)

*

15

A bed containing a stricken man. A woman enters. The man's head turns on the pillow to observe her. For a long time she looks at him, her hands loose at her sides. In her look there is pity for lost years. He succeeds in lifting his fingers from the blanket, an affirmation. She does not alter her own position as a youth enters, his limbs too active, his hands alive with impertinence. He prowls, impatient, in short moves behind her. The woman lifts her hand to assent. He pulls away her coat, and with swift and clumsy moves, takes her from behind. The woman's gaze remains on the man, even as she is rocked by the youth's aggression. Her cry comes reluctantly, half-smothered by one hand. Completed, the youth sits on the floor, his knees drawn up, rubbing his cheeks, combing his hair with his hands as if he still possessed super-abundant energy. Suddenly the woman weeps, pitifully trying to wipe away her tears with the back of her hand. The youth frets, repelled by the sound, and unable to tolerate his relative immobility, jumps to his feet and runs, first one way, then another. The woman's tears cease, and with a forlorn gesture she lies on the bed, grasping the man's hand with her own and using it to stroke her head again and again as if it might wear her away…

*

16

A sick man, stooping but unwilling to yield, approaches a house once familiar to him. He stands outside. He recovers his strength, his head lifted with an effort to the perpendicular. He knocks. He leans for support on the side of the door. Hearing the occupant approach, he leans off the door. A woman opens the door, sees him, and not certain of her reaction, folds her arms, biting her lip in her anxiety. Her arms fall to her sides. Immediately they fold again. The man simply looks, dog-like. The woman's arms fall, hang, then fold again.

MAN: I'm ill

(She looks. The remnants of love struggle in her with an instinct for self-preservation.)

I'm ill

(Her hands fall again, and hang. Her head hangs.)

So can I come back?

(She shakes her head, fast and short.)

I'm ill

(She is perfectly still.)

I'm ill

(Her mouth takes on a terrible shape as she struggles with her surging tears.)

So can I come back?

(She shakes her head slowly, continuously now.)

I'm ill

(The movement of her head extends further in each direction, so even her shoulders move with it. A second man appears. He stops. He folds his arms, putting his chin in one hand and looking patiently at the ground. Now the first man withdraws, lifting his head and feigning a confident walk. The woman's head continues to deny him…)

*

17

A servant holds a mirror, stiffly, her own body composed. A countess in hat, gloves, gown and cape, appears and walks towards the mirror, her eyes fixed, waiting for herself to be focused by it, at which point she stops and gazes at herself critically but without emotion. After some time the servant utters what is evidently a statement reiterated daily, a familiar routine.

SERVANT: If only he were here

(A few seconds pass. The countess tilts her head, plucking her veil…)

Never however

(The countess looks to the left and right in the mirror.)

Never will he be here

(The countess looks at herself, directly, her body lifted, still. The servant imitates loud weeping, convincingly, maintaining her hold on the mirror. The countess puts her gloved hands over her ears, as if she found the sound intolerable. The servant ceases abruptly, turns smartly and leaves with the mirror. The countess remains in this posture. A male servant in an apron enters, wielding a twig broom and sweeping leaves in a practised movement, to left and right. He crosses the stage. The countess is quite still…)

*

18

A man writing at a desk. His shoulders are stooped and he drives the pen from his shoulders as if he had no time in the world to reflect. He fills a page, turns it violently, rearranges his body so as to commit his last energy to complete his task, and with his face only inches from the paper, is an image of twisted concentration. So desperately does he attack his task he is unaware of the entrance of two armed men who observe him patiently from a distance, their weapons hanging loosely in their hands…

FIRST KILLER: In mid-wickedness…

(The writer hears and stops. Slowly his head lifts from the page and his eyes meet theirs. No one moves for some time. Then the writer makes a sign with one hand, asking for a fraction of time. His hand stays in the air. Receiving no response, he returns to write the final words of his testament. The only sound is the pen working the paper. But the men are bored and feel insulted. Together they make slow steps towards the writer, who sensing this, writes even quicker, the last words desperately engraved and illegible. As the men come to his shoulder he flings away the pen and making a tight shell of his body, wraps himself about the desk, thereby protecting the book, his chest drowning it and his hands locked to the legs of the desk. The spectacle gives the men pause for thought. They walk silently around the man whose eyes follow them. They are neither amused nor furious. They pass round and round, examining the desperate writer whose energy begins to ebb away. His grip weakens, his face lies on the desk, his hands hang loosely. With a gesture of surrender he lifts his hands and lets them fall again. They swing like a doll's. Without a word or glance of consultation the men walk away again. Alone, the writer is stiff with disbelief. Only slowly does he recover his position at the desk, and his head turns fearfully in the direction of the intruders.

Silently, he lifts himself off his chair. His eyes return to the book. He is afraid of it, sensing its lethal burden. He ponders leaving it behind but cannot. He stretches out his hands and lifts it off the desk in both, unnecessary given its insignificant weight. He extends it in front of him and starts to move away. Suddenly he drops it. It makes a sharp sound in the silence. He freezes. His eyes swivel in his anxiety, but no one appears. With infinite care he stoops to retrieve it. His body aches with tension. He starts to move away again but is stopped by a thought…)

WRITER: 'In mid-wickedness…'

(The title appeals to him. He continues his way…)

*

19

A park bench. Seated and stooping forward so his chin rests on his hands, his hands themselves folded on his stick, an old man, hatted and grubby. He stares into the distance. A model and a photographer enter, thrilled to be alive and conscious of their beauty. The model, a woman in her thirties, is hatted and high-heeled. The photographer snaps her even as she walks. She observes the old man and on an inspiration, sits next to him, her right leg drawn up, her left extended long in front of her. She tosses back her head as if laughing. The photographer captures her joie de vivre. She shifts to a new pose and he snaps her again. She jumps off the bench and goes behind it, posing behind the old man, drawing her dress from her breast. The old man ignores all that goes on around him. The photographer snaps the model's every pose, lying on the ground to achieve effects, putting the old man's decayed face into the same frame as the model's perfect body. The model, inebriated with her own divinity, places a long white hand against the old man's cheek. He is uncomplaining. The photographer moves in. They try one pose after another, without discussion. Now the model draws the old man back in the bench and turning, lifts her skirt so her stockinged thigh is adjacent to his head. She looks down at him as the photographer focuses the lens. He snaps. The model does not proceed to a new pose but is still as if she were herself a photograph. The photographer, kneeling, waits. The model is pained. Her hand lifts, her fingers move together, active with a growing feeling of sexual arousement. She places one hand on the old man's cheek and draws his head round so he can kiss her naked thigh. As he does so she thrusts her other hand into her mouth. She shudders in her ecstasy. The photographer fails to capture her beauty but stands, the camera idly at his side, his face twisted by dismay… no longer in control of her self the model kisses the old man with a longing that causes her eyes to widen with disbelief… her shoulders rise and fall… rise and fall… the old man's stick falls at last with a clatter. The model drags herself away from the embrace, and stands staring and biting her lip. The old man leans forward to retrieve his stick, but it is impossible for him. His hand gropes the air. The photographer picks up the stick and with a massive surge of energy, flings it far away. The old man remains fixed for a little time, then comes up, and folding his hands in front of him, waits, his eyes on the ground. All three are motionless for a little while, the photographer staring bitterly at his model. He suddenly walks away. The model fails to suppress a rising despair. She weeps. At last her weeping ceases. She gathers herself, swiftly examining her face in a compact mirror. She adjusts a stray hair, shuts the compact with a characteristic click and walks smartly away. The old man lifts his gaze from the ground. Now he weeps, he wails, he utters a curse and a prayer in the same breath, he beats himself with the flat of his hand, first on one shoulder, then the other…

*

20

An official waits, walking slowly up and down with his hands behind his back. Every so often he stops, looks at his watch, looks for the one he is expecting, continues to walk. He is suffused by an air of confidence. At last, seeing the other party to the rendezvous, he stops walking, folds his hands in front of him, and waits. A second man, lame and unkempt, half-walks, half-staggers towards him. His eyes remain on the ground until he arrives in front of the official. He stops, lifts his head and extends a hand, a formal greeting. The official disdains to shake hands, but remains upright, stiff and resolute. The second man allows his hand to fall to his side. The official turns and makes a slight sign to two others. These enter and unhurriedly advance with handcuffs. The second man, seeing their intention, throws back his chin contemptuously and folds his arms on his chest, an image of defiance. The two look at the official for instructions. The official nods once. The two advance on the second man to pinion him. Instantly the second man reveals a power of activity not discernible on his entrance, crouching and extending his hands, as if to grapple with his antagonists. The official looks fatigued.

OFFICIAL: It's all over can't you see it's all over?

All over?

All over?

(He takes out a handkerchief, white and immaculate, and blows his nose. The second man manoeuvres, shadowed by the two men. The official tucks the handkerchief away. Suddenly, as swiftly as he began, the second man relaxes, renouncing his defiance and with a grin, extends his hands to his captors. With a visible relief, they fix him, one man to each wrist. The official looks into the distance, as if observing a more interesting event, his fingers idly twirling behind his back. At his own convenience he turns to the waiting men and instructs them with the identical dip of his head. The two go to lead the prisoner away, but he is rigid, as if fixed to the ground, his eyes downcast

with determination. The chains are taut and bear on his wrists. The two men look at the official…)

OFFICIAL: It's all over can't you see it's all over?

(Suddenly the second man bursts into tears.)

All over?

All over?

(The two go to drag him, but the prisoner weeps and resists at the same time. The official is patient, and walks as if meditating a few yards in each direction, the sound of weeping rising and falling orchestrally about him. The guards look at the official, puzzled to see him sit on the ground, one knee drawn up and resting his chin on his hand, staring vaguely into the distance. The weeping stops as suddenly as it had started. The second man is resigned. The two lead him away. The official leans back, and watching the clouds, weeps…)

*

21

A woman, once a dancer, leaning on a cane. She stares into the distance, perfectly immobile. A girl fidgets beside her, pulling one hand with the other, bored and petulant. She walks up and down. She draws attention to herself.

WOMAN: Go in now

(Affecting to be piqued, the child stamps her way off. The woman remains stoically still, but some pain causes her to lift one leg a little off the ground. She allows her high-heeled shoe to fall. She repeats the action with the other foot. Less elegant but more comfortable, she maintains her position in stockinged feet. At last, sensing the futility of her vigil, she turns to follow the child. She uses her cane to retrieve a shoe, picking it off the ground, but instead of simply removing it from the cane, observes it clinically, hoisted before her eyes. Leaving it suspended in the air, she staggers into the second shoe, easing her foot into it. Now she goes to follow the child, but the disparity in the height of her heels, and a possibly arthritic hip, combine to make her moves angular and bizarre. She stops. She wonders whether to wear the second shoe, still held on the cane, or kick off the one she has replaced, and so even herself. As she struggles with the decision, a man appears, unobserved by her. He watches her pitiful irresolution. She becomes aware of him, and becomes yet stiller. The man advances and stops a little behind her, so as to remain unseen…)

MAN: Go in now

(The woman is filled with shame, and her shoulders fall. The shoe drops off the cane. Immediately the man hurries and retrieves it, but only to keep it. The woman's eyes meet his for the first time. There

is an understanding between them. She flings down the cane. Putting her hands on her hips, she walks, one foot high, one foot low. The man watches in wonder…)

*

22

A man walks with faltering steps, and stops. He waits, without moving. Slowly, a second man comes into sight and stops. The first man walks on, in the same way, going out of sight. The second man sets off, as if this were routine following. Suddenly the first man returns and confronts the second, afraid but provoked.

FIRST MAN: What is this? Who are you? Why do you follow me?

(The second man hangs his head, his hands also. The first man stares, sensing the silence of the other is absolute. He becomes larger, as his fear recedes. Almost reluctantly, he resumes his journey. The second man remains immobile, but then goes to follow. After a few paces, he sinks to the ground, dying, first onto his knees then onto his side. He lies in perfect stillness. The first man comes back, his hands in his pockets, frowning. He walks around the dead man. He extends a foot and gently prods him. He deduces the second man is dead or feigning death. He goes out, as before, and as before, hurries back in, as if he might expose a trick played on him but the second man is certainly dead. The first man sniffs, moistens his lips, thwarted. He is about to depart for the third time when he becomes aware that a third man is hovering on the edge of his vision. He casts a glance at him. This causes the third man to hang his head and his arms. The first man walks away briskly. The third man copies his decision but collides with a woman entering from the direction in which the first man had departed. She seizes him in an embrace, kissing him fervently. They slide to the ground, the dead man acting as their pillow. Her legs come apart, their passion is swiftly consummated, the third man lying spent on her shoulder. The hand of the woman lifts a compact mirror high in the air. She examines

herself. The first man returns, irritable, his fingers wildly moving. He controls this nervous anxiety by folding his arms. The woman declines to notice him. The first man kicks the ankle of the sleeping third man, but his rest is beyond disturbance. The first man is at a loss, and only accidentally observes a fourth man waiting distantly. His look causes this man to act as the previous two, his head and hands falling. The first man, charmed, continues his journey…)

*

23

A mortuary. Some bodies on slabs, covered by shrouds. A man and a woman enter. The man's arm is around the woman, to support her. They are apprehensive, they linger at the door. An attendant enters, in an overall. He is infinitely self-disciplined, his every move rehearsed, minimal and characterized by tact. He allows a few moments to pass, his hands folded in front of him, his head lowered. Then he moves forward, passing the couple at a discreet distance and positions himself at the heads of the dead row. He draws back the cloth to reveal the face of the first cadaver, lays it flat and steps back, again adopting the hands-folded posture. The man's arm falls from the woman, freeing her. They walk forward together. They look at the face of the cadaver. They simultaneously shake their heads, neither consulting nor meeting one another's eyes. The attendant covers the face and moves to the next. He repeats the operation. As if reluctantly, the couple move on, the woman first, subtly taking the initiative. She alone shakes her head. The man strokes his face in his anxiety. The attendant covers the face. As the attendant uncovers the third cadaver, the man is staring at the ceiling, unwilling to see. Thus he is a few feet away as the woman moves on, and it is her alone who shakes her head, for the first time looking at the attendant, who meets her eyes and covers the face. As he goes to the fourth, his hand reaching for the cloth, she quietly speaks.

WOMAN: Not yet

(The attendant is patient and hangs his head, his hands folding in front of him automatically. The woman tips back her head, her eyes shut, her lips tight, one of her hands lifted and active. The man cannot trespass into her pain and remains at a distance, observing her and only her. Now the woman swiftly nods, as her hand freezes. The cloth is drawn back. She makes a fist of her raised hand, and then looks into the exposed face. She is perfectly still, her expression unaltered. After some seconds she nods, and nods as if she could not stop. The man, not seeing the face because of his distance from it,

lets out a great cry that ends the woman's nodding. The attendant's chin is pressed into his chest in his discretion. He walks out, without a sound. The woman walks calmly away from the slab, as if to make way for the man. She folds her hands in front of her. The man goes to her place, but evading the viewing of the face, strokes the upturned feet, which remain covered by the shroud, over and over, as if he could warm them. She watches him, as if slightly irritated. Then she goes to him. She places her arms round his waist and lays her head on his shoulder, from the back, and is still. The man's hands work on and on...)

*

24

Moonlight and its shadows. An old man appears in slippers and a dressing gown. He walks, stops. His breath seems affected by the atmosphere.

OLD MAN: Cold enough

(He inhales, and exhales…)

Cold enough surely

(With only a moment's hesitation, he unfastens his gown, and lifting it a little in both hands, slips it off his shoulders. The effect is immediate. In his thin pyjamas, he shudders. The cold causes him to shrink no matter how he resists shrinking. He seems to lean, as if on a wind, even though it is windless. For some moments he suffers, then with measured moves, he shakes off one slipper, then the other. He puts both naked feet on the frozen ground. The cold surges up his limbs. He closes his eyes. At last his fingers grope towards his pyjama jacket, and fumble with the first button, so badly that he renounces the effort and his hand falls again. At last he summons the energy for a second attempt, frees one button but cannot attempt the second. The hand drops in the identical way. He aches. He shrinks, his head dropping. Again his hand travels to the pyjama buttons. He undoes a second, lets the hand fall and using the other hand, proceeds to fumble with the third, but it is not his natural hand and the fumbling becomes an episode, an ordeal in futility, concluded only when he jerks the jacket and the button spins away into the shadows. The pyjama jacket hangs open. With a deep breath he drags it off himself, holds it, and lets it fall. He is still, enduring the pain and the solitude. The moon travels, the shadow of the old man moves in accordance with it. At last he exclaims in a weakened voice.)

Cold enough surely?

(Deprived of his death he painfully extends an arm towards the fallen dressing gown, then falls onto his side with a small cry. He lies quite still. The moon moves on, the shadows alter. Dawn arrives in the form of the chorus. The old man lifts one arm, half-irritation, half-concession to his continuing life…)

*

25

Two rich women cycle slowly, thoughtfully, into view. They reach the edge of a high cliff. They stand, one foot on a pedal, one on the turf, identically gazing out to sea. They look at one another, for a long time. A servant cycles into the scene, discreetly dismounting some distance away, laying his cycle down, and with measured moves, shaking out a rug which he spreads behind the women for their comfort. He then retires and stands, hands folded in front of him, staring at the ground. The women now step off their cycles, laying them flat. They remove their straw hats, and toss back their hair with identical gestures. One lifts her hand to the other, who, with a suggestion of reluctance, takes it. The stronger woman draws her to the cliff edge, her eyes fixed on hers. Sensing a hazard, the servant's head lifts and he extends an arm, a warning finger raised. The women, as if rehearsed, turn their heads to him and laugh brightly, disparagingly. The servant's arm falls. The women cease laughing at once, their eyes locked. The stronger woman's grasp on the hand of the other is tightened, visibly, and she goes to leap from the cliff. The reluctance of her friend is now made obvious. She digs in her heels, pulling back her arm and breaking the momentum of the act. The stronger woman is horrified at the sabotaging of their compact. She throws her arms round the waist of the second woman and tries to throw her off the cliff, but the servant, rushing forward, likewise grabs the second woman round the waist. They struggle over her like players disputing possession of a ball. All three cry out, distinct, musical in contrast, but the strength of the man eventually tells, the stronger of the women renouncing the contest, and with her hands held out as if contaminated, flings herself weeping onto the rug and heaving great cries of despair, tosses and flails, watched by the second woman and the servant, who have not the energy to disengage. As the woman relapses into a stillness, the servant removes his hands from the waist of the second woman, and recovering his equilibrium, goes to his cycle and removes from a bag a flask. He pours out a cup, and goes to offer it to the second woman, but trips on the rug and spills it. He is still for a moment, then returns to the flask, his hand shaking so violently he fails to fill it again. Instead he sits, draws up his knees, and locking his hands together places them against his forehead. Now no one moves. The stronger woman rises from her prostration at last and leaning back on her hands, stares at the servant. Sensing this, the servant takes his hands from his face, expecting an instruction. She merely looks at him. The gulls cry. The second woman walks over to the servant and kneeling beside him, kisses him passionately on the mouth, so he falls back. The first woman watches them, unmoving, as their limbs rise and fall…

*

26

A remote place, where a wind blows unceasingly. Two men enter with bags and drift to a stop.

FIRST MAN: It's as good a place as any

(They look around the whole horizon... their eyes meet...)

As good a place as any, is it not...?

(The second man's face falls. The first man drops his bag and embraces the second, who makes pitiful, anxious noises... they remain thus for some time, then the first man withdraws from the embrace... he seems to wipe his hands on his clothes... he tightens his overcoat... he retrieves his bag. He stands looking at the second man, who forlornly nods his assent to an indisputable situation. The nodding goes on and on, a powerful sign of his reluctance which the first man breaks by shouting...)

It's as good a place as any, is it not...?

(The nodding intensifies. The first man walks swiftly away, unable to tolerate his own pity. The second man stops nodding and follows the first man with his eyes. Suddenly he falls, violently seized by a fit. His back arches. His legs kick out, he shifts about the stage in his ordeal like a broken insect... the first man hurries back in, his bag in his hand, his face taut with resentment. He watches the second man as he writhes, then begins to rain kicks on him, as if he too were seized... they move in a curious dance which ends only when the first man's anger is subdued by shame. As the second man twitches in his final throes, the first puts one hand to his head, a sign of loss... a stillness settles on the scene, and a silence but for the second man's deep breaths. The first man looks

over the land. Suddenly, thrusting his bag under his arm, he runs.

Time elapses. A woman, dirty and scavenging, observes the second man and his bag. She circles him, hyena-like, then seizing the bag, hurries to a corner to examine it. The sound of the clasps arouses the second man from his sleep. He rises onto his elbows and watches her rummage. One by one she draws out the instruments of a conjuror's trade and puzzled, lifts them into the air, silver rings, hollow books, a string of flags. With an attitude of deepening frustration she turns to meet the second man's eyes. The look is venomous. The second man makes a gesture, inviting her to keep what he no longer has a use for, but she is not placated and advancing on him, murders him with powerful hands. Dismounting his body, she aches, and feeling her years, rotates her shoulders and stretches her hands. Now she explores his clothes for valuables but sensing she is observed, lifts her eyes to see the first man has reappeared. She puts a finger to her lips, a warning to him, and completes her search, frustrated to discover her victim's pockets are perfectly empty. She climbs to her feet. She contemplates a second murder. She departs, unhurriedly. The first man is still. He seems to recollect the years. He throws his head back, smiling with fond memories. He sniffs. He wipes his face with his sleeve. He laughs. He shakes his head. He falls silent again.

*

27

A pregnant woman, an old woman, and a boy. The old woman leans on a stick. The boy holds his mother's hand. They walk to the centre of the stage. They stop. They look around them, in different ways, as if they had arrived at a rendezvous but did not expect to be met. The boy, ceasing to look, sits on the ground, his legs outstretched, lifeless, uncurious. The women scan the horizon. Now the pregnant woman sits, kicking off her shoes. The old woman, unable to sit, sinks lower on her stick. Now no one looks. They are introverted, and uninspired. The sound of castors on paving, as a man passes pushing an unwieldy table. On the table, a many-tiered wedding cake. None of the three is distracted by this. Silence returns. As if by order, the boy gets off the floor, and arranging her shoes for convenience, offers a hand to his mother. She is drawn to her feet. Already the old woman is setting off in the direction they came from. The pregnant woman and the boy follow…

*

28

A queen and her wardrobe. She paces, filled with anxiety, lifting her heavy skirts in both hands. Her maid enters swiftly, and curtsies. The queen's restless travelling stops, her gaze fixed on the mirror of the wardrobe door. The maid goes to the wardrobe and opening the door, reveals the contents without seeing for herself. Inside stands a man, naked. The maid watches the queen, the queen watches the man. The eyes, the mouth of the queen express her agony. She craves the man, and her body arches with her wanting. Swiftly the maid closes the door. The queen recovers, letting her hands hang by her sides, staring at the floor. The maid curtsies and leaves. The queen adopts the regal pose, her right hand resting on her breast, her left on her hip. A crippled courtier enters, and with agonized movements, goes down on one knee, lowering his head… the queen watches dispassionately.

QUEEN: I am far from content…

(The courtier is still.)

Far from content as you see…

(Pause.)

Do you see?

COURTIER: Madam, I see…

QUEEN: You see I am far from content…

(They remain fixed thus for some moments… then in a spasm of irritation, the queen surges to the wardrobe and plucks her hair in the mirror. She stops, then with a gasp, holds the wardrobe by its sides, and letting her forehead lean on the glass, weeps… the weeping lessens to silence…)

COURTIER: Far from content is the Queen…

(The maid returns and curtsies. The queen observes her return in the mirror, and turns to her. The maid understands her mistress. As the queen moves away, the maid goes to the wardrobe, and opens the door as before. The queen is between the naked man and

the kneeling courtier, but with her back to the open door. In her tension, the queen's hand lifts to touch her face, hangs, the fingers twirl… her breathing is deep and hard to control… Suddenly she spins to glimpse the spectacle behind her, but the maid equally swiftly closes the door. The women fix their glances on one another. Painfully, the courtier lifts his head. The scene is perfectly still until the queen, turning, offers her hand, a gesture commanding the courtier to rise. As he staggers up, the women laugh to one another, infectiously, as if unable to stop. The queen kisses formally the courtier's hand, a rare favour, smothering it in her laughter. He edges backwards from the room, still stiff, and bewildered… the laughter of the women falters… a glance is sufficient for the maid to understand she is again to open the wardrobe. She goes to it and stands with her finger to the lock, anticipating the queen's command or gesture to complete the action. The queen's hands rise involuntarily, her fingers twirl, and cease. She turns and leaves the room..)

*

29

A canvas chair, outdoors. A man seated, his arms extended down the arms of the chair, his shoulders hunched, his head still. He gazes at the horizon. A woman enters and stops. The man senses her presence behind him but refuses to acknowledge her. The woman lifts one arm from the elbow, and grasping the elbow with the opposite hand, plays with her fingers and thumb, an imitation of patience. She shifts her weight from one leg to the other, then lets her arms fall to her sides. Suddenly she goes out, denied and impetuous. For a short time the man does not move, then he lifts one arm and runs his fingers through his hair. He suffers. His legs, formerly outstretched, are retracted, lifted and wrapped in his arms. He lays his face to his knees, then gnaws them. He makes small, desperate animal sounds…

*

30

An old woman, with hat and stick, her spine distorting her walk. Behind her, in her tracks, her son, not young but infantile. He bears in either hand full bags of shopping. The old woman stops. Her son stops, a regulated distance behind her. She peers around as if contemplating a purchase. Her attitude is disdainful. She starts off again, and stops again, the man follows suit. Now she looks round at him, both hands clasped on the stick. She looks at him, as if she did not know him thoroughly.

OLD WOMAN: What when I'm gone?

(If she expects an answer, the man does not offer one. His gaze is directed at the ground. She studies him longer, as if her scrutiny could get sense from him. At last she turns and moves on. He waits, then moves after her…)

*

31

Two lines of running convicts cross the stage in opposite directions. They are barefoot and wear shorts and singlets, barely clean. Between the lines stands an officer, a cane under his arm, a whistle in his mouth. After several circuits the whistle is blown once. The convicts stop, staring ahead. The officer walks slowly about, examining them, lifting their chins with his cane if they droop, but not unkindly. He blows the whistle twice. They resume running. A pair of lovers, entwined, lost in their mutuality, drift in, stop and embrace, oblivious to the running figures. The whistle is blown. The officer repeats his routine. The loving couple continue their adoration. The whistle is blown twice. The men run, their eyes always ahead of them. Now the officer blows five shrill blasts and the men head offstage, preserving their strict order. The officer remains, the cane behind his back. His eyes on the ground. In the silence, the couple disengage. First the woman, then the man, notice the officer. They shift uncomfortably, and with a tacit understanding, depart. At once the officer races after them, disappearing offstage and returning at once, dragging the man backwards, the cane tight to his throat and held by both ends, the woman shrieking and clinging to the officer's arm. The officer lowers the half-suffocated man to the ground. The woman drapes herself over the collapsed body, lifting his head, deep moans coming from him and her together. The officer's hands hang at his sides. Nervously, he takes off his cap. He observes the consequences of his action. He drifts away, stopping, looking back, and drifting again…

*

32

A woman returns to a house where she has been happy. Her gaze travels over its surfaces, her hands resting loosely in her coat pockets. She looks at the ground. She is about to walk to the door, when a second woman appears unexpectedly behind her. The first woman turns slowly to her.

SECOND WOMAN: Nothing here is what it was

(The first woman examines the face of the second so searchingly, the second woman folds her arms defiantly. The first woman looks back at the house. Suddenly the second woman bursts into tears, her arms fall to her sides. The first woman watches this dispassionately until, with a shaking of her head, the weeping woman stops. The first woman looks at the still, distraught figure, then turns to go into the house. She stops on a thought, and is still, then she goes into the house. The second woman puts her hands together, finger tips joined and adopts a position of patience. After some moments have passed, the first woman reappears, barefoot, bare-legged, and her coat thrown over her head. She walks blindly, tripping and stopping, moving and tripping again, though never falling. The second woman chooses not to observe her ordeal. As the first woman departs, a book is flung after her from the house. It slides over the ground. The second woman cannot resist the temptation to laugh, a laughter which simultaneously fills her with shame. A second book follows the first, igniting a second eruption of laughter, as the second woman runs her hands through her hair, shaking her head, and yielding to the pleasure of it. When a third book is thrown she alters with a sudden swiftness, and ceasing to laugh, puts her hands on her hips and adopts a stance of repudiation. No book follows..)

*

33

A city park. A man early for an appointment, walks a little, turns, stands a long time, repeats the short walk. A woman, entering in a similar state of anxiety, watches him, her shoulders loose, drained of any pride but fixed in the remnants of her fascination. When the man turns, he sees her. They are still, looking with wan smiles. The desire to run to one another lives in their limbs, but is gone from their minds, and in vital seconds, dies. At last her shoulders lift in a question. His hand lifts, a fist, a substitute for already-spoken words, and falls again. His eyes fall also. The woman waits, as if still there might be a chance. She sways on her feet, caught between staying and leaving. He lends her nothing. Her own fists rise, and fall. Still she holds her place, then as if overwhelmed by a deluge, turns and strides to a second man who walks boldly in and catches her in his arms. The woman does not admit the embrace, but allowing the second man to take her by her arm, goes out with him, hurrying from the terrible place. The first man, who has watched this but only by lifting his eyes, lets his eyes fall again. He cannot move. A deep groan departs from him. He seems to sink, the groan coming again. Shrunken, he rebuilds himself, creating finally a gesture as if he lifted some cowl or helmet from his face, and letting his hands travel down his sides. He is quite still.

MAN: The man there then

(Pause. He scoffs unconvincingly. Pause.)

Always the man there

(He is able to move. He walks a few paces.)

Good

(He ponders.)

Good the man is there

(He goes to walk on. He stops, seeing it is the route he came by but more significantly, the route the woman departed on. He turns deliberately. He marches in the opposite direction.)

*

34

An old man seated on a park chair. His head is sunk between his shoulders. His hands rest on the sides on the chair, as if propping him in position. His legs are wide apart. A girl, elegant, tall, passes him reading an open newspaper, her pace varying as her concentration increases or fails. Her attention is wholly engaged by reading. She does not observe the old man. He does not react to her passage. After some time has elapsed, two young men run past, perhaps in pursuit of her. The old man seems not to perceive this either. His head lifts fractionally to watch some garden birds in his vicinity. One hand painfully reaches into his coat pocket. His shoulder, stiff and arthritic, makes the manoeuvre an ordeal. His hand emerges with breadcrumbs. With a strange twist of his arm he succeeds in spreading the crumbs in front of him. The pleasure he discovers in this is cut short as he tries to return the hand to its original position. He lets out a short, sharp cry as the arm fixes in mid-movement. His face is creased by pain. He leaves the arm in the air, familiar with its idiosyncrasies. As he maintains this crippled position, the young men return, holding the young woman aloft, one grasping her shoulders, the other her knees. They seem adept at carrying. The young woman's head hangs down, her mouth open, unconscious or possibly dead. The men move swiftly but show no sign of fear. As they depart, the old man's head slowly turns. But his shoulder fixes. Again he lets out a cry. Slowly, his body relaxes, the spasms relent. He discovers his original posture.

*

35

A chair carried on long poles, a bearer at each corner, all four in livery. In the chair a high dignitary. His head rests on a gloved hand. He watches the passing landscape with indifference. The bearers stop. They lower the chair and stand, heads bowed, hands clasped before them. The dignitary waits. He examines his fingers. He casts a glance at the sky. He lifts the skirts of his coat. He lets them fall. At last a man and a woman appear. The man carries a newly-born child, wrapped. He clasps it tenderly to his shoulder. The couple wait before the dignitary, the woman with her head lowered, the man proud. The dignitary extends a hand before him, ungloved. The woman goes to it and kisses it reverently. The hand falls. The man goes to the dignitary and extends the child to him. The dignitary kisses the forehead of the infant, and the man withdraws, leaving the woman alone. She lifts her gaze. The dignitary, attempting to suppress his tears, turns his head one way and the other, again and again. The woman, infected by his grief, heaves, and extends a hand towards him. The bearers maintain a discreet immobility. At last the dignitary's emotions overwhelm his decorum. He wails. The woman, also wailing, clasps her face in her hands. The two shudder, mutually infatuated, but yards apart. At last their pain recedes. The bearers without a sign from their master, simultaneously take up the poles. They carry away the dignitary, who, resting his chin on his hand, stares over the country…

*

36

An old servant sweeps a path. His method is characterized by its regular, unhurried discipline, two strokes to the right, two to the left. At a certain point he stops. His hand goes to his face, he grieves. He looks through his tears, through his fingers, an elbow on the handle of the broom. He recovers. He sweeps. He stops, this time against his will, holds the handle with a shuddering tightness, in both hands, and avoids weeping. His body straightens, he sweeps on. After a few more actions with the broom, his sobs overcome him, and he sinks to his knees, grasping the upright broom for support in one hand. His chest heaves. His breath is full, profound until at last his crisis passes. He does not climb to his feet but remains on his knees. He knows he must sooner or later stand but lacks the will. He looks at the path in front of him. He removes his hand from the broom which remains upright for a second, then topples. The old man's arms hang at his sides. A countess, in hat and gloves, walks swiftly by as if marching to an appointment. For a moment she does not seem to notice him. She stops abruptly. She freezes. Her head turns. She sees the servant on the edge of death. She weeps. Her shoulders heave. The servant lifts one hand, to console her. She raises one gloved hand to him.

*

37

A nun, seated. A novice enters. She waits.

NUN: You do not wish to leave it is a dread all of us experience this dread it passes

(Neither moves nor meets the other's gaze. A long time elapses. At last the nun turns to face the novice.)

All of us

(The novice is resolute.)

All of us

(And keeps her eyes on the nun.)

It passes

(The boldness of the novice's stare discomforts the nun. She stands violently as if to reprimand her, but her gaze falls. She walks a little way, stops and turns to examine the novice from the rear. The novice is still. To break the tension of the nun's stare the novice flings her starched collar to the floor, a stratagem that is ineffectual…)

All of us experience this dread

(The novice is defiant.)

All of us

All of us

(A pause, then with a flourish the novice flings off her cassock, and stands in her shift. She holds the cassock outstretched by one hand… choosing her moment, she lets it fall to the floor, leaving her hand in the air. This gesture is maintained until it visibly agonizes her… her hand falls to her side…)

All of us

All of us

(The novice spins on her heel to face the nun. Their look is long… the novice marches in her shift, worldly and a provocation… the nun hangs her head, choosing not to observe her… the novice invests more in her stride, arching her back to advertise her breasts… as she marches she loosens her hair, which falls over her shoulders… the nun keeps her eyes fixed to a spot, her pain contained… after several more turns, the novice stops. Now the nun lifts her eyes to her… the novice laughs, and stops. She weeps, and stops. The nun observes her without bitterness. Now she chooses to walk, the same route as the novice, but differently, a walk so simple it is affective and causes the novice to smile, to wipe her eyes. The nun stops, but briefly, then goes to her chair and sits. She observes the novice, her chin in one hand…)

You do not wish to leave

(The novice neither confirms nor denies this. The nun turns away. She waits, her hands folded on her knee. The novice places one hand on her heart. With the other she covers her eyes. The nun rises from her chair and leaves…)

*

38

A tram stop. A woman approaches, warily, as if it threatened her. She wears a coat, a scarf over her head, and carries a suitcase. She puts down the suitcase. Her hand, no longer occupied with the suitcase, twitches. She picks up the suitcase. She looks in both directions, as if uncertain where the tram will appear from. A man enters and stands behind her, starting a queue. He reads a newspaper. The woman puts down the suitcase and immediately picks it up again, a neurotic movement that the man observes but clandestinely. A second man enters and stands behind the first, his hands in his pockets. The woman, uncomfortable in her decision, quits the queue and takes a few steps back in the direction she came from, but stops. She seems unable to move forward or back. The second man watches. With a resolution, the woman returns but now joins the back of the queue and puts down the bag. A woman appears and stands behind her. A bell sounds in the distance. The queue looks round as one, and the woman, seeing the tram approaching strides away unhesitatingly, a move characterized by energy, decision, even elegance. The queue edges away to mount the tram. The bell clangs. When the tram has gone, the woman is seen approaching the stop with the same suspicious moves that characterized her first attempt at travelling, but now she puts the bag down, and undoing the clasps, opens it and removes a hat. She looks about her to see she is not observed and swiftly exchanges the headscarf for the hat. She closes the case. She goes to the stop. She puts down the suitcase. Again her hand writhes. She again picks it up. A couple arrive, arms around one another. They make a queue behind the woman, arms locked round one another's waists, foreheads joined, eyes staring into eyes. With a sudden move the woman places herself behind them in the queue. She looks in the direction she now expects the tram to appear from, and the clang of its bell confirms its approach. As the couple disengage to board the tram, the woman hurries off, as if summoned. The couple move away. The bell clangs. In the returning silence the woman strolls back, casual, letting her heels scrape the ground and swinging the suitcase playfully. She goes to the stop, puts down the bag and plucks her gloves. She laughs, privately. The laugh is not extinguished by the appearance of a morose youth, who stands behind her with a book. His concentration on it, perhaps a self-defence, prevents him reacting to her repetitive bending from the waist to see if a tram is approaching. The clang of its bell inspires her to pluck up her case with a blithe impatience. She seems to move up to board but in the same way swerves off and marches away, this time laughing loudly, even ecstatically. The youth looks after her with faint interest, and the tram bell clangs. The stage is empty. The woman does not reappear…

*

39

An elegant woman, the lover of a decayed man, has found a style of walking which whilst maintaining her own dignity, never outpaces his. The man moves painfully on two sticks. She preserves a parallel course, only a few feet to his left. Her head turns, alert, taking in the view, the activity of a street. His head seems rigidly directed towards the ground. As they advance, the man lets fall one of his sticks, an accident that humiliates him. He stands, despairing. The woman, accustomed to every nuance of his decay, bends with a fine movement to recover the stick and goes to replace it in his hand. The man shakes his head with despair, his hand shakes with self-loathing. The woman is patient, holding her posture. The man's hand clenches into a fist of bitterness.

WOMAN: I said I would always love you

(He shudders with self-disgust…)

I said

I said

(At last his hand closes over the stick. Only then does the woman rise from her posture. They proceed. The woman is aware that this incident has been observed by a man. She observes this without being affected by it. After a few paces the decayed man drops the same stick again. The faintest suggestion of irritation might be seen in the woman's features. In the hiatus before she bends to retrieve the fallen stick, the observing man moves swiftly and picks up the stick himself. His eyes do not meet the woman's. He stoops, offering it to the decayed man. The decayed man, sensitive to every condescension, leaves the stick in the air until the apparently kind gesture seems foolish to the man who has made it. He shrugs. His eyes rise to the woman. The woman knows full well his purpose was never altruistic. She does nothing to assist him out of his dilemma, whilst knowing her own power over him. The man's humiliation causes

him to offer the stick to her instead. She declines to relieve him. The man swallows his pride, and lays the stick down, without a sound, on the ground. The decayed man has not moved or glanced once in his direction. The man awkwardly withdraws, looking over his shoulder at what might follow. The woman repeats the operation as before, adopting the same discreet but elegant pose. The decayed man exploits his weak position by not taking the stick until the woman is uncomfortable, and provoked…)

I said

I said I would always love you

(Now the decayed man receives the stick. The woman rises. They advance…)

*

40

A throng of people, each of whom covers his eyes with a single hand. Entering from different sides, they bump together, recoil and bump again, settling at last into a tight group and craning their necks to the front like curious birds. For a long time they are silent and still. A naked woman of considerable beauty strides across what might have been their line of sight, her shoes making a characteristic sound. She makes no reference to them, nor do they seem to register her, but when she has gone, one of the throng drops his hand and stares, haunted, tortured by imagination. Time passes. The woman runs back, now wearing a hat and matching gloves. Her heels clatter like castanets. The sighted male frowns, not following her with his eyes but pained by the brief image that crossed his fixed stare. In the silence he cries, forlorn and childlike. He is uncomforted. As he at last controls his sobbing, the woman makes a third appearance, fully clothed in matching garments and holding an unfolded map, which she studies in relation to the scene, looking up, puzzled, studying again, her head turning from side to side. The sighted male, whose unmoving eyes imitate authentic blindness, senses her provocation…

MALE: My dear

My dear

(The woman, unhearing, turns the map around, squints at it, looks around again…)

My dear

My dear dear dear

(There is a loud, insolent whistle off. The woman, relieved and smiling, crushes the map in her hand and hurries away to her encounter. The sighted male replaces his hand over his eyes…)

*

WONDER AND WORSHIP IN THE DYING WARD

Characters

OSTEND	A Woman of Terrible Fidelity
ARCHITECT	A Broken Child
DOOBEE	A Mender of Women and Cars
CHILDLIKE	A Sickly Resident of a Nurseless Home
ATTO	" "
MOMPER	" "
WINDUS	" "
LOOS	" "
SLUMP	" "
PORTSLADE	" "
ONSEE	" "
ALDRINGTON	" "
BASIN	" "

A too-high window. Against it, as if to facilitiate observation, a long ladder. The sound of shuffling feet. The room fills with the pale forms of THE MORTALLY ILL *and their animals. They stare out. Their dogs mew. Their rabbits fidget.*

1

ATTO:	Oh God / darling /
MOMPER:	What? /
ATTO:	Oh God / oh God /
MOMPER:	What / darling / what? /
ATTO:	Oh God /
	Oh God /
	Oh God /

2

WINDUS:	Fuck /

3

WINDUS:	Fuck /
LOOS:	Shut up /
WINDUS:	Fuck /
LOOS:	Will you shut up /
PORTSLADE:	You /
LOOS:	Me? /
PORTSLADE:	You shut up /
LOOS:	She said silence /
PORTSLADE:	Shut up then /
WINDUS:	Fuck /
	Fuck /
PORTSLADE:	All right /

WINDUS: Fuck /

PORTSLADE: All right / all right /

WINDUS: Fuck /

LOOS: We heard you /

PORTSLADE: It's all right / it's all right /

4

CLING: Oh / Jesus /

LOOS: Silence she said / she said silence /

CLING: I know /

LOOS: Silence is silence /

SLUMP: All right /

CLING: I know /

SLUMP: All right / darling /

CLING: I know /

5

CLING: I know /

6

CLING: I KNOW /

7

CLING: I KNOW /

8

CLING: I KNOW /

MOMPER: All right /

PORTSLADE: All right / darling /

SLUMP: All right / all right /

CLING: Jesus /

PORTSLADE: All right / darling /

MOMPER: All right / all right /

SLUMP: All right /

CLING: Thank you /

SLUMP: Don't thank me /

LOOS: Silence / she said /

MOMPER: All right /

9

CLING: Thank you /

10

LOOS: Thank <u>you</u> /

11

The faint whine of an electric motor. The appearance and disappearance of a woman prostrate on a mobile bed.

12

BASIN: She hates us /

LOOS: Shut up /

PORTSLADE: You shut up /

BASIN: She hates us /

ALDRINGTON: God /
Oh God /

MOMPER: All right / darling /

CLING: Jesus /

SLUMP: All right /

CLING: Just shut up /

PORTSLADE: You /

ALDRINGTON: God /

Oh God /

CLING: Shut her up /

ALDRINGTON: Oh God /

Oh God /

CLING: Or I will /

PORTSLADE: You will /

LOOS: Ha /

CLING: Yes /

LOOS: Ha /

CLING: Yes /

WINDUS: She said silence /

13

A child, or one so shrunk as to resemble a child, is seen climbing the ladder, painfully, rung by rung.

WINDUS: Silence / she said /

14

The whimpering and fidgeting of animals. The whine of the mobile bed, which appears, passes, stops and reverses.

ARCHITECT: Coming / is she? / is she coming? /

(The CHILDLIKE hangs out the window. If it replies, the reply is inaudible. A hint of irritation in the repeated question causes a flutter of anxiety in the MORTALLY ILL.)

Coming / or not? /

LOOS Is she coming? / coming / is she? /

/CLING ETC:

(The CHILDLIKE's reply, if any reply was uttered, is lost in the wind. THE MORTALLY ILL, rigid with apprehension, stare at the prostrate ARCHITECT. The dogs mew. The rabbits fidget.)

ARCHITECT: By car / presumably / the same brown car /

(THE MORTALLY ILL, unwilling to turn to the ladder, convey the question once it is evident the CHILDLIKE has failed to respond.)

SLUMP: Car /

PORTSLADE: Brown /

SLUMP: Same brown car /

(Failing to elicit a response, THE MORTALLY ILL call shrilly.)

PORTSLADE: Car / or not? /

LOOS: Brown car / is there? /

ALDRINGTON: Car /

WINDUS: Car / darling /

ALDRINGTON: Or not? /

WINDUS: Or not? /

(The CHILDLIKE is seen idly to lift one foot off the rung of the ladder, a sign of its concentration. Fear fills THE MORTALLY ILL. The mobile bed, without haste, moves off.)

15

The CHILDLIKE turns from the window.

CHILDLIKE: Off-white /

(THE MORTALLY ILL react to this single word with a mixture of shame and curiosity.)

Off-white /

(The CHILDLIKE gazes over them, studying the backs of their heads. The dogs mew.)

16

CHILDLIKE: *(Coaxing a response.)* Off-white /

(The provocation is too much for BASIN.)

BASIN: HER SKIRT /

(The mortally-ill tremble with relief.)

CHILDLIKE: *(Gratified.)* Off-white /

ATTO/SLUMP: HER UNDERWEAR /

(A surge of mischief and delight. The dogs bark with relief. Now they all race to complete the narrative.)

WINDUS: I pressed my face /

CLING: I pressed my face to the window /

PORTSLADE: The condensation /

WINDUS: On the glass /

PORTSLADE: *(Resenting the interruption.)* The condensation /

MOMPER: On the glass / darling /

PORTSLADE: *(Affirmatively.)* The condensation on the glass /

LOOS: What was going on in there? /

SLUMP: Drowning /

ATTO: The only comparison /

ALDRINGTON: The only comparison /

MOMPER: I think /

(They are tickled by this phrase.)

ATTO: I think /

ALDRINGTON I THINK /

/BASIN:

ATTO: The only comparison /

ALL: I THINK /

(They laugh.)

ATTO: Is drowning /

WINDUS: Frost /

LOOS: Rust /

ALDRINGTON: Petrol /

LOOS: Chrome /

MOMPER: I pressed my face to the window /

WINDUS: Frost /

ATTO: Rust /

LOOS: Petrol /

ALDRINGTON: Chrome /

SLUMP: And then the door /

PORTSLADE: *(Anticipating.)* And then the door fell open /

ALL: WHY? /

(They shake with laughter.)

SLUMP: I /

LOOS: I /

BASIN: I / a child /

LOOS: A child / a little /

MOMPER: Not yet / darling /

LOOS: Not yet? /

MOMPER: *(Correcting him.)* Another door /

PORTSLADE: And then the door fell open /

SLUMP: I / a child /

MOMPER: Correct /

LOOS: *(Affirmatively.)* A child / a little child /

MOMPER: Yup /

LOOS: When the door fell open /

ALDRINGTON: Saw /

(They seem to lose the inspiration that has driven the narrative. The dogs mew. The rabbits squirm. they frown. At last BASIN mutters the word)

BASIN: My mother /

(They are reluctant to follow BASIN, who is obliged to proceed alone.)

Beautifully joyless /

(He waits for assistance.)

Beautifully joyless and /

(None comes.)

open-thighed /

CLING: *(Helpfully now.)* Darling /

BASIN: Her still grey eyes on mine /

CLING: Darling /

(Again, a reluctance, overcome at last.)

LOOS: Her stripped immensity /

ALDRINGTON: Nothing concealed /

PORTSLADE: Nothing concealed and /

MOMPER: *(Discipling PORTSLADE.)* Rust /

PORTSLADE: *(Conceding.)* Rust /

BASIN: Petrol /

CLING: Chrome /

PORTSLADE: Nothing concealed and off-white /

CHILDLIKE: Off-white /

WINDUS: Her underwear /

MOMPER: Wide-open /

CLING: Her knees /

ALDRINGTON: And me /

LOOS: Not yet /

CHILDLIKE: Off-white /

ALDRINGTON: Sorry /

ATTO: Off-white upholstery /

MOMPER: *(To ALDRINGTON.)* Now /

ALDRINGTON: And me /

SLUMP: A child /

ALDRINGTON: Properly joyless /

CLING: Her stripped immensity /

(The conclusion of the narrative leaves them tender, frail. Some bite their lips in their anxiety. The animals fidget in sympathy.)

17

In the near-silence, the whine of the electric motor precedes the appearance of ARCHITECT and the bed. CHILDLIKE scrambles to its look-out. ARCHITECT stops the bed.

ARCHITECT: A car? / A car / or not? /

CHILDLIKE: *(Turning to her.)* Brown car? /

ATTO /SLUMP ETC: BROWN / BROWN / BROWN CAR /

(CHILDLIKE gazes out. The MORTALLY ILL shift uncomfortably. They inhale and exhale. At last, ARCHITECT, permanently fixed on her right side, gives her narrative.)

ARCHITECT: And then the door fell open / why? /

(The suffers her recollection.)

Why? /

ALL: *(Raggedly.)* We can't think why /

(ARCHITECT frowns from the effort of her meditation.)

ARCHITECT: Darling / wide-open / her knees / darling / and I /

ALL: We can't think why / the door fell open /

ARCHITECT: A child /

ALL: Her eyes on mine /

ARCHITECT: Beautifully joyless /

ALL: Wide-open eyes / wide open knees /

ARCHITECT: Her stripped immensity /

(ARCHITECT struggles with the image.)

18

A woman enters, unannounced.

CHILDLIKE: *(Still at its perch.) Brown car /*

(OSTEND's measured footsteps draw CHILDLIKE's attention. She stops. ARCHITECT, paralyzed on her side, cannot observe her mother, who plays with her gloves. CHILDLIKE squirms in its frustration.)

Off-white /

OSTEND: I walked /

CHILDLIKE: UPHOLSTERY /

OSTEND: I wanted to walk / notwithstanding I am not dressed for walking / these last few yards / from the lodge to the porch / the surface of the drive / the condition of the lodge / I must say / dismayed me /

ARCHITECT: I am sorry you were dismayed /

OSTEND: Terribly dismayed / meanwhile he followed me /

ARCHITECT: He? /

OSTEND: Avoiding the pot-holes / to the best of his ability /

ARCHITECT: He? /

OSTEND: I hate alteration/ the least alteration dismays me /

ARCHITECT: I am sorry you are dismayed /

OSTEND: Sorry / are you sorry / darling? /

ARCHITECT: I think so / yes / on the other hand / to learn you are dismayed comes as no surprise to me /

CHILDLIKE: OFF-WHITE /

OSTEND: Decay is one thing /

CHILDLIKE: UPHOLSTERY /

OSTEND: Neglect is quite another /

ARCHITECT: Certainly /

OSTEND: Decay is tolerable / and not without a certain charm / neglect is irredeemably offensive /

ARCHITECT: Yes /

OSTEND: Decay arrives / neglect's invited /

ARCHITECT: I agree with that distinction /

CHILDLIKE: *(A barometer of strained atmospheres.)* AND THE DASHBOARD WALNUT /

ARCHITECT: *(Patiently.)* Neglect / I feel certain / is the effect that I intended /

CHILDLIKE: WALNUT ALSO THE LINING OF THE GLOVE COMPARTMENT /

(THE MORTALLY ILL tremble in their anxiety. Their animals whimper.)

THE SLIDE-OUT TRAY / AND THE VANITY /

(A long whine from a dog.)

SHELF /

OSTEND: *(Without evident resentment.)* So you admit you wanted me to be dismayed? /

ARCHITECT: That doesn't follow /

OSTEND: You wanted me to be dismayed and / as I have frankly confessed / I am dismayed / you have / therefore /

ARCHITECT: That doesn't follow /

OSTEND: Been wholly successful in /

ARCHITECT: NONE OF THAT CAN BE INFERRED FROM WHAT I SAID /

(Her vehemence stills the room. OSTEND plays with a glove.)

Let me see you now / let me see you / you know my field of vision / let me see you / mother /

(OSTEND delays her response.)

19

A man enters, evidently a chauffeur. He stops. OSTEND passes to the front of the mobile bed.

OSTEND: *(Gazing on her daughter.)* Darling /

DOOBEE: About the car /

OSTEND: Darling /

DOOBEE: About the car /

CHILDLIKE: *(Delighted.)* BROWN CAR /

(THE MORTALLY ILL giggle.)

DOOBEE: The car / and me /

ARCHITECT: Your hands are claws /

DOOBEE: Me / the car / and the laws of the car /

OSTEND: Darling /

DOOBEE: For example /

(He makes short, energetic pacing moves.)

The difference / the sublime and awesome difference between the front seats and the back /

ARCHITECT: Kiss / kiss /

DOOBEE: The social / psychological / and metaphysical / distinction between the front seats and the back /

(He is suddenly ugly.)

DON'T PRETEND YOU UNDERSTAND IT /

OSTEND: *(Kissing her daughter's forehead.)* Promise not to touch you with my claws / my shrunken / and prematurely senile claws /

(They laugh mildly. DOOBEE sways in his rage.)

DOOBEE: Pretending to understand / in my opinion / is vastly / vastly worse / than admitting that you don't / and you don't / you don't understand / it is a question of permission / not just who sits in the front / and who sits in the back / but who has permission /

(He marches briefly and stops.)

PERMISSION TO ENTER THE BACK /

(He frowns. His lip quivers.)

I could weep /

(He shakes his head forlornly.)

Yes / weep / not because you are ignorant / why should I care how little you understand / or how much? / but because your ignorance condemns me to an everlasting solitude /

(THE MORTALLY ILL appear suitably condign. DOOBEE seems thoughtful, then swiftly, resolved.)

Too bad / too bad /

OSTEND: *(Kindly.)* Shh /

DOOBEE: Vastly better my solitude remains inviolable / vastly better /

OSTEND: Shh /

DOOBEE: The shuttered windows / the bolted doors /

OSTEND: *(Faintly irritated.)* Doobee /

DOOBEE: Why should I want you crashing through my silence / dislodging the mirrors / vomiting on the floors? /

OSTEND: DOOBEE /

(DOOBEE is hurt by the severity of OSTEND's command. He looks at her, his mouth turned down.)

DOOBEE: It's a mansion /

OSTEND: Yes /

DOOBEE: Solitude /

OSTEND: Yes /

DOOBEE: A mansion /

(THE MORTALLY ILL shift uncomfortably. DOOBEE squirms. Suddenly he goes to move.)

I'll fetch the bags /

(He stops. he seems to consider the virtue of speaking. He inclines to it. He looks at the prostrate form of ARCHITECT.)

It's perfectly true your mother's hands are less than perfect / but in your determination to humiliate her by describing them as claws / I have to tell you / you fail utterly to understand the paradoxical character of all revelation /

ARCHITECT: *(Drily.)* Do I? /

DOOBEE: Yes / and this paradox is nowhere more subtly described than in the tide of tension that ebbs and flows between the hands of a beautiful woman and her gloves /

ARCHITECT: Is that so? /

DOOBEE: It is so / yes / a beautiful woman dares her audience / and she is never without an audience even when she is alone / dares it to assume the absolute character of her perfection / a perfection we both know and dread is logically and empirically impossible / even so / something lingers / something inextinguishable / of dream or hope / causing us / as she / with that slow and practised gesture / draws off her glove / to /

(DOOBEE swallows with difficulty.)

to /

(He aches. He sobs. OSTEND goes to him without haste and taking his head between her hands, kisses him profoundly. THE MORTALLY ILL stare. The animals fidget. The kiss ends at last.)

OSTEND: Get the bags now /

(DOOBEE obeys, his eyes fixed to the floor, but after a few paces, stops.)

DOOBEE: They don't understand /

OSTEND: No /

DOOBEE: *(Shaking his head.)* No one ever / ever / understands /

(He lifts his eyes to OSTEND. He goes out, only to swiftly return.)

THE LESS-THAN-PERFECT HAND / AT THE MOMENT OF ITS REVELATION /

(The spectacle of DOOBEE now provokes a ripple of half-suppressed laughter in THE MORTALLY ILL. Their animals bark or whimper.)

/ FAR FROM DIMINISHING THE BEAUTY OF THE WOMAN / TESTIFIES TO HER / HER /

(THE MORTALLY ILL are now infected with derision.)

PORTSLADE: *(To SLUMP.)* All right / darling /

WINDUS: All right / all right /

(They shudder.)

DOOBEE: TESTIFIES / YES / TESTIFIES /

LOOS: *(To THE MORTALLY ILL.)* All right /

CLING: *(Collapsing.)* Oh no /

LOOS: Steady /

CLING: Sorry / sorry /

(CHILDLIKE, choking on laughter, turns to hang out the window.)

DOOBEE: TO AN EXQUISITE FRAILTY / DOES IT NOT? /

(As THE MORTALLY ILL tremble and rock, forcing their hands into their mouths, DOOBEE stands at bay.)

DOES IT NOT? /

(His defiance at last subdues THE MORTALLY ILL. OSTEND watches without intervening as they discover the shame of the infants' class. In the restored silence, the motor of the mobile bed produces its characteristic sound. In a gesture of disdain, ARCHITECT is drawn from the room.)

20

CHILDLIKE: *(Turning on the ladder.)* Neglect it's /

MOMPER: Shh /

CHILDLIKE: Everywhere /

MOMPER: Shh /

CHILDLIKE: Everywhere / neglect /

ALDRINGTON: Us /

LOOS: Especially /

MOMPER: Shh /

LOOS: Especially us /

CLING: Ulcers /

LOOS: Scabies /

CLING: Scabies and ulcers /

LOOS: Show them / show them your legs /

SLUMP: Horrible legs /

PORTSLADE: As for the facilities /

LOOS: *(As CLING reveals her wounds.)* I can't look /

ATTO: *(Turning away.)* Oh God /

LOOS: I can't look /

PORTSLADE: The bathroom /

(DOOBEE, nauseated, departs to fetch the bags.)

LOOS: Can I / darling? / I can't look /

PORTSLADE: Is sordid /

SLUMP: She's infected /

PORTSLADE: Verminous /

SLUMP: Isn't she / infected again? /

PORTSLADE: And a hotbed of disease /

BASIN: Then there's the rash /

LOOS: The rash /

ATTO: Show her the rash /

BASIN: Everybody has the rash /

WINDUS: Not me /

ATTO: Show her / show her /

WINDUS: For some reason /

BASIN: *(Pulling aside his shirt.)* Chest /

WINDUS: Not me /

BASIN: And back /

ALDRINGTON: Behind the knees / in my case /

PORTSLADE: As for the bed linen /

LOOS: Show her /

PORTSLADE: The bed linen is stiff /

MOMPER: Oh God / darling /

PORTSLADE: Stiff /

MOMPER: It's weeping

PORTSLADE: Stiff /

ALDRINGTON: And beneath the arms /

MOMPER: It's weeping / darling /

ALDRINGTON: Under the arms / behind the knees /

PORTSLADE: As for the lavatory /

MOMPER: *(Grimacing.)* That's bad / Michael / that is very / very / bad / darling /

PORTSLADE: The one and only /

LOOS: God / oh God /

PORTSLADE: Functioning lavatory /

ATTO: Show her / she can't see /

(As THE MORTALLY ILL present their symptoms to OSTEND, CHILDLIKE begins to shudder with laughter.)

PORTSLADE: This single lavatory is situated /

WINDUS: Undo the bandage /

PORTSLADE: On the fourth floor /

WINDUS: Let her see /

PORTSLADE: Not the second / or the third /

BASIN: *(Squirming.)* Don't touch /

ATTO: Darling / she can't see /

PORTSLADE: THE FOURTH /

(The animals are squirming and yelping.)

MOMPER: It's stuck / the bandage / it's all stuck /

LOOS: I'm not looking /

SLUMP: Help him / somebody /

PORTSLADE: THE FOURTH FLOOR /

21

CHILDLIKE: *(Nimbly descending the ladder.)* Neglect is not decay /

(It addresses OSTEND.)

Did you say that? /

OSTEND: I said that / yes /

CHILDLIKE: They are not synonymous / certainly / and yet there could be no decay / could there / without neglect? /

(OSTEND gazes on CHILDLIKE with disdain.)

Please argue / argument is ecstasy / no one argues here / not surprisingly / the dying are not dialectical / if they were ever curious / they are curious no longer /

(He experiences a spasm.)

OFF-WHITE UPHOLSTERY /

(OSTEND regards CHILDLIKE with a certain sympathy.)

Please argue / however brief the argument / argue with me /

(OSTEND is measured.)

OSTEND: Look at me /

CHILDLIKE: Yes /

OSTEND: Are you looking at me? /

CHILDLIKE: Yes /

OSTEND: No / scrutinize / scrutinize me /

(CHILDLIKE concentrates.)

Do I look neglected? /

CHILDLIKE: No / I would not say so /

OSTEND: Rather the contrary /

CHILDLIKE: The contrary / yes /

OSTEND: Then you know /

(CHILDLIKE is puzzled.)

CHILDLIKE: Do I? /

OSTEND: And argument / in this / as in so many instances / is redundant /

CHILDLIKE: I don't follow / what is it I know? /

(DOOBEE appears, holding baggage from the car.)

Say / please say /

OSTEND: The First Law of Existence is decay /

(CHILDLIKE studies OSTEND in a manner simultaneously mischievous and diffident.)

CHILDLIKE: The law becomes you /

(OSTEND regards CHILDLIKE for a moment, then strides from the room.)

22

DOOBEE watches but does not follow OSTEND. Her footfalls fade. Sensing he is the focus of their collective regard, DOOBEE turns to THE MORTALLY ILL.

DOOBEE: I'm afraid /

(They pity him. Their animals fidget.)

Always / always afraid /

(He ponders, then rants.)

NOT OF THE WOMAN / NOT OF THE WOMAN / YOU THINK I'M AFRAID OF THE WOMAN /

(He tosses his head with contempt.)

It's not the woman / it's not the woman makes me afraid /

(He fathoms. He frowns.)

It's in the room now / the thing that makes me afraid /

(He creates a thin smile.)

She's the same / she's equally afraid / oh yes / for all her /

(He pulls a face.)

Call it what you like / her /

(He shakes his head.)

Supreme /

(He bites his lip.)

EQUALLY AFRAID /

(He resolves.)

I'd better go / she's on her own / it isn't fair / some damp room / cracked mirrors / squalid bed / and it's already there / it went in with her / like a dog / it runs ahead / then turns to look at you / sometimes we hardly dare /

(He is agonized.)

Touch /

(THE MORTALLY ILL suffer with DOOBEE. He makes to go again.)

I WISH I COULD SAY IT SIMPLY /

(They seem to sway as tree tops in a wind. DOOBEE seems fixed.)

CHILDLIKE: And then the door fell open /

(DOOBEE looks at CHILDLIKE.)

Why? /

(DOOBEE's mouth moves silently. He hoists the baggage and marches in the direction taken by OSTEND. THE MORTALLY ILL, unsupervized, relapse into cascades of laughter.)

23

ATTO: Oh God /

WINDUS: Fuck / fuck /

CLING: Jesus /

SLUMP: Oh God /

(They choke and splutter, the dogs bark, the rabbits fidget.)

24

LOOS: Joyless and beautiful /

ALDRINGTON: Oh God /

MOMPER: Joyless /

BASIN: Her stripped /

(He chokes on the words.)

CLING: Jesus /

SLUMP: Oh God / oh God /

BASIN: Her stripped /

LOOS: Joyless /

BASIN: IMMENSITY /

(Each proposition intensifies the laughter.)

MOMPER: Joyless / I said /

(They heave and howl, rendering the faint whine of the mobile bed inaudible. Consequently ARCHITECT has arrived and is stationary even as they rock and squeal. Slowly, they become aware of her presence. They fall silent. They are both embarrassed and afraid.)

25

ARCHITECT: They went up /

(A dog mews.)

Did they? /

(THE MORTALLY ILL are stiff with apprehension.)

To the room? /

(Their reluctance makes her vehement.)

THE DESIGNATED ROOM? /

PORTSLADE: We think so / yes /

ARCHITECT: THE ROOM WHICH / AS A CONSEQUENCE OF BEING DESIGNATED THEIRS / BECOMES THEIR ROOM? /

PORTSLADE: Yes /

ARCHITECT: *(For her own pleasure.)* THEY WENT UP TO THEIR ROOM /

(She meditates. They tremble.)

Six words I think / yes / six / six words / all single syllables / say them now / the six words /

(THE MORTALLY ILL, accustomed to her methods, satisfy ARCHITECT.)

Good /

(She frowns.)

Good / considering how tired you are / standing when you would much prefer / I know / to be lying on your beds / but these words are / oh / so / so /

(She marvels. She seizes on an idea.)

AND SHE PRECEDED HIM /

(She bites her lip.)

DID SHE? / DID SHE? / DID SHE GO FIRST? /

CHILDLIKE: Yes /

ARCHITECT: UP / UP / UP TO THEIR ROOM /

CHILDLIKE: Yes /

ARCHITECT: UP TO THEIR ROOM / AND SHE WENT FIRST /

ATTO: He carried the cases /

ARCHITECT: He carried the cases / yes /

CHILDLIKE: *(Serving ARCHITECT.)* AND SHE WENT FIRST /

ARCHITECT: *(Simultaneously ravished and tortured.)* Describe it /

CHILDLIKE: Describe it? /

ARCHITECT: DESCRIBE IT / YES / THE ASCENT OF THE STAIRS /

(The animals whimper.)

I know you're tired / I know how tired you are /

(Her face is shaped by despair.)

DESCRIBE THE WOMAN ON THE STAIRS / THE EFFECT OF THE STAIRS ON THE WOMAN /

(THE MORTALLY ILL look to CHILDLIKE to satisfy ARCHITECT.)

26

CHILDLIKE: The common form of the erotic consists in some oscillation of the hips /

ARCHITECT: Why common? /

CHILDLIKE: Lifting / tilting / gyrating the hips /

ARCHITECT: What's common about it? /

CHILDLIKE: *(Only briefly distracted.)* As if inviting copulation /

(THE MORTALLY ILL suffocate their giggles.)

Yet simultaneously withholding it /

ARCHITECT: What renders an action common / or uncommon / is the discernment that is brought to it / surely? /

(CHILDLIKE compresses its lips.)

The rather few positions a human body might adopt / its limited repertoire / need not diminish its capacity for creating / in the one privileged to contemplate it / breathless wonder / is breathless wonder common? /

CHILDLIKE: No / yes / no / I /

ARCHITECT: IT IS NOT COMMON /

CHILDLIKE: No / not common / possibly / not common and /

ARCHITECT: IT IS NOT COMMON AND I AM RIGHT /

CHILDLIKE: *(Browbeaten.)* Yes /

ARCHITECT: *(In a surge of pain.)* THE SKIRT TIGHT ON MY MOTHER'S ARSE / HER EXTENDED THIGH / HER LIFTED HIP / AND HIM / AND HIM /

(She cries out.)

HIS WONDER ARRIVING AGAIN /

(She shudders. THE MORTALLY ILL utter in unison.)

MORTALLY ILL: AND THEN THE DOOR FELL OPEN /

ARCHITECT: WHY? / WHY? /

(The heaving of ARCHITECT's body subsides. In the silence, her deep sobbing. The electric motor whines. ARCHITECT departs. THE MORTALLY ILL seem drained of strength and support one another as they limp from the room. CHILDLIKE hangs back, observing them.)

27

CHILDLIKE: Brutal / if only she was /

28

CHILDLIKE: Mild her hurting /

29

CHILDLIKE: Mild / and as a consequence / they erode / they do not die /

(It skips.)

When dying is the point / I know / I was dying in the womb / hereditary defects / cross infections / unknown blood groups / impossible to save me / consensus of the specialists / absurd to try / my mother was relieved / a one-eyed hermaphrodite / not to everybody's taste / but the expected / the predicted / the desired / oh / the sheer frustration / I failed to die /

(It laughs. It skips.)

Still I / still I /

(It is suddenly still.)

HAUNT THE GATE /

(It seems bemused.)

And they rush by / the actors / footballers / astronauts / their plane crashes / their lost battles with tumours / I'm shoved aside / I'm sick / I say / I always was / as far as mortal sickness goes I'm over-qualified /

(It reflects.)

No / she hurts in a tepid way / Miss Architect /

30

OSTEND enters. Her fingers twitch against her sides.

OSTEND: I fell three floors /

31

CHILDLIKE looks puzzled.

OSTEND: Metaphorically / three floors /

(She laughs. Shortly, with a toss of her head.)

I was not / however / impaled on the railings /

(DOOBEE appears, with the baggage.)

Was I? /

(DOOBEE shakes his head.)

Metaphorically impaled? /

DOOBEE: You were not /

OSTEND: I was not / I was not /

(She gazes on DOOBEE.)

DOOBEE: I'll put the bags in the car /

OSTEND: Darling /

(DOOBEE is half-shy of her.)

Darling /

(He goes out. OSTEND plucks her gloves.)

I forgot the layout of the rooms / the landings / half-landings / and so on / it was only when I got inside the /

(She falters.)

What? / what shall we call it? / the museum / I recognized / whose room it was /

(She moves her fingers anxiously.)

And the car /

CHILDLIKE: Brown car /

OSTEND: The car / when I looked out the window / was parked / oh /

(She shakes her head.)

As if we had colluded in this / this / what shall we call it? / archaeology / the car was parked in exactly the same spot /

(She laughs, unrealistically. CHILDLIKE, as if delighted by her account, utters.)

CHILDLIKE: OFF-WHITE UPHOLSTERY /

(OSTEND looks at CHILDLIKE for some moments.)

OSTEND: Tell my daughter / I fell three floors /

CHILDLIKE: Three floors? /

OSTEND: Metaphorically / the dolls / the toys / the little bed / three floors of memory / but then / I stopped / as it were / in mid-air /

(She tightens her lips.)

And Mr Doobee being there /

(She is adamant.)

I was comforted /

(She lets the idea hang in the air. DOOBEE appears.)

DOOBEE: Bags in the car /

OSTEND: *(Her eyes on CHILDLIKE still.)* Darling /

(She turns to go with DOOBEE.)

CHILDLIKE: THE DOOR FELL OPEN / WHY? /

(OSTEND stops. She turns to face CHILDLIKE.)

OSTEND: You know why /

(She injures CHILDLIKE with her gaze, then departs.)

CHILDLIKE: I DON'T / I DON'T KNOW WHY /

(The whine of the electric motor announces ARCHITECT's appearance.)

ARCHITECT: Don't let them go /

CHILDLIKE: *(Instinctively obedient.)* DON'T GO /

ARCHITECT: No / follow them /

CHILDLIKE: Follow them? /

ARCHITECT: THEY MAY NOT GO /

(CHILDLIKE hastens after OSTEND.)

CHILDLIKE: NOT TO GO /

(As CHILDLIKE's voice travels from outside, PORTSLADE enters, pale and clasping a pet.)

PORTSLADE: Belinda's dying /

ARCHITECT: *(Supremely indifferent.)* Belinda? /

PORTSLADE: Belinda / yes /

(ARCHITECT manoeuvres the bed closer to the door.)

ARCHITECT: *(Calling to CHILDLIKE.)* BEG THEM / BEG /

PORTSLADE: On the first floor / was a dancer /

ARCHITECT: *(To PORTSLADE.)* He can't hear me /

PORTSLADE: Survived a plane crash /

ARCHITECT: Can he? /

PORTSLADE: In a jungle /

ARCHITECT: *(Calling to CHILDLIKE.)* LIE DOWN IN FRONT OF THE CAR /

(ARCHITECT strains to hear the result of her instructions.)

PORTSLADE: That Belinda /

(ARCHITECT ignores PORTSLADE. Her face is a mask of tension. After some seconds have elapsed, DOOBEE walks in.)

32

DOOBEE: *(Patiently.)* Your mother senses the futility of persisting with a reconciliation which /

ARCHITECT: It wasn't you /

DOOBEE: Is so one-sided /

ARCHITECT: Was it? / It wasn't you /

DOOBEE: She wonders therefore if you would consent to /

ARCHITECT: You must have been a boy /

DOOBEE: Her staying in a hotel? /

33

ARCHITECT: He was obscure / possibly because I consigned him to obscurity / or equally possibly / his obscurity was literal / he was unilluminated / the time of day / the time of year / it was January / and an afternoon / in any case / I knew / by intuition / his utter insignificance / you too are insignificant / I am not critical / I am not denigrating you /

PORTSLADE: She doesn't want a doctor / Belinda / she wants a priest /

DOOBEE: My significance / if I have any / is better understood / I daresay / by your mother /

PORTSLADE: Unlikely / I said / you will be satisfied on that score / but I would ask anyway /

ARCHITECT: No priest /

PORTSLADE: No priest / that is what I said you'd say /

ARCHITECT: *(To PORTSLADE.)* Waiting for the appearance of a priest merely delays the dying /

PORTSLADE: I have observed that /

ARCHITECT: Whereas / convinced no priest can possibly appear /

PORTSLADE: They hasten on their way /

ARCHITECT: Say I am adamant /

PORTSLADE: I will do /

(PORTSLADE shuffles, stops.)

Oh / and she says thank you /

(He departs. DOOBEE gazes at ARCHITECT, who cannot observe him.)

DOOBEE: To the extent that / on that particular / and terrible day /

ARCHITECT: Not terrible /

DOOBEE: *(Deflected.)* Not terrible? /

(He fathoms ARCHITECT's dissent.)

Not terrible / that day? /

(She is silent.)

Forgive me / I allowed myself / in an unguarded moment / to be conventional in describing as terrible a day in which a child / flinging herself from a window three storeys from the ground / became impaled on railings / I am properly corrected for my presumption / you / and you alone / are qualified to say how terrible the day was / or if it was not terrible at all /

(He is satisfied.)

As for my insignificance / and the insignificance of him who sat beside your mother in the rear seats of the car / you may be right there too / but in describing him as obscure / unilluminated / I think / was your description / I wonder if you have not yourself indulged a prejudice / as if all afternoons were dark / which is not strictly true / whilst it was winter / there was snow on the ground / thin snow / and snow both intensifies light / and reflects it / so / far from being lost in the penumbra / his face may have been lurid / I don't know /

ARCHITECT: You were not there /

DOOBEE: I was not there / but even so /

ARCHITECT: You were not there /

DOOBEE: No /

ARCHITECT: You were a child /

DOOBEE: I was /

ARCHITECT: A hundred miles away /

DOOBEE: Or more /

ARCHITECT: A hundred / two hundred / and blissfully unaware of /

(The sound of a car horn. Instinctively DOOBEE goes to obey its summons.)

DOOBEE: She's calling me /

ARCHITECT: Yes / but you need not go /

DOOBEE: *(Puzzled.)* Need not go? /

ARCHITECT: So swiftly /

DOOBEE: Not go so swiftly / no / I suppose I need not /

ARCHITECT: I have to know if /

(The horn repeated. The sound acts like a shock to DOOBEE.)

DON'T GO /

(Her command stops DOOBEE in his tracks.)

Going up to your room /

(The phrase causes ARCHITECT to frown.)

Going up /

(She frets. Her face is strained from the extent of her concentration.)

GOING UP TO YOUR ROOM YOU /

34

OSTEND enters. The sound of her heels on the tiles alerts ARCHITECT, who emits a single, stricken sound, half-sob, half-jeer. OSTEND stops.)

OSTEND: A situation is developing /

DOOBEE: *(Sensing a rebuke.)* Yes / yes / I /

OSTEND: A situation of extraordinary stupidity / you know how I hate that / to be in stupid situations /

DOOBEE: Yes /

OSTEND: Especially when the stupidity is imposed on me by someone else /

DOOBEE: Yes /

OSTEND: If I wish to be inveigled into a stupid situation / I will contrive the circumstances myself /

DOOBEE: Yes / I was explaining to /

OSTEND: I am talking / I am talking / Doobee /

DOOBEE: Yes /

OSTEND: *(Patiently.)* I am seated in the car / not in the rear seats / in the front / the one-eyed individual who claims to enjoy arguing has draped itself across the bonnet and is staring at me through the glass /

DOOBEE: I'm so sorry /

OSTEND: This might be tolerable / but I discover / happening to glance in the mirror / we have acquired an audience / at every window / these faces / no / not faces / masks / masks of morbid curiosity /

DOOBEE: I am so sorry /

OSTEND: *(Swiftly.)* WHY? / WHY SORRY / DOOBEE? / DID THE SITUATION ORIGINATE IN YOU? /

DOOBEE: *(Stung into a stern defence.)* Obviously it did not originate in me / but I should have acted in such a way as to prevent this situation / any situation / developing which discomforts or embarrasses you /

(OSTEND admires DOOBEE.)

OSTEND: Yes / perhaps you should / now / bring in the bags again /

DOOBEE: But we /

OSTEND: The bags / darling /

DOOBEE: The hotel in the village / we /

OSTEND: DO NOT ARGUE / KISS / KISS /

(The urgency of OSTEND's plea draws DOOBEE to her lips.)

Don't argue /

DOOBEE: No /

(They resume the kiss.)

OSTEND: Don't / don't /

DOOBEE: Never / never argue /

(DOOBEE frees himself from OSTEND and goes out. OSTEND is thoughtful. ARCHITECT gazes.)

35

ARCHITECT: Beautifully joyless /

36

ARCHITECT: Her thighs so spread /

37

ARCHITECT: And this / oh / this immensity / of hair / of flesh /

(She wonders.)

If she had only said /

(She strains to imagine.)

The joy / darling / the joy in this /

(She tightens her mouth.)

A child of six might /

(DOOBEE enters, with the baggage. He stops.)

Possibly / have understood that this flayed animal / all hanging out her clothes / vivisected / posed for an atrocity / was in the throes of something adult / ugly obviously / but so much is ugly that is adult / a child of six already knows / instead /

(She stops. DOOBEE, uncomfortable, starts to move.)

She gazed /

(DOOBEE stops.)

Beautiful and joyless her grey gaze / as if / as if /

(ARCHITECT ceases at the point of her speculation.)

If you're not happy with the single bed / the woman called Belinda / once a dancer / has no further use for hers / she's dead /

(DOOBEE casts a glance at OSTEND, and proceeds to the staircase.)

38

OSTEND: I so nearly fled /

ARCHITECT: I stopped you /

OSTEND: You stopped me /

ARCHITECT: For which I know you'll thank me /

OSTEND: I think so /

ARCHITECT: If not today /

OSTEND: Tomorrow / probably /

ARCHITECT: To come / and then to go /

OSTEND: Silly /

ARCHITECT: I want my mother to know peace /

OSTEND: Thank you /

ARCHITECT: To walk in quiet ways / with lowered head / her hands disposed as the wind disposes them /

OSTEND: Penitent /

ARCHITECT: If necessary / yes /

(OSTEND declines to engage her daughter, and turns to follow DOOBEE.)

Mr Doobee called the day terrible /

(OSTEND stops.)

Is that how it was described to him? /

39

OSTEND judges her riposte.

OSTEND: I have a sense that in recalling it for Mr Doobee's benefit / and I keep nothing from him / I should have emphasized the exquisite character of the thing that took place in the car that afternoon / and not its consequence /

(ARCHITECT, gazing away from OSTEND, who is not visible to her, is icily still. After a moment's consideration, OSTEND proceeds.)

But Mr Doobee is a sensitive man / uncommonly sensitive in one so young /

and if I impressed on him one form of the terrible / the terrible wonder a mother knew on those rear seats / he is perfectly capable of finding differently terrible the spectacle of her daughter spiked and writhing on that fence /

(The effort of articulation shakes OSTEND's resolution.)

I CAN / BELIEVE ME / LOWER MY HEAD / I CAN /

(She trembles.)

LOWER MY HEAD /

(Far from doing so, OSTEND tosses her head and marches away in the direction taken by DOOBEE. ARCHITECT is aware much of this has been observed. CHILDLIKE emerges from the obscurity of the doorway.)

40

ARCHITECT: The brown car /

CHILDLIKE: Hard /

ARCHITECT: Hard / was it? /

CHILDLIKE: And slippery /

ARCHITECT: Polished / I expect /

CHILDLIKE: Polished / certainly / but also wet / so whereas I had no difficulty in clambering on the bonnet / it was altogether harder maintaining my position there / the higher I climbed / the further I slid /

ARCHITECT: *(Inspired.)* The windscreen wipers /

CHILDLIKE: Yes /

ARCHITECT: Cling to the windscreen wipers /

CHILDLIKE: Exactly / exactly what I did / and all the time she glared at me /

ARCHITECT: To no effect /

CHILDLIKE: A peculiar proximity / on one side of the glass / a decaying queen / and on the other / a one-eyed monkey / one-eyed and half-dead /

ARCHITECT: You are not half-dead /

CHILDLIKE: The smell of steel / of petrol / and off-white upholstery /

(CHILDLIKE goes to leave, but stops.)

Beautifully kept / the brown car /

ARCHITECT: Yes /

CHILDLIKE: It rarely moves / I think / and surely / it has never crashed? /

ARCHITECT: Mr Doobee would know that /

(CHILDLIKE withdraws, thoughtfully.)

41

Two women of THE MORTALLY ILL enter, one with towels and basin, one with a jug of warm water. They hesitate.

WINDUS: All right / now? /

MOMPER: Is now all right? /

42

ARCHITECT: I am not sure /

WINDUS: We know you're not /

ARCHITECT: I am not sure if I should be washed /

MOMPER: *(Proceeding to the BASIN.)* It's the ethical dimension /

(WINDUS folds down ARCHITECT's gown.)

ARCHITECT: Not hot /

WINDUS: Never hot / darling /

ARCHITECT: Tepid /

WINDUS: It is tepid /

(As MOMPER fills the BASIN from the jug.)

Isn't it / darling? / tepid? /

MOMPER: The ethical dimension / creates a dilemma / not only for you /

WINDUS: *(Preparing ARCHITECT.)* Towel /

MOMPER: *(Approaching with the BASIN.)* Also for us /

(WINDUS arranges the towel. MOMPER attends.)

There is hygiene /

(WINDUS squeezes a sponge.)

Which is not ambiguous /

(WINDUS proceeds to wash ARCHITECT's naked back.)

And there is love /

WINDUS: Tepid enough? /

MOMPER: We wash ourselves / that's hygiene /

WINDUS: Arm /

MOMPER: But when another washes us /

WINDUS: Hand /

MOMPER: We can't help wondering /

WINDUS: Back /

MOMPER: If we are loved enough /

WINDUS: Back of hand /

MOMPER: If they deserve this /

WINDUS: *(Taking the towel.)* Cover up now / cover up /

MOMPER: *(Placing the bowl on the floor.)* Intimacy /

(She proceeds to towel ARCHITECT's upper body.)

Intimacy must be earned /

(WINDUS exposes the lower part of ARCHITECT's body.)

I am saying / it might be preferable / to be abandoned to one's dirt /

WINDUS: More than tepid now /

MOMPER: Than be offered up for loveless washing /

WINDUS: *(Sweetly.)* These little feet /

MOMPER: I don't know / I am only thinking / is that the ethical dimension? /

WINDUS: *(Sponging.)* Child's feet /

MOMPER: And hands /

WINDUS: So pretty / darling /

MOMPER: After the accident / I think I'm right in saying this / only the extremities ceased to grow /

WINDUS: So pretty /

MOMPER: Dry / dry now /

WINDUS: *(Replacing the cover on ARCHITECT.)* All done /

MOMPER: And off we go /

(MOMPER is shocked to find her wrist is tightly gripped by ARCHITECT. She casts a glance at WINDUS, who is chilled.)

ARCHITECT: Say a cruel thing /

(MOMPER is puzzled. Her gaze stays on WINDUS, who bites her lip.)

MOMPER: *(To give herself time.)* A cruel thing? / a cruel thing? / what kind of thing? /

(ARCHITECT declines to help MOMPER.)

That hurts /

(THE MORTALLY ILL are seen to enter the room, holding or leading their pets. They gather, inquisitive, trembling.)

All right I'll / that hurts / that so hurts /

(She appeals to WINDUS with her eyes. The pain inspires her.)

THROW YOURSELF OUT OF THE WINDOW /

(ARCHITECT's grip tightens.)

ONTO THE RAILINGS / GO ON / GO /

(MOMPER winces.)

ARCHITECT: Not cruel /

MOMPER: *(Horrified.)* Not cruel? / that kind of thing / though? /

(She regards the audience.)

Along the lines of /

(ARCHITECT hurts her more.)

SO YOUR MOTHER HAD HER LEGS OPEN / THAT'LL TEACH LITTLE GIRLS TO GO /

(She shakes her head in despair.)

Spying on /

(She is hurt more and utters shrilly.)

FUCKING IN A CAR / THAT'S SOMETHING YOU'LL NEVER KNOW /

(She is hurt even more.)

IN A CAR OR OUT OF ONE /

(She weeps as ARCHITECT's grip tightens.)

THE PISS RAN DOWN HER LEGS SHE WAS SO /

(MOMPER cannot proceed. ARCHITECT frees her wrist. MOMPER nurses her injury, unable to lift her eyes from the floor. A tremor runs through the MORTALLY ILL. The pets whimper. The sound of

the electric motor precedes the departure of ARCHITECT. A strained silence holds the MORTALLY ILL in suspension for some time.)

43

WINDUS: *(Going to MOMPER.)* Lie down / darling / lie down /

(MOMPER, bursting into tears, runs from the room.)

44

THE MORTALLY ILL, sensing it is safe to do so, begin to laugh, at first guiltily, then without control. The dogs bark in sympathy. When at last they cease, they are transformed.

LOOS: The door did not fall open / let us be scrupulous in our use of language /

ATTO: The handle was depressed / and from the inside /

LOOS: The inside / certainly /

ATTO: Nothing was accidental / therefore /

LOOS: The sequence of events / beginning with the opening of the door /

ATTO: And ending with the impaling of a child upon a fence /

LOOS: Was at every stage / deliberate /

ATTO: And must be talked of in the active / and not in the passive / tense /

(They are quite still. CHILDLIKE frowns with concentration.)

CHILDLIKE: It follows / possibly you are not aware of this / that once we admit the door did not fall open /

LOOS: We have admitted it /

CHILDLIKE: You have admitted it / in which case what I am about to say is possibly superfluous / you simultaneously commit yourselves / not only to describing this event / but to understanding the reasons which determined it /

(It is satisfied by the prospect.)

Dense and complex argument lies ahead of us / scholarly and dialectical / which /

(It is thrilled.)

Given our state of health / we cannot expect to see the end of /

(It is exultant.)

So / taking the single proposition we now regard as self-evident /

(He proposes the subject with gravity.)

SHE OPENED THE DOOR /

(He bites his lip in his excitement. He looks from one to the other.)

SHE / OPENED / THE / DOOR /

(Like a besotted teacher, he poses his question.)

Why? /

(THE MORTALLY ILL frown with concentration. The pets mew.)

45

DOOBEE wanders in, hands in pockets, preoccupied.

SLUMP: *(From the back.)* Caroline's been sick again /

ALDRINGTON: Oh God /

BASIN: Oh God / darling /

ALDRINGTON: Caroline /

SLUMP: Fuck / oh fuck /

PORTSLADE: All right / all right /

ALDRINGTON: *(Assisting CLING.)* Caroline /

ATTO: Steady / sweetheart /

(THE MORTALLY ILL, to the accompaniment of wailing pets, shuffle out, watched by DOOBEE with a mixture of horror and disgust.)

CHILDLIKE: *(Interpreting DOOBEE's expression.)* There are no nurses here /

(DOOBEE frowns.)

They have a tendency to interfere with natural processes / dying for example /

(DOOBEE stares.)

Medical intervention / misplaced philanthropy / and so on /

(He taunts DOOBEE.)

Only adds years to lives which /

(He is mischievous.)

Argue with this if you want to /

(He smiles.)

Are worthless even to those condemned to struggle with the decaying remnants of them /

(He fails to provoke DOOBEE.)

This is Miss Architect's opinion / you might want to disagree / but then / you have whole life / whereas we / we are fragments /

(DOOBEE looks at CHILDLIKE.)

Whole life / and a car /

(CHILDLIKE gazes on DOOBEE. DOOBEE shifts uneasily.)

DOOBEE: Yes /

CHILDLIKE: A brown car /

DOOBEE: Brown / or to be precise / umber /

CHILDLIKE: *(Pondering this.)* Umber /

(It plays with the word.)

Umber / umber car / umber with /

(It is triumphant.)

OFF-WHITE UPHOLSTERY /

(It smiles.)

I cannot say I have examined it closely / but crawling on it /

(Its smile deepens.)

I gained the impression that / despite its age / this umber car is in perfect order / rust-free / uncorroded / immune / it appears / immune to decay /

(Its eyes taunt DOOBEE.)

I imagine / sitting in the rear seats / it seems like only yesterday /

(It stops. It hangs its head, a different provocation.)

She /

(It breaks the tension.)

DECAY / THE FIRST LAW OF EXISTENCE / DID SHE NOT SAY? /

(CHILDLIKE seems to waver as OSTEND idly enters the room. She stops. Without lifting its head, CHILDLIKE flees.)

46

DOOBEE: She desires me /

(OSTEND drifts back and forth, and stops.)

Not for my appearance / nor my voice / nor anything I say /

(OSTEND resumes walking.)

Strictly speaking / who I am plays little or no part in it / I am insignificant / or to put it another way / the huge significance I have acquired exists without reference to me / this kind of desire is the worst / I don't think we can stay /

(OSTEND regards DOOBEE.)

Can we? / how can we stay? /

(And regards him longer.)

You want to stay /

(DOOBEE purses his lips.)

I don't / I don't / but you do / you want to stay so who /

OSTEND: Doobee /

DOOBEE: Cares for my opinion? /

OSTEND: Doobee /

DOOBEE: *(Petulantly.)* A SITUATION IS DEVELOPING /

(He fixes her with a stare.)

A situation which / I am reluctant to say this /

OSTEND: Say it /

DOOBEE: I hate to argue /

OSTEND: We both do /

DOOBEE: YOU CAN ONLY HAVE ANTICIPATED /

(His fingers work.)

And which / kiss me / delights or gratifies you / kiss me / darling /

(OSTEND is thoughtful.)

OSTEND: We'll go /

DOOBEE: *(Transformed.)* I'll get the bags down / kiss me /

OSTEND: And if some dwarf clings to the bonnet /

DOOBEE: I'll throw him off / kiss me / kiss me / I'm so /

OSTEND: Fetch the bags / Doobee /

DOOBEE: Kiss me /

OSTEND: *(Brutally.)* NO / NO / NO KISSING / NO /

(DOOBEE stares at OSTEND. Swiftly he smacks her face. She smarts. Immediately his head hangs, his hands make fists at his sides. A single deep sob comes from him. He stares at the floor.)

DOOBEE: There have been priests / and these priests /

(He suffers. He lifts his gaze to OSTEND.)

knew more of God / than God Himself did /

(OSTEND frowns.)

not a good thing / not a good thing / probably /

(He turns to go. She pulls him strongly to her and grasping him by the back of his head with one hand, kisses him firmly, not letting his mouth part from hers even as the sound of the electric bed announces their imminent discovery.)

47

The mobile bed cruises into the room. ARCHITECT's routine posture deprives her of any visual means of establishing the presence of the lovers. Nevertheless she senses it. The bed stops. DOOBEE squirms. OSTEND holds him in the kiss.

ARCHITECT: Smell you /

(The lovers are stock still.)

48

ARCHITECT: Smell you / and you might think / in this miasma of corruption nothing could be distinguished / but all would be suffocated in the odour of the sick / an odour thick as furnishing / draperies of nausea / tapestries of stench /

(She is exquisitely provocative.)

But there is rot and rot /

(She insinuates her cruelty.)

Rot and rot / and some so sweet / oh / they smother putrefactions that might dare compete / the decay of love / really / I can scarcely breathe /

(ARCHITECT smiles. OSTEND, not removing her mouth from DOOBEE's, with her free hand begins to remove his clothes. He is discomforted but dares not protest. Acutely sensitive to sound, ARCHITECT is fascinated but wary.)

I think too much / that is the worst pain of paralysis / at least for me /

(She frowns, listening.)

Whereas as a child I thought hardly at all / and my life was shaped / cruelly some would say / by spontaneity /

(Having removed DOOBEE's jacket, OSTEND with a deliberate gesture, flings it over the mobile bed. It is registered by ARCHITECT.)

Now I think too much / nothing is obvious /

(She detects OSTEND stripping the shirt from DOOBEE's back.)

What might be clear as daylight to another is / oh / a sunless maze of discrepancy to me / for example /

(The shirt is flung on the bed. ARCHITECT registers its arrival. OSTEND proceeds to unbutton DOOBEE's trouser. Again ARCHITECT senses, with a frown of concentration, what transpires beyond her field of vision. DOOBEE suffers but does not resist.)

The nakedness of Mr Doobee /

(DOOBEE's trousers fall.)

Whilst representing itself as a gift /

(OSTEND nimbly slips off his underwear.)

Cannot be a thing freely and wholeheartedly donated / is any gift? /

(DOOBEE is naked.)

For example /

(ARCHITECT creates a small and insincere laugh.)

I keep saying for example / excuse my classroom manner /

(She smiles.)

It might be apology /

(The last word acts as a closing bracket to OSTEND's long kiss.)

49

OSTEND walks out, her footsteps disappearing into silence.

DOOBEE: I'm not a gift /

(He squirms.)

I'm not a gift / a gift is given / I can't be given / I'm not property /

ARCHITECT: But naked / you are naked / Mr Doobee? /

DOOBEE: Naked / yes / naked but not property /

(Suddenly.)

Not entirely naked / I have socks on / I have shoes /

ARCHITECT: Socks spoil nakedness /

DOOBEE: I agree /

(He is uncomfortable.)

ARCHITECT: Remove the socks then / Mr Doobee /

DOOBEE: Remove them? / I could remove them / I could do that / yes /

(He fails to act.)

Alternatively / I could dress /

ARCHITECT: Don't dress / Mr Doobee /

(DOOBEE tightens his mouth.)

DOOBEE: Everybody tells me what to do /

ARCHITECT: Show me what my mother loves / show me /

(He is recalcitrant.)

SHOW ME /

(ARCHITECT is pitiful.)

SHOW /

(DOOBEE affects reluctance.)

DOOBEE: I do not like it here /

ARCHITECT: No /

DOOBEE: It is a vile and sordid place /

ARCHITECT: Is it? /

DOOBEE: You know it is /

(ARCHITECT is coy.)

If I do what you ask / you must not hinder our departure / you must let us go /

(ARCHITECT is taut, unyielding.)

Promise /

ARCHITECT: NO SHOES OR SOCKS / DOOBEE /

DOOBEE: Promise /

(She frowns in her chagrin.)

Promise /

ARCHITECT: *(Crossly.)* YOU PROMISE /

DOOBEE: I do /

(He tugs at his shoe laces.)

Now you /

(The shoes clatter. He strips away his socks and tosses them down.)

NOW YOU /

ARCHITECT: *(Archly.)* Did you know / if when you make a promise / at the same time / you curl up your toes / the promise is not binding? /

DOOBEE: Nothing below your neck works / Miss Architect / does it? / so /

ARCHITECT: *(Shrill with frustration.)* SHOW / SHOW /

(He is adamant.)

I promise /

(She is innocent as a child.)

Promise /

(DOOBEE, with the slightest anxiety, walks from behind the mobile bed and entering the line of her sight, presents himself to ARCHITECT. She studies him with a sense of wonder. The wonder endures. She is agonized by longing. At last she puts an end to her own suffering by flight. The electric motor whines as the bed sweeps out of the room. DOOBEE, also in a condition of disbelief, awakes to his own precarious state.)

DOOBEE: My clothes / my clothes /

(He goes to run after the bed, sees his socks and shoes, grabs them up, and follows ARCHITECT. A sound of wailing from an upstairs room insinuates itself, and its pity draws OSTEND into the room, as if she recognized its tone.)

50

CHILDLIKE appears discreetly, and observes the concentration of OSTEND.

CHILDLIKE: It's Marjorie /

(OSTEND turns to observe CHILDLIKE.)

Caroline is dying / but it's Marjorie making the noise /

(OSTEND looks blankly at CHILDLIKE.)

Marjorie and Caroline are friends /

(OSTEND's indifference encourages CHILDLIKE.)

Says Marjorie / without Caroline life's meaningless /

(It delays its account, gazing at OSTEND.)

Marjorie says she wishes she'd gone first /

(Pause.)

And so on /

(Pause.)

Caroline and Marjorie have animals /

(Pause.)

Caroline has a spaniel /

(Pause.)

Marjorie has a bird /

(Pause.)

What about my bird / says Marjorie / when I'm gone? /

(Pause.)

Etcetera /

(Pause. CHILDLIKE emits a strange laugh. Its head hangs. It shakes it. DOOBEE enters, a bag in each hand. He looks at CHILDLIKE, who leaves. DOOBEE goes to carry the bags ot the car, and stops.)

DOOBEE: Actually / I don't want to /

(He lingers, then turns a glance to OSTEND. OSTEND merely regards him. DOOBEE is intimidated, turns and walks a few more steps. He stops. He puts down the bags, decisively.)

I don't want to go /

(OSTEND looks at the back of DOOBEE's head.)

OSTEND: It was you who /

DOOBEE: Yes /

51

OSTEND: Darling /

DOOBEE: No /

OSTEND: Darling /

DOOBEE: No /

OSTEND: Darling /

(Now DOOBEE just shakes his head, compulsively. They are still for a long time.)

Doobee / I don't drive / as you well know /

So if you don't / how can I go? /

(DOOBEE denies her a reply. OSTEND walks a few paces, stops, and opens her mouth to speak. She is interrupted on her first syllable.)

DOOBEE: No /

(OSTEND closes her lips.)

I'm saying no / I'm saying no and only no / in saying no I'm saying everything that could be said / but which / in actual fact / need not be said / since the outcome is determined / and is not susceptible to modification/ interrogation / ratification / or any other thing /

(He tilts up his chin.)

So / no /

(OSTEND seems to contemplate arguing, but instead turns on her heel. She goes to march from the room but is stopped by the sound of DOOBEE's sudden and mournful weeping, a tone counter-pointed by the wails which travel down from above. She returns a few paces. She regards him, not without sympathy.)

OSTEND: Being mine / and being hers / is it very different / Doobee? /

(DOOBEE, in conformity with his decision, shakes his head fiercely. Again OSTEND goes to leave.)

DOOBEE: *(From the depths of his soul.)* I KNOW / I KNOW / I KNOW MY INSIGNIFICANCE /

(OSTEND is moved by DOOBEE's sacrifice.)

OSTEND: Darling /

DOOBEE: No /

OSTEND: Darling /

DOOBEE: No /

OSTEND: *(An adieu.)* Darling /

(OSTEND looks at DOOBEE with an expression almost maternal in the depths of its love. DOOBEE squirms, and in his discomfort plucks up the bags without knowing what to do with them. He dithers, half-extending one to OSTEND, and when she declines to relieve him, going as if to place it in the car. At the door he stops, seems to ponder the purpose of his decision, and returns. He places the bag at OSTEND's feet. He stares for a moment at the floor, and then decisively carries his own upstairs.)

52

OSTEND gazes at the bag, her fingers working in her agony. Again, CHILDLIKE's presence is intuited by her. She turns her head.

CHILDLIKE: Driving / anyone can do it /

OSTEND: Including you? /

(CHILDLIKE lifts its shoulders in a self-deprecating gesture.)

CHILDLIKE: It's a big car /

OSTEND: It's a big car / and you're a dwarf /

CHILDLIKE: Norman tested racing cars /

OSTEND: Norman? /

CHILDLIKE: In his youth /

OSTEND: Ask Norman if he would be so kind as to /

CHILDLIKE: Norman's bed-ridden /

(OSTEND looks cruelly at CHILDLIKE, who is not rebuked.)

Some would say / not me / it's a pity you don't drive the brown car yourself /

(It returns her critical stare.)

The brown car with the off-white upholstery /

(It is coy.)

Not me / not me / however / if I know one thing about cars / I know this /

(It seems to experience a spasm.)

THE FRONT SEATS AREN'T THE BACK /

(It laughs, as if something were liberated in it.)

The door did not fall open / the handle was depressed /

(It gazes at OSTEND. She is unperturbed.)

OSTEND: That's obvious /

CHILDLIKE: Yes / so I have always argued / the handle was depressed / and from the inside /

OSTEND: By me /

CHILDLIKE: BY YOU / BY YOU / YES /

(CHILDLIKE seems gratified. OSTEND, by contrast, is blasé. CHILDLIKE stares at the floor, its three fingers compressed in its palm and frowning. OSTEND observes its efforts.)

And yet / and yet /

(It raises its eyes to OSTEND.)

As so often with these things / what once seemed crucially significant / once it is established / fails to bring us one step nearer the explanation we so desperately seek /

OSTEND: Explanation for what? /

(CHILDLIKE frowns.)

What is it that requires explaining? /

(CHILDLIKE looks into OSTEND as if it might read her thoughts. The sound of the electric motor announces the return of ARCHITECT.)

53

CHILDLIKE: OFF-WHITE / OFF-WHITE / OFF-WHITE UPHOLSTERY /

(It runs out as the electric bed cruises into the room and stops.)

54

ARCHITECT: Thank you for Doobee /

(OSTEND chooses not to reply.)

In this man / extraordinary depth / breathtaking complexity /

(She gazes as if ravished.)

OSTEND: *(Coolly.)* I could never have kept Doobee / his reverence for women requires some exercise of pity / I might have leapt ten floors / still I think you /

(OSTEND contemplates her own tactlessness.)

You would have held the greater fascination /

(The women are still, fortified.)

ARCHITECT: Show me yourself /

(OSTEND is hesitant.)

I want to see how loss describes itself in you /

(OSTEND bides her time.)

SHOW ME THE LOSS / MOTHER / COME INTO VIEW /

(In her own time, OSTEND walks round the bed and stands for ARCHITECT's inspection. Her posture does not yield to scrutiny.)

OSTEND: Doobee /

ARCHITECT: *(Pleading.)* Shh /

(OSTEND submits to further study.)

OSTEND: *(At the end of her patience.)* Doobee knew everything there is to know /

ARCHITECT: Oh / shh /

(By way of reply to ARCHITECT's plea, OSTEND walks out of her vision.)

OSTEND: About gear-boxes / brake-linings / and so on /

(She plucks her gloves.)

Finding parts for old cars / not easy nowadays / rather few men / I think / know what lies beneath the bonnet / my father did / my dear father / he / with rolled-up sleeves he /

(She falters. In the silence, the distant sound of a dog in an upstairs room.)

ARCHITECT: Buy a new one /

55

The suggestion menaces OSTEND.

OSTEND: Buy a new car? /

(She affects nonchalance.)

But the old one is in perfect order / a speck of rust / the slightest blemish in the chrome / he / Doobee / not Doobee / not Doobee now / Doobee previously / he /

(She disciplines her thoughts.)

And the other three / devoted to its preservation / immediately they /

(She is assured.)

attended it / oh /

(She shakes her head.)

With cloths and fragrant polishes /

(She makes a slight gesture.)

My own decay I can't conceal / the car / however / might be perpetuated /

(ARCHITECT calculates.)

Endlessly /

(ARCHITECT frowns.)

Presumably /

ARCHITECT: The car is not a car /

OSTEND: Not a car? / what is it / then? /

(ARCHITECT's silences are deliberate.)

It sounds like a car / it smells like a car /

ARCHITECT: Yes /

OSTEND: It stops / and goes / like a car /

ARCHITECT: It has all the characteristics of a car /

OSTEND: So how can it be said /

ARCHITECT: *(Condescendingly.)* Shh /

OSTEND: Of a thing / which satisfies in all respects the terms of its definition /

ARCHITECT: Shh / shh /

OSTEND: *(With a spasm of resentment.)* DON'T HUSH ME / DON'T CHILD ME LIKE THAT / DON'T /

(ARCHITECT is gratified by OSTEND's frustration. OSTEND discovers a mild tone.)

That it is / notwithstanding it fulfils / and possibly surpasses / these exacting criteria /

(She stops. She laughs.)

It's not a car /

ARCHITECT: It's a temple /

OSTEND: It's a temple / yes /

ARCHITECT: And these men /

OSTEND: Whilst being men /

ARCHITECT: By all the usual /

OSTEND: Objective /

ARCHITECT: Usual and objective /

OSTEND: Criteria of maleness / masculinity /

ARCHITECT: Etcetera /

OSTEND: Are also /

ARCHITECT: Priests / scholars / doctors of theology / who practise their devotions on the back seats /

(They seem to share a moment of assent. OSTEND walks back into ARCHITECT's line of sight.)

So frayed the relic / so frantic the priest /

(They look into one another.)

Say sorry to me /

(The shape of OSTEND's shoulders suggests she is contemplating this, but ARCHITECT wilfully obliterates the prospect.)

Doobee says / hear Doobee / Doobee says my mouth is ten cunts / ten cunts tight / ten cunts deep /

(ARCHITECT glares at her mother, who lifts a hand to her, but seeing it is gloved, tears off the glove with her free hand and flings it to the floor.)

HEED DOOBEE /

(ARCHITECT engages the electric motor and swiftly glides from the room. OSTEND is left with her hand in the air.)

56

The sound of whimpering and mewing pets is heard.

ATTO: *(The first to enter.)* It's all over with Caroline /

OSTEND: Is it? /

ATTO: I couldn't watch / no more could Marjorie /

SLUMP: *(Entering.)* Oh God / oh God / Billy /

ATTO: *(To SLUMP.)* And Marjorie was like a sister to her / wasn't she? /

SLUMP: Oh God /

ATTO: A sister to Caroline? /

SLUMP: One by one we left / we didn't stay to see /

OSTEND: What? / what did you not stay to see? /

WINDUS: *(Entering.)* It's not over /

ATTO: *(Horrified.)* It's not? / it's not over? /

SLUMP: Oh God /

WINDUS: *(To BASIN, who enters.)* It's not over / is it / darling? /

BASIN: *(Disgusted.)* The noise /

WINDUS: The noise of it /

BASIN: *(Parodying his horror.)* This uuaagh / this uuaagh /

WINDUS: It's the vomiting that gets to me /

ATTO: And you liked Caroline /

BASIN: I liked Caroline /

WINDUS: Some can take it /

BASIN: Others can't / me / I can't /

SLUMP: Is anybody with her? /

WINDUS: Nobody /

ATTO: Nobody's with her /

BASIN: This uuaagh / this uuaagh /

SLUMP: Poor bloody Caroline /

ATTO: Oh dear / oh dear /

BASIN: Vomiting /

WINDUS: And dying /

ATTO: And not a soul /

WINDUS: Not even Marjorie /

ATTO: Nobody near /

57

CHILDLIKE: *(Entering.)* Marjorie's lying down /

(THE MORTALLY ILL look to CHILDLIKE.)

The collapse of Caroline has / inexorably resulted in the collapse of Marjorie /

(THE MORTALLY ILL sigh and groan in a spasm of sympathy. OSTEND goes to surge upstairs.)

PLEASE /

(CHILDLIKE's vehemence stops OSTEND.)

Don't violate her wretchedness / her perfect wretchedness / with your dubious sympathy /

OSTEND: It is not dubious /

CHILDLIKE: DO YOU KNOW CAROLINE? /

OSTEND: I don't know Caroline /

CHILDLIKE: YOU DON'T KNOW CAROLINE /

OSTEND: Neither Caroline nor Marjorie / I do not require to know them in order to /

CHILDLIKE: You are fraudulent /

(OSTEND senses the scrutiny of THE MORTALLY ILL.)

Here we die differently /

OSTEND: Alone /

CHILDLIKE: In unheated rooms / unconsoled / and undeceived /

(CHILDLIKE's single eye is fixed on OSTEND. To her own surprise, she suddenly dissolves into tears, heaving and sobbing. The pets respond, wailing and fidgeting. The MORTALLY ILL are uncomfortable but at the same time, prurient. They lean, they gather. Only the appearance of the electric bed distracts them, causing them to stagger back. ARCHITECT stops, briefly, to observe the crisis of OSTEND, then continues on her way. OSTEND shows no awareness of her passage. Swiftly, OSTEND restores herself.)

58

OSTEND: I attach no significance to my own tears /

(She pulls a handkerchief from her sleeve.)

And when others attach significance to them /

(She dries her eyes.)

They are invariably wrong /

(She tucks away the handkerchief and concealing her lack of a destination by the decisiveness of her manner, turns to go, first in one direction then immediately in the other. CHILDLIKE detects her confusion and on an impulse seizes her violently by the wrist. She is stopped.)

59

OSTEND: Let go of me /

(CHILDLIKE is unrelenting and fixing its eye to the floor, seems braced. THE MORTALLY ILL watch with fascination.)

Let go of me /

(CHILDLIKE is adamant.)

You are stronger than you think /

(OSTEND suddenly pulls but ineffectively.)

That hurts /

(CHILDLIKE is mineral.)

Listen / I am not a young woman and I have thin skin / if you bruise me /

(She affects a laugh and tries another tack.)

I will smack you /

(THE MORTALLY ILL enjoy her initiative and laugh, not without sympathy.)

I will give you such a smack in a minute /

(Nothing avails.)

Such a smack /

(Pause.)

I hate situations / situations not of my own making / and with people looking on / it's /

(She falters. She looks to THE MORTALLY ILL.)

Speak to him / please /

(THE MORTALLY ILL decline to intervene. CHILDLIKE is tenacious as a dog.)

All right / I'll smack you /

(THE MORTALLY ILL laugh. OSTEND's free hand is the ungloved. She aims and delivers a blow. The MORTALLY ILL laugh and applaud as if spectators at a circus. CHILDLIKE is unmoved, OSTEND frustrated.)

For someone who claims to believe so passionately in argument this is /

(She delivers a fierce blow to CHILDLIKE's face. The MORTALLY ILL are thrilled and jump up and down, their pets barking in sympathy. Not expecting CHILDLIKE to capitulate, OSTEND rains futile blows on it. As soon as she stops, it releases her. The MORTALLY ILL fall silent. OSTEND lifts her freed hand and nurses her wrist. In the peculiar stasis that follows, PORTSLADE enters.)

PORTSLADE: It's all over with Caroline /

(No one heeds this information.)

At last /

(The tension is unbroken. The entire focus of the MORTALLY ILL remains on the spectacle of OSTEND and CHILDLIKE, CHILDLIKE rigid and still gazing at the floor, OSTEND slowly massaging her injury.)

She fell out of bed /

(PORTSLADE now shares the curiosity of the others.)

That did it /

(CHILDLIKE moves at last, to retrieve the glove thrown down by OSTEND, and offers it to her. She accepts it.)

CHILDLIKE: I'll wait in the car /

OSTEND: *(Indifferently.)* Will you? /

CHILDLIKE: The brown car /

OSTEND: Is there any other? /

CHILDLIKE: The back seats of the brown car /

(OSTEND stares at CHILDLIKE, who walks away.)

THE MORTALLY ILL: BROWN CAR / OFF-WHITE UPHOLSTERY /

(They collapse in fits of giggling. The pets mew and fidget. OSTEND is neither conciliatory nor indignant.)

60

OSTEND: He has not seduced me /

(Embarrassment and mischief combine to excite THE MORTALLY ILL to further laughter, which falters in the face of OSTEND's peculiar resolution.)

Really / I am not seduced /

(They watch her nervously. As if with decision, she turns to follow CHILDLIKE, but stops.)

MOMPER: Don't go /

(OSTEND is fixed to the spot.)

ATTO: If you don't want to /

MOMPER: Say no / darling /

PORTSLADE: Say no / say no /

(OSTEND seems to contemplate their advice. Suddenly she looks up at them, frowning with incomprehension.)

OSTEND: I came here for a reason /

(They pity her. They gaze on her.)

MOMPER: What reason? /

(OSTEND shakes her head frantically and briefly like an animal.)

ATTO: What was the reason / darling? /

OSTEND: I don't know /

(She lifts her eyes to them, pitifully.)

So a dying dwarf could strip my clothes from me / perhaps / so his one eye / and his one hand / like thirst-stricken travellers / could go through the shrivelled land of me /

(She hunches.)

I DON'T KNOW / I DON'T KNOW /

(A certain dread overtakes OSTEND, which the MORTALLY ILL detect.)

LOOS: The door did not fall open / let us use language scrupulously / the door did not fall open / the handle /

OSTEND: I have said so /

LOOS: The handle was depressed /

ATTO: And from the inside /

OSTEND: FROM THE INSIDE / YES /

(She scrutinizes them, trying to ascertain their sympathies. The animals fidget. OSTEND frowns. A distant door bangs in a draught.)

LOOS: *(At last.)* We believe in you /

(OSTEND is puzzled.)

OSTEND: Believe in me? /

THE MORTALLY ILL: *(As if acclaiming her.)* BELIEVE IN YOU / YES /

(OSTEND creates an uncanny smile.)

OSTEND: You believe in me / and believing in me / does that make me a god? /

(They laugh like children.)

I mean to say / you /

(They shake and shudder in their delight, as if confessing an adored secret. OSTEND is infected by their mischief.)

You don't believe / or disbelieve / my answer to your question / the truth as such / it's /

(She shrugs.)

Irrelevant /

(She is charged.)

OF COURSE THE DOOR DID NOT FALL OPEN.

(THE MORTALLY ILL are inspired.)

LOOS: It did not /

ALDRINGTON: It did not /

OSTEND: CERTAINLY IT DID NOT /

(They rock and giggle.)

I put my hand to it / I depressed the handle / it swung open noiselessly / on oiled hinges / in rushed a draught / this draught was like a cold tongue /

THE MORTALLY ILL: *(Charmed.)* A COLD TONGUE /

OSTEND: A cold tongue on my legs /

ATTO: *(Helpfully.)* Bare legs /

OSTEND: Bare legs / yes /

ATTO: Wide open /

OSTEND: WIDE OPEN AND BARE LEGS / and there /

(The pace of her narrative is broken.)

Stood a child / and this child stared / my own child / in the bright glare of the snow /

(Pause.)

How long this stare endured / I don't know / but a long time / until at last the man beside me said / the man /

(Pause.)

The man who / given his age / given that this was long ago / is certainly dead /

(THE MORTALLY ILL gaze on OSTEND with love or wonder. The car horn is heard, and ignored.)

I had to show /

(They smile.)

I HAD TO SHOW / AND IF SOME VOICE ASSURED ME / YOUR CHILD WILL FLING HERSELF THREE FLOORS / AND HANG / TWITCHING / FROM RAILINGS / IT COULD HAVE MADE NO DIFFERENCE /

(THE MORTALLY ILL hesitate for a little time, then spontaneously applaud. OSTEND shrinks.)

It was not bravado /

(She shakes her head.)

Listen / you / you /

(The car horn, repeated, seems to excite the MORTALLY ILL into a state of euphoria.)

THE MORALLY ILL: *(Mischievously.)* DON'T GO / DON'T GO /

OSTEND: You think / you think / she is so /

(The pets squirm and bark.)

SO BRAZEN /

(In her frustration OSTEND can only raise a hand, staring at the floor, a picture of solitude. At last the excitement subsides. THE MORTALLY ILL attend on OSTEND, impatient as a class. OSTEND's hand falls.)

The door fell open / not because I opened it / but because it was impossible it should stay closed / there had to be witness / the witness was my child / my child /

(She is impaled on the word.)

My child /

(She squirms.)

My child then chose /

(OSTEND lifts her gaze.)

To render her life loathsome / and thereby / cause me to loathe my own /

(The pets, discerning the sound of the mobile bed, fidget and whimper.)

61

ARCHITECT enters, and stops. THE MORTALLY ILL are drained of their delight.

OSTEND: *(Not turning to address her daughter.)* I say chose / can it be said / of any six-year old / the child chose? /

62

ARCHITECT is perfectly silent. The car horn sounds. In the leaden atmosphere, a sense of alarm.

ONSEE: Maurice /

(A pet writhes.)

Maurice /

BASIN: What? /

ONSEE: Help me upstairs / Maurice / please /

(BASIN is unwilling. A disastrous event unfolds in private.)

MAURICE /

(A wave of movement. A pet yelps.)

SLUMP: Maurice /

BASIN: *(Ill-temperedly.)* Maurice yourself /

MOMPER: All right / darling /

WINDUS: All right / all right /

PORTSLADE: Someone help Jane /

BASIN: You /

WINDUS: *(To ONSEE, who is stricken.)* Steady / steady darling /

BASIN: You help Jane /

MOMPER: Steady / steady /

BASIN: If you think Jane needs help /

(The car horn.)

PORTSLADE: Not nice / Maurice /

BASIN: I'M DOING SOMETHING /

PORTSLADE: Not a nice attitude /

(The collapse of ONSEE absorbs the entire strength of THE MORTALLY ILL, who topple one way, then the other. They groan, the pets squeal. The car horn sounds again.)

ARCHITECT: *(To OSTEND.)* GO TO THE CAR /

(THE MORTALLY ILL variously support ONSEE and stagger her away, leaving only BASIN as witness.)

WHY DON'T YOU GO TO THE CAR? /

63

OSTEND gazes on her daughter, half-resistant, half-conciliatory. With decision, she turns and goes as instructed. BASIN, shocked by her resolution, limps after her.

BASIN: She doesn't have to / she doesn't have to go /

(He stops. He stares. He turns back, frowning with incomprehension. His hands move strangely, then seem to petrify.)

64

ARCHITECT: Oh /

(She laughs, briefly.)

Oh /

(She seems suddenly profoundly unhappy.)

With the woman called my mother / it is impossible to know what's pain / and what's /

(She sobs.)

Imitation /

(She breathes deeply.)

It's ambiguous / I know / I know the ambiguity of sacrifice / NO ONE MORE SO / now / climb the ladder /

(BASIN looks appalled.)

Climb / I said /

(He hesitates.)

This grotesque parody of passion / perch and tell / how misted are the windows / and so on /

(BASIN is agonized.)

Listen / if you fell and broke your neck /

BASIN: It wouldn't matter /

ARCHITECT: Would it? /

BASIN: It wouldn't / no /

(He shakes his head.)

ARCHITECT: You are stricken / and incurable /

BASIN: I DON'T LIKE HEIGHTS /

ARCHITECT: PLEASE / PLEASE /

BASIN: *(Who would like to satisfy her.)* I'm so / I'm so /

(Neither BASIN nor ARCHITECT have observed DOOBEE's entrance. He goes to BASIN and

taking him kindly by the shoulders, manoeuvres him away from the foot of the ladder. BASIN is profoundly relieved. DOOBEE proceeds to climb the rungs, and arriving at the window, to observe the car. BASIN makes his escape.)

65

DOOBEE: Condensation /

ARCHITECT: *(Gratified.)* Always /

DOOBEE: Condensation / yes / and yet /

ARCHITECT: *(More so.)* AND YET /

DOOBEE: These so-dim /

ARCHITECT: SO-DIM / YES /

DOOBEE: So-dim figures /

ARCHITECT: As if drowning /

DOOBEE: Drowning the only comparison / yes /

(DOOBEE stares. ARCHITECT waits. DOOBEE imagines.)

Her knees / on the tide of their /

(He fails to discover the word.)

Her knees / drift / wide open / and she is fluid /

ARCHITECT: Wet to his one palm / wet to his one wrist / Loose-lipped /

DOOBEE: Her mouth /

ARCHITECT: Like something ripped /

DOOBEE: Terrible mouth / her whole head tipped /

ARCHITECT: Back /

DOOBEE: Her hat / her veil /

ARCHITECT: Slipped /

DOOBEE: Squirming hips /

ARCHITECT: And spreading / this spreading /

DOOBEE: Immensity /

ARCHITECT: And him /

DOOBEE: And him /

ARCHITECT: His one eye racing /

DOOBEE: Mad eye /

ARCHITECT: Mad-eyed as a tortured horse /

DOOBEE: From breast to belly /

ARCHITECT: Arse to thigh /

DOOBEE: His three fingers /

ARCHITECT: Pitiless /

DOOBEE: As if /

ARCHITECT: Pitiless three fingers /

DOOBEE: As if he clung / then slid / from knowing to unknowing /

ARCHITECT: Her body in decay / and him a dwarf /

DOOBEE: The condensation /

ARCHITECT: A sordid parody of love /

DOOBEE: The condensation /

ARCHITECT: Her glove /

DOOBEE: Makes it hard to say /

ARCHITECT: Her pants /

DOOBEE: What's happening /

ARCHITECT: Her handkerchief /

(DOOBEE looks down to ARCHITECT. She simply gazes out of her paralysis. He descends a rung but she senses this and reprimands him.)

STAY / STAY /

(He resumes his observation.)

The soiled stuff of her fornication / like leaves / like litter / I SAID STAY /

DOOBEE: I am staying /

ARCHITECT: The door will open /

DOOBEE: Obviously /

ARCHITECT: Obviously /

(She is suddenly seized by an anxiety.)

HOW WILL SHE LEAVE THE CAR / DOOBEE? / BEFORE OR AFTER HIM? /

DOOBEE: *(Turning his gaze to ARCHITECT.)* After /

ARCHITECT: After? / after is her way / is it? /

DOOBEE: She makes up /

ARCHITECT: She makes up /

DOOBEE: In the mirror / she makes up her face /

ARCHITECT: Which mirror? /

DOOBEE: The driving mirror /

ARCHITECT: The driving mirror / isn't it too far away? /

DOOBEE: She leans / it strains her skirt / 'LET ME WATCH YOU / PLEASE' / I say /

ARCHITECT: You want to watch? /

DOOBEE: I want to watch / but she refuses / I climb out / there's a delay / and then /

ARCHITECT: How long? / How long is this delay? /

DOOBEE: Long / a long delay / and then she /

(He is nostalgic.)

As if / who'd know she / her hair / her veil / who'd know she / immaculate / no hint of / in her face / or in her clothes / no hint of /

(He pulls a face of loss.)

And leaves the door for me to close /

(DOOBEE is turned on the ladder to look at ARCHITECT. ARCHITECT's prostrate position denies her a view of him. Consequently neither detects the entrance of CHILDLIKE who itself whilst seeing ARCHITECT on the electric bed, does not perceive a figure at the top of the ladder. For a moment all are still.)

66

CHILDLIKE: *(A cry of faith.)* OFF-WHITE UPHOLSTERY /

(It is thoughtful.)

Faint traces of / the so-faint traces / sponged but not expunged / by Mr Doobee /

(It laughs.)

OFF-WHITE NO WONDER / I SAID YOUR SMEAR / I SAID YOUR SMEAR / THE OFF-WHITE MORE OFF HERE / THAN HERE /

(It laughs. It frowns. It closes its eye. It bites its lip.)

An enjoyable conversation / during which /

(He shakes his head.)

It became clear to me / that whilst to say the door fell open is / strictly speaking / contradictory / our understanding of this immaculate / and profoundly

(CHILDLIKE strains for the word.)

SACRED /

(Its fist tightens.)

Sacred / moment in your history / is not advanced one iota /

(It shakes its head like an animal.)

And always I suspected this /

(It smiles, a pitiful smile.)

WITH REVELATION / ARGUMENT'S A CUL-DE-SAC /

(It flagellates itself with its single arm.)

GOODBYE TO WHY / GOODBYE TO WHY /

(Its ecstasy subsides.)

She had to show / your mother / it was not possible she could not show / and you / who stood there / impossible you could not know /

(He is melancholy.)

And knowing / throw yourself three storeys / Miss /

67

ARCHITECT seems to meditate on CHILDLIKe's exposition.

ARCHITECT: Abortion / you stink of her /

(CHILDLIKE is motionless.)

Hermaphrodite /

CHILDLIKE: We had a lengthy conservation /

ARCHITECT: You stink /

(ARCHITECT is inundated by tears. DOOBEE rapidly descends the ladder. CHILDLIKE, for the first time aware of DOOBEE's presence, turns and seizes him as he makes to comfort ARCHITECT. CHILDLIKE's strength shocks DOOBEE who struggles but is constrained.)

CHILDLIKE: The sacrifice cannot be compensated /

(DOOBEE lurches and sprawls.)

Mr Doobee /

(DOOBEE climbs to his feet and makes to go to ARCHITECT again. Again CHILDLIKE frustrates him.)

BEAUTIFULLY JOYLESS / MR DOOBEE /

(CHILDLIKE suddenly abandons his struggle.)

IS THE SACRIFICE /

(DOOBEE's nightmare of loss, rage and moral indignation compels him to rain kicks on the now unresisting dwarf, whose body flaps like a doll. The stronger attraction of ARCHITECT's misery draws him to the mobile bed.)

DOOBEE: Darling /

(He seems helpless, gazing on her, his hands suspended.)

Darling /

(CHILDLIKE lifts itself, then collapses.)

Darling /

68

Obedient to an impulse he barely understands, DOOBEE pulls the covering from the mobile bed, exposing the nakedness of ARCHITECT. He gazes on her, then as if by some tacit accord, sweeps her up into his arms. ARCHITECT's expression is one of appalled anticipation.

69

DOOBEE goes to carry ARCHITECT into the house, but the sound of OSTEND's footsteps spoils his resolution. He stops. His body is an arch of tension.

OSTEND: Fling her / Doobee / fling her on the railings / it's what she wants /

(DOOBEE turns to face OSTEND, and in doing so, turns ARCHITECT's regard also. In conformity with DOOBEE's description, OSTEND is newly-made up. Her gaze falls on the lifeless body of CHILDLIKE. As if to reinforce a contrived objectivity, she draws on a glove.)

DOOBEE: *(As if thwarted.)* How swiftly you have dressed /

OSTEND: I was never undressed /

DOOBEE: *(Brutally.)* ALL RIGHT / HOW SWIFTLY YOU HAVE REARRANGED YOUR CLOTHES /

OSTEND: They never were disturbed /

(She lifts her eyes to the lovers.)

What happened thirty years ago is only fit for parody / so /

(She returns her gaze to CHILDLIKE.)

We had a conversation /

(And back to DOOBEE.)

And if / as a consequence / I'm too swift to leave the car / you're too slow to reach the third floor / Doobee / let alone to throw my daughter out / one apotheosis / only one / I know / oh /

(She pulls her mouth tight.)

I KNOW /

(DOOBEE feels the rebuke. His eyes falter. OSTEND agonizes.)

The door /

(She wills herself on.)

The door which /

(She discovers the only phrase.)

HAD TO BE OPENED /

(She shakes her head slowly.)

By the same law / needed to be closed / I could not close it / snow notwithstanding / draught on my naked legs / no strength / no will / so / he leant across me / I smelled his hair / it clicked / it did not close / no / that isn't shut / darling / not shut / he muttered some oath / not about the door / he didn't curse the door / he praised my thigh / darling / I was /

(She suffers.)

Oh / what was I? / he stretched / he strained / he hauled it back again / across me like an unslung Christ / it clicked / it shut / the second time / shut now / the door / dead now / the man / and then / her cry / her cry /

(OSTEND shakes her head in a slow, tortured manner.)

As if closing the door God closed my eye /

(She loses her physical integrity.)

If I apologize I'll die /

(Her shoulders are decayed.)

I apologize /

70

DOOBEE, with ARCHITECT in his arms, suffers the wound of OSTEND's capitulation. A killed animal drops from high and smacks the floor. DOOBEE's horrified gaze lifts to the heart of the house. A second animal plunges. OSTEND turns to DOOBEE, as if oblivious of what now becomes a rain of pets.

OSTEND: I'll drive /

(She extends a hand as if for the keys of the car.)

I can't drive /

(A bird cage descends, bounces, rolls away.)

I'll drive /

(Rabbits, dogs, cascade, as ostend's hand remains outstretched.)

*

www.ingramcontent.com/pod-product-compliance
Ingram Content Group UK Ltd.
Pitfield, Milton Keynes, MK11 3LW, UK
UKHW031249020325
455689UK00008B/141

9 781783 190874